WILEY TRADING ADVANTAGE

Cybernetic Trading Strategies
Developing a Profitable Trading System with State-of-the-Art Technologies

Murray A. Ruggiero, Jr.

JOHN WILEY & SONS, INC.
New York • **Chichester** • **Weinheim** • **Brisbane** • **Singapore** • **Toronto**

Library of Congress Cataloging-in-Publication Data:

Ruggiero, Murray A., 1963–
    Cybernetic trading strategies : developing a profitable trading
  system with state-of-the-art technologies / by Murray A. Ruggiero,
  Jr.
        p.   cm. — (Wiley trading advantage)
    Includes index.
    ISBN 0-471-14920-9 (cloth : alk. paper)
    1. Investment analysis.   2. Electronic trading of securities.
  I. Title.   II. Series.
  HG4529.R84   1997
  332.6'0285—dc21   96-53326

Printed in the United States of America.

10 9 8 7 6 5 4 3

Foreword

As we approach the end of one millennium and the beginning of another, computers have changed the way we think and act. In the field of financial market analysis, the changes have been nothing short of revolutionary. Some of us remember when analysts charted the performance of markets without the aid of computers. Believe me, it was slow and no fun at all. We spent hours constructing the charts before even getting to the fun part—analyzing them. The idea of experimenting with indicators and optimizing them was still decades away.

The computer has removed the drudgery of market analysis. Any investor can buy a computer and some inexpensive software and, in no time at all, have as much data at his or her fingertips as most professional money managers. Any and all markets can be charted, manipulated, over-laid on one another, measured against one another, and so on. In other words, we can do pretty much anything we want to with a few keystrokes. The popularity of computers has also fostered a growing interest in technical market analysis. This visual form of analysis lends itself beautifully to the computer revolution, which thrives on graphics.

Up to now, however, the computer has been used primarily as a data-gathering and charting machine. It enables us to collect large amounts of

---

Mr. Murphy is CNBC's technical analyst, and author of Technical Analysis of the Futures Markets and Intermarket Technical Analysis. His latest book, The Visual Investor (Wiley, 1996), applies charting techniques to sector analysis and mutual fund investing.

market information for display in easily understood chart pictures. The fact is, however, most of us have only been scratching the surface where the computer is concerned. We've been using it primarily as a visual tool.

Enter Murray A. Ruggiero, Jr., and Cybernetic Trading Strategies.

I first became aware of Murray's work when he published an article titled "Using Neural Nets for Intermarket Analysis," in *Futures Magazine*. I subsequently did a series of interviews with him on CNBC in which he developed his ideas even further, for a larger audience. I've followed his work ever since, with growing interest and admiration (and occasionally offered a little encouragement). That's why I'm delighted to help introduce his first book. I do so for some selfish reasons: Murray's research validates much of the work I helped develop, especially in the field of intermarket analysis. Murray's extensive research in that area not only validates my earlier writings in that field but, I believe, raises intermarket analysis to a higher and more practical level.

Not only does he provide statistical evidence that intermarket linkages exist, but he shows numerous examples of how to develop trading systems utilizing intermarket filters. Most traders accept that a positive correlation exists between bonds and stocks. How about utilizing a moving-average filter on the bond market to tell us whether to be in the stock market or in T-Bills? One such example shows how an investor could have outperformed the S&P500 while being in the market only 59 percent of the time. Or how about utilizing correlation analysis to determine when intermarket linkages are strong and when they are weak? That insight allows a trader to use market linkages in trading decisions only when they are most likely to work. I was amazed at how useful (and logical) these techniques really were. But this book is more than a study of intermarket analysis.

On a much broader scale, traditional technical analysts should applaud the type of work done by Murray and young writers like him. They are not satisfied with relying on subjective interpretations of a "head and shoulders pattern" or reading Elliott Waves and candlestick patterns. They apply a statistical approach in order to make these subjective methods more mechanical. Two things are achieved by this more rigorous scientific methodology. First, old techniques are validated by historical backtesting. In other words, Ruggiero shows that they do work. Second, he shows us how to use a more mechanical approach to Elliott Waves and candlesticks, to make them even more useful. Murray does us all a favor by validating what many of us have known for a long time—technical market analysis does work. But it can also be made better.

There's much more to this book, having to do with state-of-the-art thinking—for starters, chaos theory, fuzzy logic, and artificial intelligence—which leads us to some new concepts regarding the computer itself. The computer can do more than show us pretty pictures. It can optimize, backtest, prove or disprove old theories, eliminate the bad methods and make the good ones better. In a way, the computer almost begins to think for us. And perhaps that's the greatest benefit of *Cybernetic Trading Strategies*. It explores new ways to use the computer and finds ways to make a valuable machine even more valuable.

Technical analysis started being used in the United States around the beginning of the 20th century. Over the past 100 years, it has grown in both value and popularity. Like any field of study, however, technical analysis continues to evolve. *Intermarket Technical Analysis*, which I wrote in 1991, was one step along that evolutionary path. *Cybernetic Trading Strategies* is another. It seems only fitting that this type of book should appear as technical analysis begins a new century.

JOHN J. MURPHY

Preface

Advanced technologies are methods used by engineers, scientists, and physicists to solve real-world problems that affect our lives in many unseen ways. Advanced technologies are not just rocket science methods; they include applying statistical analysis to prove or disprove a given hypothesis. For example, statistical methods are used to evaluate the effectiveness of a drug for treating a given illness. Genetic algorithms have been used by engineers for many different applications: the development of the layout of micro processors circuits, for example, or the optimization of landing strut weights in aircraft. In general, complex problems that require testing millions or even billions of combinations to find the optimal answer can be solved using genetic algorithms. Another method, maximum entropy spectral analysis or the maximum entropy method (MEM), has been used in the search for new oil reserves and was adapted by John Ehlers for use in developing trading strategies. Chaos, a mathematical concept, has been used by scientists to understand how to improve weather forecasts. Artificial intelligence was once used only in laboratories to try to learn how to capture human expertise. Now, this technology is used in everything from cars to toasters. These technologies—really just different ways of looking at the world—have found their way to Wall Street and are now used by some of the most powerful institutions in the world. John

Deere Inc. manages 20 percent of its pension fund money using neural networks, and Brad Lewis, while at Fidelity Investments, used neural networks to select stocks.

You do not need to be a biophysicist or statistician to understand these technologies and incorporate them into your technical trading system. *Cybernetic Trading Strategies* will explain how some of these advanced technologies can give your trading system an edge. I will show you which technologies have the most market applicability, explain how they work, and then help you design a technical trading system using these technologies. Lastly, but perhaps most importantly, we will test these systems.

Although the markets have no single panacea, incorporating elements of statistical analysis, spectra analysis, neural networks, genetic algorithms, fuzzy logic, and other high-tech concepts into a traditional technical trading system can greatly improve the performance of standard trading systems. For example, I will show you how spectra analysis can be used to detect, earlier than shown by classical indicators such as ADX—the average direction movement indicator that measures the strength of a trend—when a market is trending. I will also show you how to evaluate the predictive value of a given classical method, by using the same type of statistical analysis used to evaluate the effectiveness of drugs on a given illness.

I have degrees in both physics and computer science and have been researching neural networks for over eight years. I invented a method for embedding neural networks into a spreadsheet. It seemed a natural extension to then try and apply what I have learned to predicting the markets. However, my early models were not very successful. After many failed attempts, I realized that regardless of how well I knew the advanced technologies, if I didn't have a clear understanding of the markets I was attempting to trade, the applications would prove fruitless. I then spent the greater part of three years studying specific markets and talking to successful traders. Ultimately, I realized that my systems needed a sound premise as their foundation.

My goals are: to provide you with the basics that will lead to greater market expertise (and thus a reasonable premise on which to base your trades) and to show you how to develop reliable trading models using so-called advanced technologies.

HOW TO GET THE MOST OUT OF THIS BOOK

This book will introduce you to many different state-of-the-art methods for analyzing the market(s) as well as developing and testing trading systems. In each chapter, I will show you how to use a given method or technology to build, improve, or test a given trading strategy.

The first of the book's five parts covers classical technical analysis methodologies, including intermarket analysis, seasonality, and commitment of traders (COT) data. The chapters in Part One will show you how to use and test classical methods, using more rigorous analysis.

Part Two covers many statistical, engineering, and artificial intelligence methodologies that can be used to develop state-of-the-art trading systems. One topic I will cover is system feedback, a concept from systems control theory. This technology uses past results to improve future forecasts. The method can be applied to the equity curve of a trading system to try to predict the results of future trades. Another topic is cycle-based trading using maximum entropy spectra analysis, which is used in oil exploration and in many other engineering applications. I apply this method to analyzing price data for various commodities and then use this analysis to develop mechanical trading strategies.

Part Three shows how to mechanize subjective methods such as Elliott Wave and candlestick charts. Part Four discusses development, implementation, and testing of trading systems. Here, I explain how to build and test trading systems to maximize reliability and profitability based on particular risk/reward criteria.

Finally, in Part Five, I show how to use many different methods from the field of artificial intelligence to develop actual state-of-the-art trading systems. These methods will include neural networks, genetic algorithms, and machine induction.

I would like to point out that many of the systems, examples, and charts have different ending dates, even in the same chapter. This occurs because the research for this book is based on over one year of work, and not all of the systems and examples in each chapter were compiled at the same time.

As you read the book, don't become discouraged if you don't understand a particular concept. Keep reading to get a general sense of the subject. Some of the terminology may be foreign and may take some getting used to. I've tried to put the concepts in laypersons' terminology, but the fact remains that jargon (just like market terminology) abounds. After you get a general feel for the material, reread the text and work through the examples and models. Most of the examples are based on real systems and models being used by both experienced and novice traders. It has been my goal to present real-world, applicable systems and examples. You won't find pie-in-the-sky theories here.

MURRAY A. RUGGIERO, JR.

East Haven, Connecticut
May 1997

Acknowledgments

Whatever my accomplishments, they have resulted from the people who have touched my life. I would like to thank all of them. First, my loving wife Diana, who has stood beside me my whole career. While I was building my business, she worked full-time and also helped me on nights and weekends. Early in 1996, she left her job at Yale University so we could work together. We make a great team, and I thank God for such a wife, friend, and partner. I also thank my son, Murray III, for understanding why his daddy needs to work and for giving me focus. I know that I must succeed, so that he can have a better life. Next, I thank my parents, who raised me to work hard and reach for my dreams. I am also indebted to Ilias Papazachariou for spending several weekends helping me with researching, organizing, collecting, and editing the material in this book.

Several of my professors and colleagues have helped me become who I am. Dr. Charlotte LeMay believed in me more than I believed in myself. It has been 12 years since I graduated from Western Connecticut State University and she is still a good friend. She made me believe that if I could dream it, I could do it.

Many friends in the futures industry have also helped me along the way. I thank Ginger Szala, for giving me the opportunity to share my research with the world in *Futures Magazine*, and John Murphy for giving me a chance to meet a larger audience on CNBC, for being a good friend and colleague, and for agreeing to write the Foreword of this book.

Finally, I thank Larry Williams. Larry has been very good to me over the years and has helped me understand what it takes to be successful in this business. *Inside Advantage*, my newsletter, began based on a suggestion from Larry Williams. Larry has been a valued colleague, but, most importantly, he is a friend whom I can always count on.

I know that I am forgetting people here; to everyone else who has helped me along the way: Thank You!

M.A.R.

Contents

PART THREE   MAKING SUBJECTIVE METHODS MECHANICAL

PART FOUR   TRADING SYSTEM DEVELOPMENT AND TESTING

PART FIVE   USING ADVANCED TECHNOLOGIES TO DEVELOP TRADING STRATEGIES

Introduction

During the past several years, I have been on a quest to understand how the markets actually work. This quest has led me to researching almost every type of analysis. My investigation covered both subjective and objective forms of technical analysis—for example, intermarket analysis, Elliott Wave, cycle analysis, and the more exotic methods, such as neural networks and fuzzy logic. This book contains the results of my research. My goal was to discover mechanical methods that could perform as well as the top traders in the world. For example, there are technologies for trading using trend following, which significantly outperform the legendary Turtle system. This book will show you dozens of trading systems and filters that can increase your trading returns by 200 to 300 percent. I have collected into this volume the best technologies that I have discovered. This overview of the book's contents will give you the flavor of what you will be learning.

Chapter 1 shows how to use intermarket analysis as a predictive tool. The chapter first reviews the basics of intermarket analysis and then, using a chartist's approach, explains the many different intermarket relationships that are predictive of stocks, bonds, and commodities. That background is used to develop fully mechanical systems for a variety of markets, to show the predictive power of intermarket analysis. These markets include the S&P500, T-Bonds, crude oil, gold, currencies, and more. Most of these systems are as profitable as some commercial systems costing thousands of dollars. For example, several T-Bond trading systems have averaged over $10,000 a year during the analysis period.

Chapter 2 discusses seasonal trading, including day-of-the-week, monthly, and annual effects. You will learn how to judge the reliability of a seasonal trade and how to develop reliable and profitable seasonal in-dexes. Several winning methods for using seasonality were developed using a walk forward approach in which the seasonal is calculated only using prior data for trading stocks, bonds, and corn. This means that these results are more realistic than the standard seasonal research normally available and are very profitable. The chapter also discusses several issues relating to the proper use of seasonality. For example, in some mar-kets, such as corn or other commodities that are grown, all of the available data should be used to calculate a seasonal. In markets like T-Bonds, where seasonal forces are influenced by the release of government re-ports, only the past N years are used because these dates change over time. Finally, several new seasonal measures are presented, beginning with the Ruggiero/Barna Seasonal Index. This new indicator combines the win percentage (Win%) and returns into one standardized measure that outperforms standard ways of selecting which seasonal patterns to trade. For example, 71 percent of our trades can be won by using the Rug-giero/Barna Seasonal Index to trade T-Bonds using walk forward analy-sis. Next, two other new indicators are explained: (1) seasonal volatility and (2) the seasonal trend index based on the trading day of the year. The seasonal volatility measure is valuable for setting stops; for example, when seasonal volatility is high, wider stops can be used, and when it is low, tighter stops can be used. This measure is also good for trading op-tions, that is, for selling at premium when seasonal volatility is falling. I use my seasonal trend index to filter any trend-following system. The power of this seasonal trend index was exhibited when it predicted the trend in T-Bonds starting in mid-February of 1996. By taking the down-side breakout in T-Bonds during that month, when our seasonal trend in-dicator was crossing above 30, I caught a short signal worth about $9,000.00 per contract in only a month and about $13,000.00 in only eight weeks.

Chapter 3 shows how fundamental factors such as inflation, consumer confidence, and unemployment can be used to predict trends in both in-terest rates and stocks. For example, one market timing model has been 90 percent accurate since August 1944, and would have produced better than the standard 10 to 12 percent produced by buy and hold and was in the market about half the time.

Chapter 4 discusses traditional technical analysis, beginning with why some people say technical analysis does not work and why they are wrong. Several powerful trading strategies based on technical analysis are used by professional traders to exploit inefficiencies in the markets and make money. These strategies range from position to day trading.

Chapter 5 explains what the commitment of traders (COT) report is, how it is reported, and how to use it to develop market timing models. Several system examples are provided.

Chapter 6 is an overview of how general statistical analysis can be applied to trading. To make you a more profitable trader, the following statistical measures are discussed:

Mean, median, and mode.

Types of distributions and their properties.

Variance and standard deviation.

Interrelation of gaussian distribution, mean, and standard deviation.

Statistical tests that are of value to trading system developers.

Correlation analysis.

This chapter serves as a background to much of the rest of the book. Chapter 7 first explains the nature of cycles and how they relate to real-world markets. Later, you will see how cycles can be used to develop actual trading strategies using the maximum entropy method (MEM), or maximum entropy spectral analysis. MEM can be used to detect whether a market is currently trending, or cycling, or is in a consolidation mode. Most important, cycles allow discovery of these modes early enough to be of value for trading. A new breakout system, called adaptive channel breakout, actually adapts to changing market conditions and can therefore be used to trade almost any market. During the period from 1/1/80 to 9/20/96, this system produced over $160,000.00 on the Yen with a draw-down of about $8,700.00. Finally, the chapter tells how MEM can be used to predict turning points in any market.

Chapter 8 shows how combining statistics and intermarket analysis can create a new class of predictive trading technology. First, there is a revisit to the intermarket work in Chapter 1, to show how using Pearson's correlation can significantly improve the performance of an intermarket-based system. Several trading system examples are provided, including systems for trading the S&P500, T-Bonds, and crude oil. Some of the systems in this chapter are as good as the high-priced commercial systems. The chapter also discusses a new indicator, predictive correlation, which actually tells how reliable a given intermarket relationship currently is when predicting future market direction. This method can often cut draw-down by 25 to 50 percent and increase the percentage of winning trades. Intermarket analysis can be used to predict when a market will have a major trend. This method is also good at detecting runaway bull or bear markets before they happen.

Chapter 9 shows how to use the current and past performance of a given system to set intelligent exit stops and calculate the risk level of a given trade. This involves studying adverse movement on both winning and losing trades and then finding relationships that allow setting an optimal level for a stop.

In Chapter 10, system control concept feedback is used to improve the reliability and performance of an existing trading strategy. You will learn how feedback can help mechanical trading systems and how to measure system performance for use in a feedback model. An example shows the use of a system's equity curve and feedback to improve system perfor-mance by cutting drawdown by almost 50 percent while increasing the average trade by 84 percent. This technology is little known to traders but is one of the most powerful technologies for improving system per-formance. The technology can also be used to detect when a system is no longer tradable—before the losses begin to accumulate.

Chapter 11 teaches the basics of many different advanced technolo-gies, such as neural networks, machine induction, genetic algorithms, sta-tistical pattern recognition, and fuzzy logic. You will learn why each of these technologies can be important to traders.

The next three chapters tell how to make subjective analysis mechani-cal. Chapter 12 overviews making subjective methods mechanical. In Chapter 13, I explain Tom Joseph's work, based on how to identify me-chanical Elliott Wave counts. Actual code in TradeStation's EasyLanguage is included. In Chapter 14, I develop autorecognition software for identi-fying candlestick patterns. A code for many of the most popular forma-tions, in EasyLanguage, is supplied.

The next topic is trading system development and testing. Chapter 15, on how to develop a reliable trading system, will walk you through the de-velopment of a trading system from concept to implementation. Chap-ter 16 then shows how to test, evaluate, and trade the system that has been developed.

In the final chapters, I combine what has been presented earlier with advanced methods, such as neural networks and genetic algorithms, to develop trading strategies.

Chapter 17 discusses data preprocessing, which is used to develop models that require advanced technologies, such as neural networks. The chapter explains how to transform data so that a modeling method (e.g., neural networks) can extract hidden relationships—those that normally cannot be seen. Many times, the outputs of these models need to be processed in order to extract what the model has learned. This is called postprocessing.

What is learned in Chapter 17 is applied in the next three chapters. Chapter 18 shows how to develop market timing models using neural networks and includes a fully disclosed real example for predicting the S&P500. The example builds on many of the concepts presented in earlier chapters, and it shows how to transform rule-based systems into supercharged neural network models.

Chapter 19 discusses how machine learning can be used to develop trading rules. These rules assist in developing trading systems, selecting inputs for a neural network, selecting between systems, or developing consensus forecasts. The rules can also be used to indicate when a model developed by another method will be right or wrong. Machine learning is a very exciting area of research in trading system development.

Chapter 20 explains how to use genetic algorithms in a variety of financial applications:

Developing trading rules.

Switching between systems or developing consensus forecasts.

Choosing money management applications.

Evolving a neural network.

The key advantage of genetic algorithms is that they allow traders to build in expertise for selecting their solutions. The other methods presented in this book do not offer this feature. Following a discussion of how to develop these applications, there is an example of the evolution of a trading system using TSEvolve, an add-in for TradeStation, which links genetic algorithms to EasyLanguage. This example combines intermarket analysis and standard technical indicators to develop patterns for T-Bond market trades.

Part One

CLASSICAL MARKET PREDICTION

1

Classical Intermarket Analysis as a Predictive Tool

WHAT IS INTERMARKET ANALYSIS?

Intermarket analysis is the study of how markets interrelate. It is valuable as a tool that can be used to confirm signals given by classical technical analysis as well as to predict future market direction. John J. Murphy, CNBC's technical analyst and the author of *Intermarket Technical Analysis* (John Wiley & Sons, 1991), is considered the father of this form of analysis. In his book, Murphy analyzes the period around the stock market crash of October 19, 1987, and shows how intermarket analysis warned of impending disaster, months before the crash. Let's examine some of the intermarket forces that led to the 1987 stock market crash.

Figure 1.1 shows how T-Bonds began to collapse in April 1987, while stocks rallied until late August 1987. The collapse in the T-Bond market was a warning that the S&P500 was an accident waiting to happen; normally, the S&P500 and T-Bond prices are positively correlated. Many institutions use the yield on the 30-year Treasury and the earnings per share on the S&P500 to estimate a fair trading value for the S&P500. This value is used for their asset allocation models.

T-Bonds and the S&P500 bottomed together on October 19, 1987, as shown in Figure 1.2. After that, both T-Bonds and the S&P500 moved in a trading range for several months. Notice that T-Bonds rallied on the

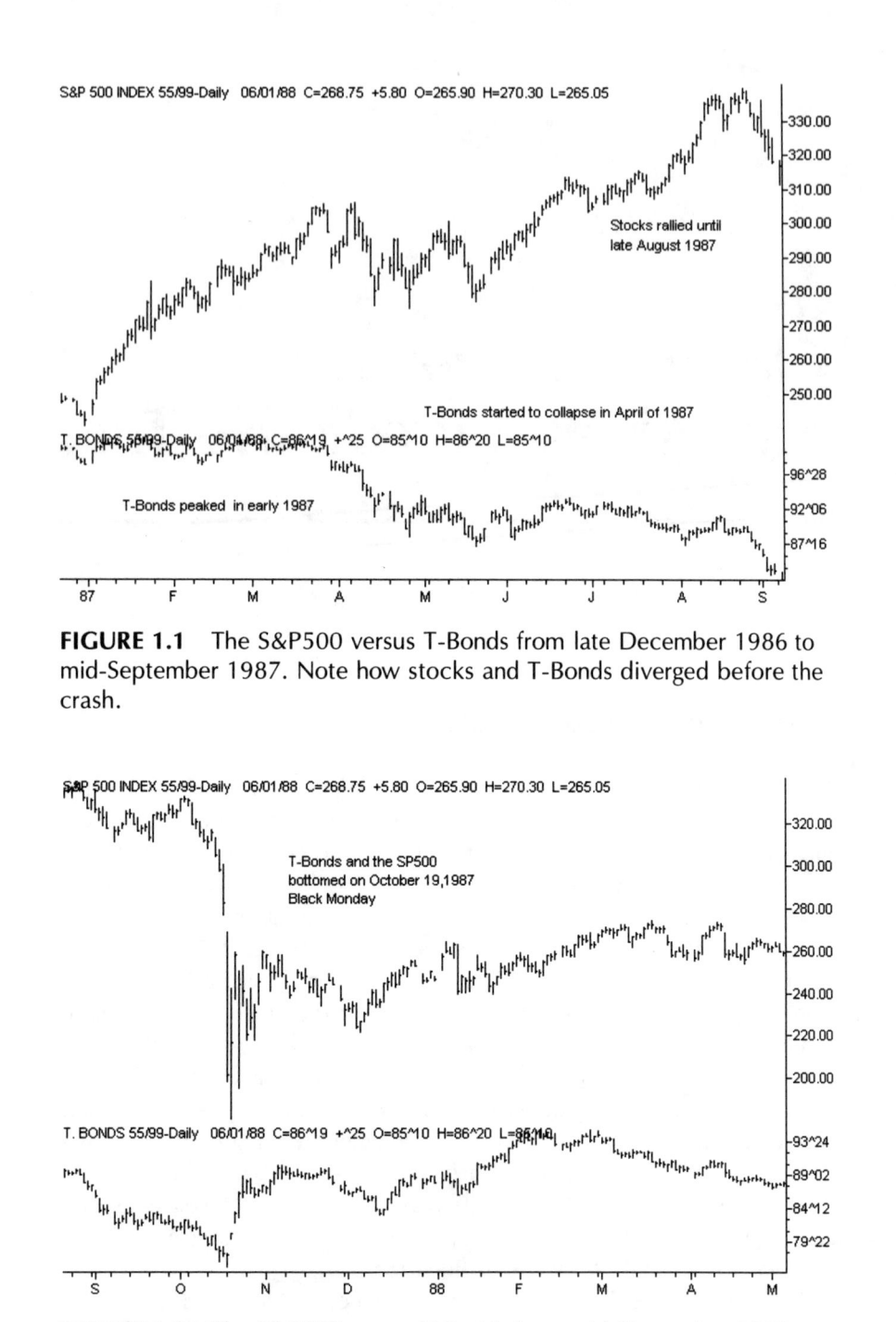

FIGURE 1.1 The S&P500 versus T-Bonds from late December 1986 to mid-September 1987. Note how stocks and T-Bonds diverged before the crash.

FIGURE 1.2 The S&P500 versus T-Bonds from mid-September 1987 to early May 1988. T-Bonds bottomed on Black Monday, October 19, 1987.

day of the crash. This was because T-Bonds were used as a flight to safety.

T-Bond yields are very strongly correlated to inflation; historically, they are about 3 percent, on average, over the Consumer Price Index (CPI). Movements in the Commodity Research Bureau (CRB) listings are normally reflected in the CPI within a few months. In 1987, the CRB had a bullish breakout, which was linked to the collapse in the T-Bond market. This is shown in Figure 1.3. The CRB, a basket of 21 commodities, is normally negatively correlated to T-Bonds. There are two different CRB indexes: (1) the spot index, composed of cash prices, and (2) the CRB futures index, composed of futures prices. One of the main differences between the CRB spot and futures index is that the spot index is more influenced by raw industrial materials.

Eurodollars, a measure of short-term interest rates, are positively correlated to T-Bonds and usually will lead T-Bonds at turning points. Figure 1.4 shows how a breakdown in Eurodollars preceded a breakdown in T-Bonds early in 1987.

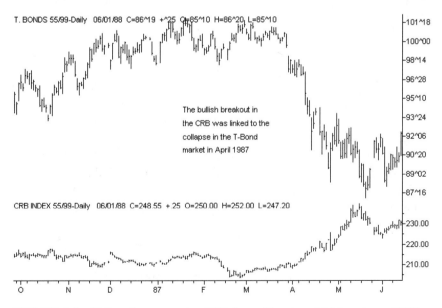

FIGURE 1.3   T-Bonds versus the CRB from October 1986 to June 1987. The bullish breakout in the CRB in late March 1987 led to the collapse in the T-Bond market in April 1987.

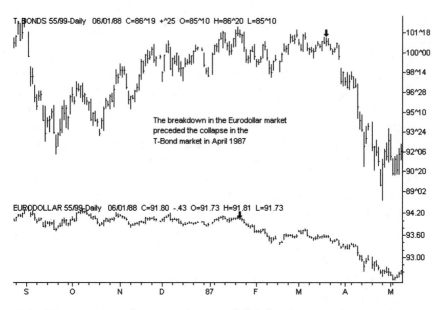

FIGURE 1.4 T-Bonds versus the Eurodollar for the period September 1986 to May 1987. The breakdown in Eurodollars in late January 1987 preceded the collapse in the T-Bond market in April 1987.

Figure 1.5 shows how the gold market began to accelerate to the upside just as Eurodollars began to collapse. Gold anticipates inflation and is usually negatively correlated with interest-rate-based market rates such as the Eurodollar.

Analysis of the period around the crash of 1987 is valuable because many relationships became exaggerated during this period and are easier to detect. Just as a total solar eclipse is valuable to astronomers, technical analysts can learn a lot by studying the periods around major market events.

Given this understanding of the link between the S&P500 and T-Bonds, based on the lessons learned during the crash of 1987, we will now discuss intermarket analysis for the S&P500 and T-Bonds in more detail.

Figure 1.6 shows that T-Bonds peaked in October 1993, but the S&P500 did not peak until February 1994. The collapse of the bond market in early 1994 was linked to the major correction in the S&P500, during late March.

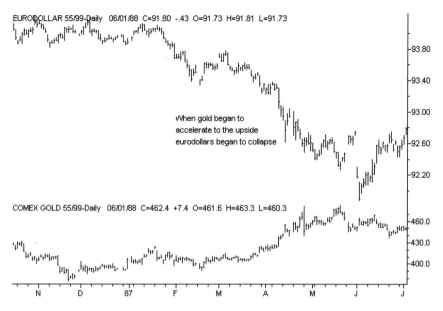

FIGURE 1.5 Eurodollars versus Comex gold for the period mid-October 1986 to July 1987. Eurodollars collapsed as gold began to accelerate to the upside.

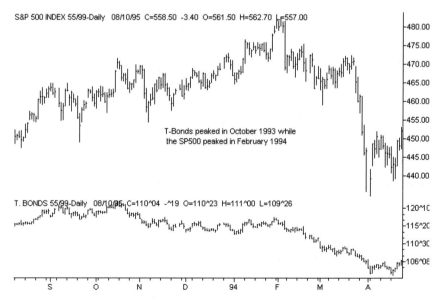

FIGURE 1.6 The S&P500 versus T-Bonds for the period August 1993 to April 1994. The 1994 bear market in T-Bonds led to the late March correction in the S&P500.

13

T-Bonds continued to drop until November 1994. During this time, the S&P500 was in a trading range. The S&P500 set new highs in February 1995 after T-Bonds had rallied over six points from their lows. This activity is shown in Figure 1.7.

Figure 1.8 shows the Eurodollar collapse very early in 1994. This collapse led to a correction in the stock market about two weeks later. This correction was the only correction of more than 5 percent during all of 1994 and 1995.

Figure 1.9 shows that the Dow Jones Utility Average (DJUA) also led the S&P500 at major tops. The utilities topped in September 1993—a month before bonds and five months before stocks.

Figure 1.10 shows that the S&P500 and DJUA both bottomed together in November 1994.

With this background in intermarket relationships for the S&P500, let's now discuss the T-Bond market.

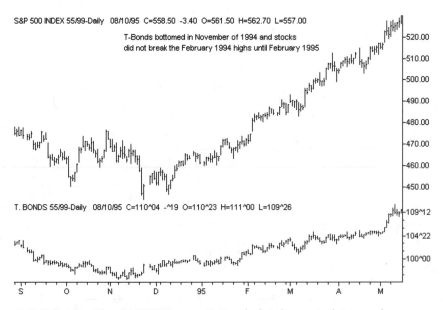

FIGURE 1.7 The S&P500 versus T-Bonds for the period September 1994 to May 1995. When T-Bonds bottomed in November 1994, stocks did not break the February 1994 highs until February 1995.

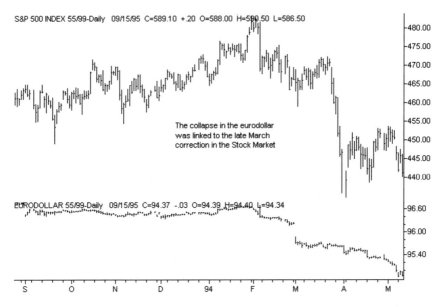

FIGURE 1.8 The S&P500 versus Eurodollars for the period September 1993 to May 1994. The collapse in Eurodollars was linked to the late March 1994 correction in the stock market.

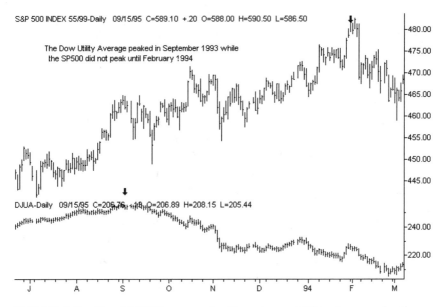

FIGURE 1.9 The S&P500 versus the Dow Jones Utility Average for the period July 1993 to March 1994. The DJUA peaked in September 1993. Stocks did not peak until February 1994.

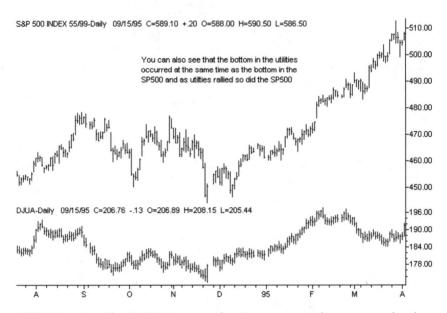

FIGURE 1.10   The S&P500 versus the Dow Jones Utility Average for the period August 1994 to April 1995. The S&P500 and the DJUA bottomed together in November 1994 and rallied together in 1995.

Figure 1.11 shows that the Dow Jones Utility Average (DJUA) led the bond market at the top during several weeks in late 1993. The DJUA is made up of two different components: (1) electrical utilities and (2) gas utilities. Before T-Bonds turned upward in late 1994, the electrical utilities began to rally. This rally was not seen in the DJUA because the gas utilities were in a downtrend. This point was made during the third quarter of 1994 by John Murphy, on CNBC's "Tech Talk." Figure 1.12 shows how the electrical utilities are correlated to T-Bond future prices.

One of the most important things that a trader would like to know is whether a current rally is just a correction in a bear market. The Dow 20 Bond Index, by continuing to make lower highs during 1994, showed that the rally attempts in the T-Bond market were just corrections in a bear market. This is shown in Figure 1.13. The Dow 20 Bond Index is predictive of future T-Bond movements, but it has lost some of its predictive power for T-Bonds because it includes some corporate bonds

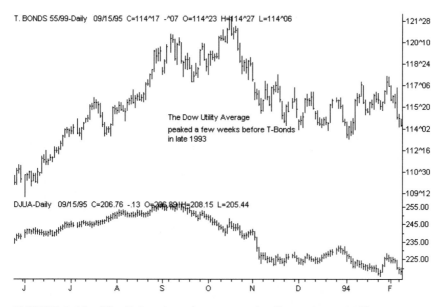

FIGURE 1.11   The T-Bond market versus the Down Jones Utility Average. The DJUA peaked a few weeks before T-Bonds in late 1993.

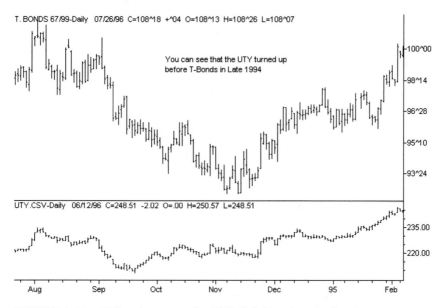

FIGURE 1.12   T-Bonds versus the Philadelphia electrical utility average for the period August 1994 to February 1995. The electrical average turned up before T-Bonds in late 1994.

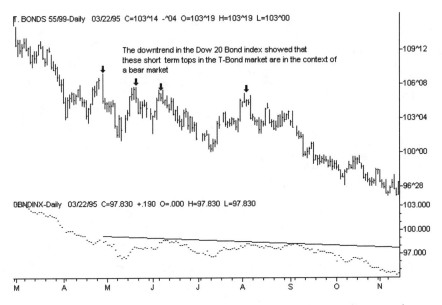

T. BONDS 55/99-Daily 03/22/95 C=103^14 -^04 O=103^19 H=103^19 L=103^00

The downtrend in the Dow 20 Bond index showed that
these short term tops in the T-Bond market are in the context of
a bear market

109^12
106^08
103^04
100^00
96^28

DBNDINX-Daily 03/22/95 C=97.830 +.190 O=.000 H=97.830 L=97.830

103.000
100.000
97.000

M   A   M   J   J   A   S   O   N

FIGURE 1.13 T-Bonds versus the Dow 20 Bond Index for the period
March 1994 to November 1994. The Dow 20 Bond Index is in a
downtrend, and short-term breakouts to the upside fail in the T-Bond
market.

that are convertible to stock. This property also makes the Dow 20 Bond
Index a very good stock market timing tool.

Copper is inversely correlated to T-Bonds, as shown in Figure 1.14.
The chart shows that copper bottomed in late 1993, just as the T-Bond
market topped. The copper–T-Bond relationship is very stable and reliable; in fact, copper is a more reliable measure of economic activity than
the CRB index.

Many other markets have an effect on T-Bonds. One of the most important markets is the lumber market. Lumber is another measure of the
strength of the economy. Figure 1.15 shows how T-Bonds have an inverse
relationship to lumber and how lumber is predictive of T-Bonds.

Crude oil prices, another measure of inflation, are inversely correlated
to both T-Bonds and the Dollar index. The inverse correlation of crude oil
and T-Bonds is depicted in Figure 1.16.

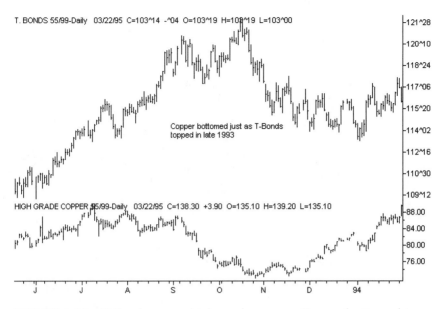

FIGURE 1.14 T-Bonds versus high-grade copper. Copper bottomed in late 1993 just as T-Bonds topped.

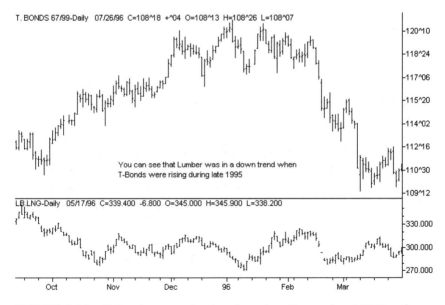

FIGURE 1.15 T-Bonds versus lumber from late September 1995 to the end of March 1996. Lumber was in a downtrend during late 1995 while T-Bonds were rising.

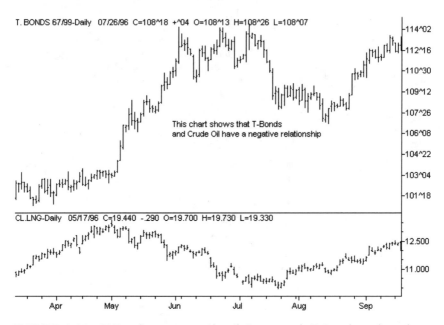

FIGURE 1.16   T-Bonds versus crude oil. In general, T-Bonds and crude oil have a negative relationship.

Many other markets are predictive of T-Bonds. For example, many of the S&P500 stock groups have strong positive or negative correlation to T-Bond prices. Some of these groups and their relationships are shown in Table 1.1.

We will now discuss the Dollar, which is normally negatively correlated with the CRB and gold. Figure 1.17 shows that the breakout in gold in early 1993 led to a double top in the Dollar. Later, when gold and the CRB stabilized at higher levels, the Dollar had a major decline, as shown in Figure 1.17.

Let's now look at foreign currencies. The Deutsche Mark (D-Mark) was in a major downtrend during 1988 and 1989 and so was Comex gold. The D-Mark and gold broke out of the downtrend at the same time, as shown in Figure 1.18.

Another intermarket that has a major effect on the currencies is T-Bonds. In the December 1993 issue of *Formula Research,* Nelson Free-burg discussed the link between T-Bonds and the currencies. T-Bonds and

TABLE 1.1 T-BONDS VERSUS VARIOUS INTERMARKETS.

Stock Group	Relationship to T-Bonds
S&P500 Chemical Group	Negative
S&P500 Aluminum Index	Negative
S&P500 Group Steel	Negative
S&P500 Oil Composite	Negative
S&P500 Saving and Loans	Positive
S&P500 Life Insurance	Positive

foreign currencies are positively correlated. On a longer-term basis, this relationship makes sense. When interest rates drop, Dollar-based assets become less attractive to investors and speculators. Foreign currencies gain a competitive edge, and the Dollar begins to weaken. Freeburg's research has also shown that the link between T-Bonds and foreign currencies is

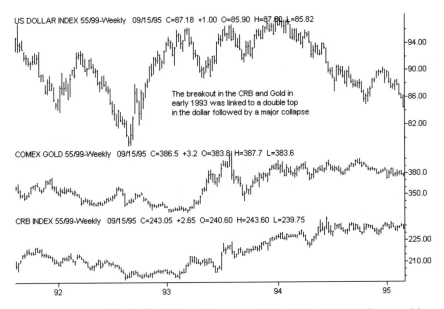

FIGURE 1.17 The Dollar index, Comex gold, and the CRB index weekly from mid-1992 to early 1995. The breakout in the CRB and gold in early 1995 was linked to a double top and then a collapse in the Dollar.

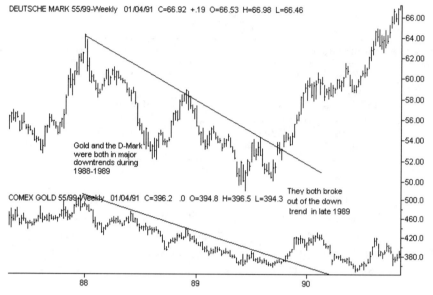

DEUTSCHE MARK 55/99-Weekly 01/04/91 C=66.92 +.19 O=66.53 H=66.98 L=66.46

Gold and the D-Mark
were both in major
downtrends during
1988-1989

COMEX GOLD 55/99-Weekly 01/04/91 C=396.2 .0 O=394.8 H=396.5 L=394.3

They both broke
out of the down
trend in late 1989

FIGURE 1.18   The weekly chart of the D-Mark versus Comex gold for the period early 1988 to late 1990. Both the D-Mark and gold were in a downtrend that was broken in late 1989.

stronger than the link between T-Bills or Eurodollars and currencies. Figure 1.19 shows the link between the Yen and T-Bonds.

Our next subject is the precious metals—gold, silver, and platinum. Figure 1.20 shows that, on a weekly basis, gold, silver, and platinum move together, and silver and platinum usually turn a few days before gold at major turning points.

Let's now see how the gold stocks can be used to predict gold prices. The XAU (Philadelphia gold and silver index) usually leads gold at major turning points. Figure 1.21 shows that the gold stocks bottomed about three months before gold did. The gold stocks also had a bigger percentage of increase because the gold stocks are leveraged. For example, if XYZ Mines has a production cost of $330.00 per ounce and gold is selling for $350.00, then XYZ will make $20.00 an ounce. If gold rises to $370.00 an ounce, XYZ has doubled its profits.

Figure 1.22 shows that the double top in gold stocks contributed to the breakdown in gold.

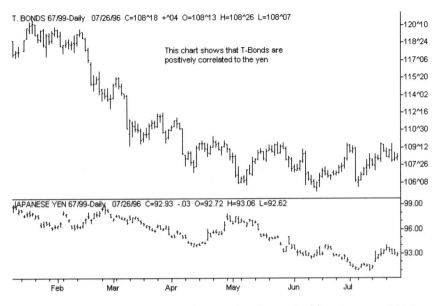

FIGURE 1.19 T-Bonds versus the Yen for the period late January 1996 to late July 1996. T-Bonds and the Yen are positively correlated.

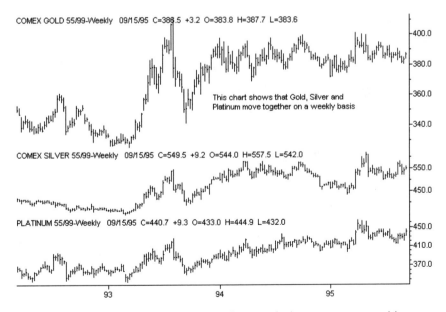

FIGURE 1.20 Comex gold, Comex silver, and platinum on a weekly basis for the period early 1993 to late 1995. The three metals move together.

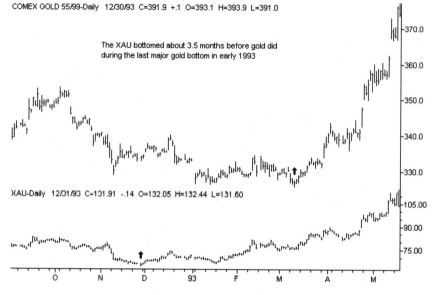

FIGURE 1.21 Comex gold versus the XAU index for the period September 1992 to May 1993. The XAU bottomed 3.5 months before gold in early 1993.

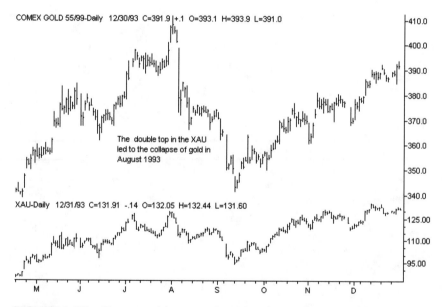

FIGURE 1.22 Comex gold versus the XAU during the period May 1993 to December 1993. A double top in the XAU led to the collapse of gold in August 1993.

Turning now to crude oil, Figure 1.23 shows that crude is negatively correlated to the Dollar. Notice that the rally in the Dollar during late 1993 was linked to the collapse of crude oil down to its lows around $14.00 a barrel.

When the Dollar collapsed during early 1994, it caused crude to rally to over $20.00. When the dollar stabilized, crude prices dropped, as shown in Figure 1.24.

We will now examine the link between oil stocks and crude oil. As Figure 1.25 shows, the XOI (Philadelphia oil stock index) turns either with or a few days ahead of crude oil.

Figure 1.26 shows that the XOI link to crude can disappear. The XOI rose as part of a bull move in the general market during 1995. When the dollar bottomed and began to stabilize, crude collapsed even though the XOI was rallying.

Now that you have a basic understanding of intermarket relationships for various markets, let's apply it to developing subcomponents for mechanical trading systems. Most intermarket relationships between the

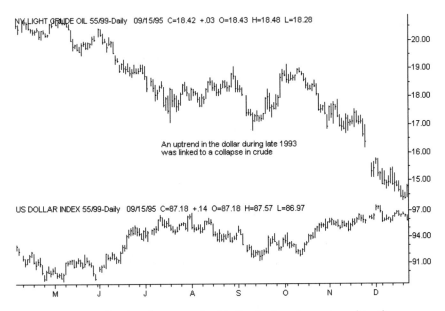

FIGURE 1.23   Crude oil versus the Dollar index. An uptrend in the Dollar during late 1993 was linked to a collapse in crude.

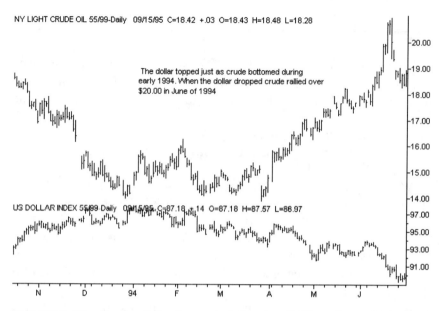

FIGURE 1.24   Crude oil for the period October 1993 to June 1994. As the dollar topped, crude began to bottom and then rallied to over $20 a barrel in June 1994.

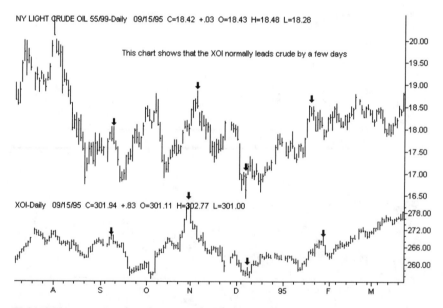

FIGURE 1.25   Crude oil versus the XOI from late July 1994 to March 1995. The XOI normally leads turns in the crude oil market.

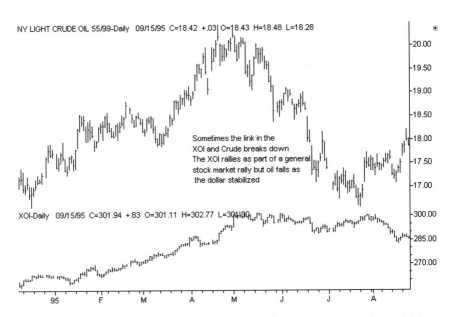

NY LIGHT CRUDE OIL 55/99-Daily 09/15/95 C=18.42 +.03| O=18.43 H=18.48 L=18.28

Sometimes the link in the
XOI and Crude breaks down
The XOI rallies as part of a general
stock market rally but oil falls as
the dollar stabilized

XOI-Daily 09/15/95 C=301.94 +.83 O=301.11 H=302.77 L=304.00

FIGURE 1.26   Crude oil versus the XOI for the period December 1994 to August 1995. Sometimes the link between crude and the XOI can break down. Here, the XOI decoupled from oil as part of a stock market rally.

market you are trading (Traded Market) and another commodity (X) can be classified as shown in Table 1.2.

Having gained an understanding of the theory behind how different markets may interact, let's use these interactions to develop trading methodologies that give us an edge.

USING INTERMARKET ANALYSIS TO DEVELOP FILTERS AND SYSTEMS

The S&P500 futures contract rose about 410.55 points during its 3,434-day trading history as of early February 1996. This represents an average rise of about 0.120 point per day or $60.00 per day on a futures contract. Let's now examine how the S&P500 has done when T-Bonds are above or below their 26-day moving average. The theory is: You should be long

TABLE 1.2   TYPES OF INTERMARKET RELATIONSHIPS.

Event	Action
X is in an uptrend	Buy Traded Market
X is in a downtrend	Sell Traded Market
X is in an uptrend	Sell Traded Market
X is in a downtrend	Buy Traded Market
X is up and Traded Market is down	Buy Traded Market
X is down and Traded Market is up	Sell Traded Market
X is down and Traded Market is down	Buy Traded Market
X is up and Traded Market is up	Sell Traded Market
If X/Traded Market > average (X/Traded Market)	Buy Traded Market
If X/Traded Market < average (X/Traded Market)	Sell Traded Market
If X/Traded Market < average (X/Traded Market)	Buy Traded Market
If X/Traded Market > average (X/Traded Market)	Sell Traded Market

X is an intermarket used in your study.

only when you are above the moving average, and be short only when you are below it. We are using the 67/99 type back-adjusted continuous contract supplied by Genesis Financial Data Services, without slippage and commissions. Using these simple rules, you would have been long 2,045 days and short 1,389 days. During this time, the market rose an average of 0.204 point per day when you would have been long, and fell an average of −0.0137 point when you would have been short. This means that you would have outperformed the S&P500 while being in the market only 59 percent of the time. During the other 41 percent of the time, you would have been in a money market earning interest risk-free. By subdividing the market, based on whether T-Bonds were trending up or down, we produced two subsets of days, and their distributions are very different from those of the complete data set.

We can also use the ratio between two markets. As an example, let's look at the ratio of T-Bonds to the S&P500. When this ratio is above its 28-day average, you buy; when it's below, you sell. Once again, this simple method would have outperformed buy and hold. This simple ratio test made 424.00 points on the long side in 1,740 days, or 0.2437 point per day. It also made 47.75 points on the short side in 1,650 days, or −0.028 point per day.

When it was long, the market moved higher 70 percent of the time; when it was short, it moved lower 56 percent of the time.

Let's now look at how we can use the relationship between Eurodollars and the S&P500, employing the ratio of Eurodollars/S&P500. We would have been bullish when the ratio was above its 10-day moving average, and bearish when it was below. When this ratio was above its average, the market rose 457.85 points in only 1,392 days, or 0.3289 point per day. When it was bearish, the market fell 91.35 points in 1,903 days, or −0.048 point per day. You would have outperformed buy and hold by 11.6 percent while being in the market only about 40 percent of the time. When this model is bullish, the market rises 77 percent of the time; when it is bearish, it falls 66 percent of the time.

How can simple intermarket relationships be used to give us a statistical edge in the bond market? Using the Philadelphia Utilities average as an example, we will buy T-Bonds when this average crosses above its moving average and sell when it crosses below. By using these simple rules, a 40-day simple moving average works best. During the period from 1/4/88 to 5/13/96, this simple model produced $72,225.00 on 133 trades—an average trade of $543.05, after $50.00 slippage and commissions. The drawdown was high (almost −$15,000.00), but it does show that this data series is predictive of T-Bonds.

Let's now discuss trading crude oil. We showed earlier that crude oil is inversely correlated to the Dollar. How can we use this information to help predict crude oil? We will buy crude when the Dollar is below its moving average and sell it when it is above. We tested parameters for this moving average between 10 and 50, in steps of 2. We will use a continuous backadjusted contract for our analysis.

All but four of these parameters were profitable on both sides of the market. Over three-fourths of them made more than $40,000.00. The best combination, based on both performance and robustness, was a 40-day moving average.

Table 1.3 shows the results using a 40-day moving average for the period from 11/20/85 to 5/17/96, with $50.00 deducted for slippage and commissions.

USING INTERMARKET DIVERGENCE TO TRADE THE S&P500

Divergence is a valuable concept in developing trading systems. Combining divergence and intermarket analysis, we define *intermarket divergence* as the traded market moving in an opposite direction to what was

TABLE 1.3   SIMPLE CRUDE/DOLLAR SYSTEM.

Net profit	$56,421.00
Profit long	$42,200.00
Profit short	$4,221.00
Win%	49
Average trade	$316.97
Drawdown	-$11,290.00
Profit factor	2.02

Profit factor = Gross profit/Gross losses.

expected. If we trade the S&P500, for example, T-Bonds rising and the S&P500 falling would be divergence. On the other hand, if we trade T-Bonds, gold rising and T-Bonds rising would also be defined as divergence because these two markets should be negatively correlated.

Using an add-in we developed for both SuperCharts™ and Trade-Station™, we were able to easily test intermarket divergence as a method that would yield a statistical edge.

We tested two different types of intermarket divergence. The first is a simple momentum of both the intermarket and the market being traded. The second compares the current prices of both the intermarket and the traded market to their respective moving averages.

Let's now analyze how divergence between T-Bonds and the S&P500 can be used to build trading systems for the S&P500. We will optimize across the complete data set in order to simplify our examples. Normally, when these types of systems are developed, there are at least two sets of data. One is used for developing parameters and the second is used to test them on new data. We used backadjusted continuous contracts for the period from 4/21/82 to 2/7/96. During the data period used, buy and hold was about $193,000.00.

Let's first analyze how divergence between the S&P500 and T-Bonds can give an edge for forecasting the S&P500. Table 1.4 shows the top four overall moving average lengths (MALen) relative to prices used for developing divergence patterns between the S&P500 and T-Bonds, with $50.00 deducted for slippage and commissions.

Table 1.4 shows that simple intermarket divergence is a powerful concept for developing a trading system for the S&P500.

When we used our tool for TradeStation and SuperCharts to analyze the effect of T-Bonds, T-Bills, and Eurodollars on longer-term movements in

TABLE 1.4   S&P500/T-BOND DIVERGENCE MODEL POSITION TRADING.

MALen S&P500	MALen T-Bonds	Net Profit	Long Profit	Short Profit	Drawdown	Trades	Win%
16	26	$348,175.00	$267,225.00	$80,950.00	−$28,525.00	130	68%
12	30	344,675.00	265,475.00	79,200.00	−26,125.00	124	69
12	26	341,275.00	263,775.00	77,500.00	−26,125.00	130	68
14	26	333,975.00	260,100.00	73,825.00	−31,675.00	130	68

the S&P500, we discovered some very valuable relationships. First, among all of the markets we have used as intermarkets to predict the S&P500, T-Bond futures are the best for developing systems that hold overnight positions. We also found that using the moving average rather than the price momentum between the two markets works better for these longer-term systems. Our results were very robust, and similar sets of parameters gave us very similar results.

For longer holding periods, T-Bonds are the most predictive of the S&P500. Let's analyze the effect of T-Bonds, T-Bills, or Eurodollars on predicting whether the S&P500 will close higher or lower than its opening average.

This is the same period we used earlier, so once again buy and hold is about $193,000.00. Let's look at our results, with $50.00 deducted for slippage and commissions.

Our research showed that Eurodollars are better than T-Bonds for predicting price movements on an open-to-close basis. We also found that using simple differences in our divergence patterns, rather than prices above or below a moving average, worked better for this type of short-term trading. Table 1.5 examines the best overall sets of parameters, with $50.00 deducted for slippage and commissions, over the period from 4/21/82 to 2/7/96. In the table, LenTr is the period used in the momentum for the S&P500, and LenInt is the period used in the momentum for intermarket analysis.

The best two sets of parameters, one on the long side and one on the short side, used the difference between a price and its moving average. T-Bills produced the best profit on the long side, and T-Bonds, the best profit on the short side. The best long-and-short combination is as follows,

**TABLE 1.5   S&P500 AND INTERMARKET
DIVERGENCE OPEN TO CLOSE.**

Intermarket	LenTr	LenInt	Net Profit	Long Profit	Short Profit	Drawdown	Trades	Win%
Eurodollars	8	12	$133,710.00	$108,500.00	$25,210.00	−$20,775.00	1,337	54%
Eurodollars	8	8	132,810.00	102,600.00	30,219.00	−22,900.00	1,306	54
Eurodollars	10	12	131,160.00	117,875.00	13,285.00	−22,825.00	1,322	54
T-Bills	8	8	130,660.00	111,900.00	18,760.00	−26,175.00	1,400	54
Eurodollars	12	8	129,635.00	124,425.00	5,210.00	−27,675.00	1,370	54

where LenTr is the length of the moving average for the S&P500, and LenInt is the length of the moving average of the intermarket:

Best long:

Intermarket	LenTr	LenInt	Long Profit	Drawdown	Trades	Win%
T-Bills	18	10	$135,675.00	−$20,000.00	667	56%

Best short:

Intermarket	LenTr	LenInt	Short Profit	Drawdown	Trades	Win%
T-Bonds	2	8	$39,435.00	−$44,300.00	821	52%

PREDICTING T-BONDS WITH INTERMARKET DIVERGENCE

Let's now use divergence between Eurodollars and the T-Bonds for predicting T-Bonds. T-Bonds and Eurodollars are positively correlated, and divergence between them can be used to develop either trading filters or a trading system. We will trade T-Bonds using these rules:

1. If T-Bonds close below average (T-Bond close,LenTB) and Eurodollars close above average (Eurodollar close,LenEuro), then buy at open.

2. If T-Bonds close above average (T-Bond close,LenTB) and Eurodollars close below average (Eurodollar close,LenEuro), then sell at open.

We tested this basic relationship using different lengths of LenTB and LenEuro for the period from 1/2/86 to 2/7/96. Our research indicated that divergence between Eurodollars and T-Bonds normally resolved itself in the direction of the Eurodollar market. We tested over 500 different combinations of moving average lengths and, based on both profit and stability, we found that a Eurodollar length of 32 and a T-Bond length of 24 worked best. The results for these parameters, with $50.00 allowed for slippage and commissions, are shown in Table 1.6.

Besides the relationship between Eurodollars and T-Bonds, many other commodities are predictive of T-Bonds. We tested over 4,000 combinations of divergence using crude oil, lumber, XAU, gold, and copper. Because all of these commodities or indexes have a negative correlation to T-Bonds, we would define divergence as the commodities moving in the same direction; that is, if T-Bonds were rising and so was the XAU, that pattern would be defined as divergence and we would expect T-Bonds to fall shortly.

Our tests showed that using a price relative to a moving average produces the best results for systems that hold overnight positions. We also found that the XAU is the most predictive of these five markets. For example, 39 of the top 40 most profitable combinations used the XAU. The only non-XAU combinations of parameters were sets of parameters using copper. The best overall set of parameters using copper used an 8-day moving average for T-Bonds and a 10-day moving average for copper. One of the best sets of parameters used the XAU and was chosen based on both profitability and robustness. Data were: T-Bond moving average length = 6; XAU moving average length = 34.

Our results during the period from 1/1/86 to 3/18/96, with $50.00 allowed for slippage and commissions, are shown in Table 1.7.

TABLE 1.6   INTERMARKET DIVERGENCE SYSTEM T-BONDS/EURODOLLARS.

Net profit	$63,593.75
Profit long	$55,431.25
Profit short	$8,275.00
Win%	59
Average trade	$1,447.87
Drawdown	−$13,331.25
Profit factor	2.57

TABLE 1.7   INTERMARKET DIVERGENCE
T-BONDS/XAU.

Net profit	$101,250.00
Profit long	$74,250.00
Profit short	$27,000.00
Trades	110
Win%	66
Average trade	$920.45
Drawdown	-$16,793.75

These results are not good enough for stand-alone trading, but they make a great indicator to give you an edge.

Another nontradable but very interesting set of parameters uses a 2-day moving average for both T-Bonds and the XAU index. This combination made $95,668.75 during our development-and-testing period and won 61 percent of its trades. What makes it interesting is that it trades once a week. The drawdown is high (over $35,000.00), but this is a good short-term directional filter. Our research shows that, based on the divergence found, lumber is the next most predictive market after the XAU, and gold is a distant third. Crude oil was the least predictive of all of the markets studied.

We also tested the divergence between the CRB cash and the CRB futures and found that the CRB futures have been more predictive of T-Bonds. Using a simple model that was bullish when T-Bonds and the CRB were below their moving average, and bearish when T-Bonds and the CRB were above their moving average, we found that using 10 days for the moving average of T-Bonds and 16 days for the moving average of the CRB futures produced both profitable and stable results. This combination produced over $92,000.00 in net profit from 1/12/86 to 3/18/96 while winning 67 percent of its trades. The maximum drawdown was about -$13,000.00. These divergence models based on the CRB performed badly in 1989, 1993, and 1994, and very well in the other years.

Earlier in this chapter, we saw how the Philadelphia electrical utility average was predictive of T-Bonds (see Figure 1.12). Let's now see how using intermarket divergence between this average and T-Bonds can produce great results for trading T-Bonds. We optimized the period from 6/1/87 to 6/18/96 for both price difference and price, relative to a

TABLE 1.8   INTERMARKET DIVERGENCE T-BONDS/UTY.

Net profit	$98,937.50
Trades	90
Win%	64
Average trade	$1,099.31
Maximum drawdown	−$9,506.25
Profit factor	3.08

moving average from 2 to 30 in steps of 2. Over 25 percent of these combinations generated more than $10,000.00 a year; 165 of them produced 65 percent or more winning trades. On the basis of our analysis for both profitability and robustness, we selected a set of parameters that used price relative to a moving average. The moving average used an 8-day period for T-Bonds and a 24-day period for the UTY index. This was not the most profitable set of parameters—in fact, it was seventh on our list. Four other sets of parameters produced more than $100,000.00 during this period. Table 1.8 shows the results during the analysis period for the selected set of parameters.

PREDICTING GOLD USING INTERMARKET ANALYSIS

Let's now discuss the gold market. Using divergence, we will examine the relationship between gold and both the XAU and the D-Mark. The XAU is an index of American gold mining stocks and is positively correlated to gold, as is the D-Mark. We begin by testing the following relationship:

1. XAU up, gold down, D-Mark up = buy gold.
2. XAU down, gold up, D-Mark down = sell gold.

We defined *up* and *down* as a given market's being above or below its *N*-day exponential moving average (EMA). Our test rules have been tested in the period from 1/3/84 to 2/8/96 using backadjusted continuous contract data. The rules are:

1. If XAU is greater than XAverage (XAU,Len1), gold is less than XAverage (Gold,Len2), and the D-Mark is greater than XAverage (D-Mark,Len3), then buy at open.

2. If XAU is less than XAverage (XAU,Len1), gold is greater than XAverage (Gold,Len2), and the D-Mark is less than XAverage (D-Mark,Len3), then sell at open.

We tested these rules using different values for Len1, Len2, and Len3 over the period from 1/3/84 to 2/8/96. This period was selected because 1/3/84 was the starting point for the XAU Index. We found that the intermarket relationship among these three data series was very stable and profitable during the selected time period.

We tested Len1 and Len2 from 10- to 20-day periods, and Len3 from 16- to 24-day periods. We found that all 121 tests we ran were profitable. On the long side, 106 of them made money, and all of them made money on the short side. About half of them made more than $40,000.00 in net profit, and almost 75 percent of them had drawdowns of less than −$10,000.00. We found that the best parameters were 12, 10, and 20. Using this set of parameters, with $50.00 deducted for slippage and commissions, the results over our test period were as shown in Table 1.9.

USING INTERMARKET DIVERGENCE TO PREDICT CRUDE

Earlier in this chapter we showed how a simple moving average of the Dollar index could be used to predict crude oil (see Figure 1.23). Let's now use divergence between the Dollar and crude oil to trade the crude. We found that using a moving average relative to price-type divergence

TABLE 1.9   RESULTS OF INTERMARKET DIVERGENCE PREDICTING GOLD USING GOLD, XAU, AND D-MARK.

Net profit	$60,360.00 + $1,980.00 open
Trades	54 + open
Win%	65
Average trade	$1,117.78
Drawdown	−$6,910.00
Profit factor	4.54

performed well. This type of divergence model traded much more than our simple moving average model and had a much higher winning percentage. For example, a 12-day moving average for crude oil and an 18-day moving average for the Dollar proved to be a robust pair of parameters that performed very well. The results for this set of parameters for the period from 1/2/86 to 5/17/96, with $50.00 deducted for slippage and commissions, are shown in Table 1.10.

This set of parameters was picked for its profitability and stability. It was not the most profitable set of parameters; for example, a 12-day average for crude and an 8-day average for the Dollar produced over $50,000.00. This relationship between the Dollar and crude was very stable for 78 out of the 90 tests, won more than 60 percent of the trades, and had a positive net profit in every test but one. The net profits of all of the pairs of parameter values cluster between $40,000.00 and $50,000.00; in fact, 30 of them made more than $40,000.00 and 65 of them made more than $30,000.00.

The Dollar index is not the only intermarket that can be used with the concept of divergence to predict crude. The XOI index, an index of oil stocks, is also predictive of crude oil. We use prices related to a moving average as our measure of an uptrend or a downtrend. When the XOI is up and crude is down, then buy crude; when the XOI is down and crude is up, then sell crude. We found that a moving average length of 2 days for crude and 16 days for the XOI produced good results during the period from 11/7/84 to 5/17/96. This combination produced $49,271.00 during this period and had 63 percent winning trades. It is not tradable as a system because the drawdown is much too high (−$19,000.00), but it does show that the XOI is predictive of future oil prices. The XOI is not the

TABLE 1.10   RESULTS OF INTERMARKET DIVERGENCE CRUDE/DOLLAR INDEX.

Net profit	$46,171.00
Profit long	$38,180.00
Profit short	$7,991.00
Trades	134
Win%	68
Average trade	$344.56
Drawdown	−$11,690.00

only index that is predictive. The S&P500 oil-based stock groups are very predictive of the future oil price; in fact, some of these groups are used in systems that we have developed for our clients.

PREDICTING THE YEN WITH T-BONDS

We showed earlier that T-Bonds are positively correlated to the currencies. Let's now see what happens when we use divergence between the Yen and T-Bonds to predict the Yen. They are positively correlated, so we would want to buy the Yen when T-Bonds rise and the Yen falls. Using a 67/99 type for the period from 1/1/80 to 3/18/96, we found that a simple difference worked better at predicting the Yen than prices relative to a moving average. We tested parameter lengths between 12 days and 40 days for both types of divergence and found that all of the top 84 sets of parameters used system difference between prices and not a moving average. On the basis of our analysis, we found that a 34-day difference between both T-Bonds and the Yen produced both profitable and stable results. Our results with this pair of parameters, allowing $50.00 for slippage and commissions, are shown in Table 1.11.

These results are impressive except for the drawdown, which was caused by two large losing trades. One closed in 1989 and the other in 1995. These large losses occurred because this is a stop-and-reverse system and the market did not produce a divergence between the Yen and T-Bonds for 8 months and a little over a year, respectively.

TABLE 1.11   RESULTS OF INTERMARKET DIVERGENCE YEN/T-BONDS.

Net profit	$97,875.00
Profit long	$67,162.50
Profit short	$30,712.50
Win%	71
Average trade	$1,075.55
Drawdown	−$20,312.50

USING INTERMARKET ANALYSIS ON STOCKS

Intermarket analysis is also a valuable tool when you trade some individual stocks. A classic example is the inverse relationship between Eastman Kodak and silver, shown in Figure 1.27. The relationship is based on Kodak's use of silver for processing film.

Let's now use the concept of intermarket divergence to try to predict the future direction of Kodak stock. Because Kodak and silver are negatively correlated, we can develop a system for trading Kodak using divergence between silver and Kodak. Our rules are as follows:

1. If Kodak **is less than** Kodak [Len1] and silver **is less than** silver [Len2], then buy at open.

2. If Kodak **is more than** Kodak [Len1] and silver **is more than** silver [Len2], then sell at open.

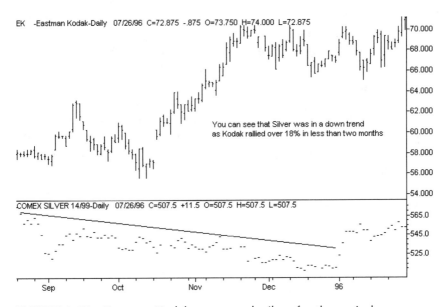

FIGURE 1.27   Eastman Kodak versus cash silver for the period September 1995 to January 1996. As silver was in a downtrend, Kodak rallied.

We tested 256 different sets of parameters for Len1 and Len2. Of these, all of the parameters between 10 days and 40 days were profitable during the period from 7/29/80 to 4/22/94. We started in 1980 because the relationship between silver and Kodak was upset during the Hunt Crisis* of the late 1970s. During this time, silver rose to over $50.00 an ounce.

The results of our tests were very stable, and we found that 18 days and 48 days were the best parameters for Len1 and Len2. During our testing of 256 sets of parameters in this range, we found that all of them outperformed buy and hold on this stock. Another impressive fact was that this divergence pattern had between 63 percent and 78 percent winning trades across all 256 combinations. The number of trades varied from 75 to 237 during this 14-year period, using different sets of parameters.

The results for the selected set of parameters, without any allowance for slippage and commission, are shown in Table 1.12. Amounts are for only one share of stock.

Many life insurance companies and financial institutions are positively correlated to interest rates; as an example, let's look at U.S. Life Corporation and T-Bonds. Using divergence measured by a 22-day moving average for U.S. Life and a 28-day moving average for T-Bonds produced good results. This combination gained more than $31.00 a share and rose 73 percent of the time when the market was set up for bullish divergence.

In another example, we will use T-Bond futures to predict Pegasus gold. Our research has shown that Pegasus gold has a positive correlation to T-Bonds. This might sound odd, but it does make some sense. Gold stocks normally lead gold prices at major turning points. For example, the biggest move in the XAU was produced when T-Bond futures rose to all-time highs during 1993. Lower interest rates are viewed as a stimulus to the economy. This will lead to a rise in gold prices. We used a 12-day moving average for Pegasus and a 30-day moving average for T-Bonds. During the period from 4/17/86 to 3/8/96, this stock rose from $6.25 to $15.00; using our selected parameters would have produced a profit of $51.72 per share while winning 67 percent of its trades. Profits, equally divided on the long and short sides, represented over 80 percent per year before slippage and commissions.

---

* During the late 1970s, the Hunt family tried to corner the silver market. The government sold silver and caused a collapse from $50 an ounce to less than $4.

**TABLE 1.12   RESULTS OF INTERMARKET
DIVERGENCE KODAK/SILVER.**

Net profit	$117.87
Profit long	$64.91
Profit short	$52.97
Win%	70
Average trade	$0.74
Drawdown	−$16.56

These impressive results show that intermarket analysis is powerful even when trading certain individual stocks.

The above examples show that intermarket analysis does have predictive value. We optimized some of the parameters used in the examples. If we were developing real trading systems, we would have split our data into three sets: (1) a development set, (2) a testing set, and (3) an out-of-sample set. We would have optimized on the development set, and then tested on the testing and out-of-sample sets. Furthermore, we would not have selected only the most profitable sets of parameters. The parameters selected should offer both good returns and neighboring sets of parameters that produce similar results. The flatter the profit surface, the more likely the system will be robust. These intermarket relationships are so strong that even the most profitable set of parameters is surrounded by other very profitable pairs. For this reason, the parameters selected should be reasonably robust and should hold up well into the future. These intermarket relationships will reappear in later chapters, when we develop trading systems using advanced technologies such as neural networks and genetic algorithms.

2
Seasonal Trading

Many commodities, and even some individual stocks or stock groups, have recurring fundamental factors that affect their prices. These forces can be seen by analyzing a market by day of week, day of month, or day of year. This is called *seasonal trading*.

TYPES OF FUNDAMENTAL FORCES

Three types of fundamental forces cause seasonal trading patterns. The first type is based on events that have fixed or relatively fixed dates. Examples are: The pollination of corn in late June and early July, and the filing of federal tax returns on April 15.

Many seasonal forces are related to events for which the date could change—for example, the government's release of the current unemployment numbers. If these dates remain fairly constant for many years, then seasonal effects can be identified. If these dates change slightly, it may look as if the seasonal pattern has changed when, in actuality, the seasonal bias relative to the reports has not changed. For example, the Thursday before the monthly unemployment number is scheduled to be announced has a downward bias in the T-Bond market.

The third type of fundamental forces is based on human psychological factors. For example, in the stock market, Mondays have an upward bias because many traders exit their positions on the preceding Friday and reenter them on Monday. This Monday bias has existed at least since the

42

1970s, but it has been magnified since the 1987 Black Monday crash. For example, since the 1987 crash, Mondays have had an upward bias of over .60 point per trade, or about $300.00, on a futures contract on an open-to-close basis. Before the crash, the bias was about $138.00 per trade. The crash magnified the fear of hold positions over a weekend. This fear enhanced the upward bias on Mondays and changed the psychology of the market.

CALCULATING SEASONAL EFFECTS

Now that we understand why seasonal trading works, let's discuss different ways of calculating these measures.

The simplest method is to use price changes—different prices from open to close or from close to close. This type of seasonal analysis works very well for day-of-week and day-of-month analyses. When calculating seasonality on a yearly basis, price changes or several other methods can be used to capture the effects of these recurring fundamental forces.

One alternate method is to calculate the seasonal effect using a de-trended version of the data. The simplest way to detrend a price series is to subtract the current price from a longer-term moving average. Another popular method for calculating seasonality is to standardize the data on a contract-by-contract or year-by-year basis—for example, by identifying the highest or lowest price on each contract or year and using it to create a scaled price.

MEASURING SEASONAL FORCES

Let's first discuss measuring these seasonal forces based on the day of the week. Day-of-week forces can be measured in several ways. The first way is to measure the change on an open-to-close or a close-to-close basis—for example, measure the close-to-open change every Monday on the S&P500. Another, even more powerful, variation is to compare only one day of the week throughout a month—Mondays in December, for example. As we will see later, this type of analysis can produce amazing results.

Using another form of day-of-week analysis, you would map where the high and low for a given week will occur. This information can help you pinpoint when, during a given week, you should take a position historically. On a shorter-term basis, it can tell you how strong the bear or bull market is. In bull markets, the high occurs later in the week; in bear markets, the high is earlier in the week.

The final form of day-of-week analysis is conditional day-of-week analysis. Buying or selling is done on a given day of the week, based on some condition—for example, buy on Tuesday when Monday was a down day. This type of analysis can produce simple and profitable trading patterns.

Larry Williams, a legendary trader, developed the concept of trading day-of-month analysis. This concept is very powerful for discovering hidden biases in the markets. There are two major ways to use this type of analysis: (1) on an open-to-close or close-to-close basis, and (2) more often, by buying or selling on a given trading day of the month, and holding for N days. When a holding period is used, this type of analysis can produce tradable systems by just adding money management stops.

Let's now discuss three methods for calculating seasonality on a yearly basis. The first method originated in the work of Moore Research, which calculates seasonality on a contract-by-contract basis, using a calendar day of the year. Moore Research converts prices into a percentage of yearly range and then projects this information to calculate the seasonal.

The second method is the work of Sheldon Knight, who developed a seasonal index he calls the K Data Time Line. The calculation involves breaking down each year according to the occurrences on a given day of the week in a given month. The steps for calculating the K Data Time Line are shown in Table 2.1.

TABLE 2.1   CALCULATING THE K DATA TIME LINE.

1. Identify the day-of-week number and the month number for each day to be plotted—for example, the first Monday of May.
2. Find the 5-year price changes in the Dollar for that day, in each of the years identified.
3. Add the 5-year average price change for that day to the previous day's time line value. The full-year time line value starts at zero.
4. Trade by selecting the tops and bottoms of the time line for your entries and exits. Buy the bottoms of the time line and sell the tops.

The final method is one that I use in my seasonal work. I call it the Ruggiero/Barna Seasonal Index. This index is part of a product we call the Universal Seasonal, a TradeStation or SuperCharts add-in that automatically calculates many different measures of seasonality if the historical data are available. This tool will work on all commodities and even on individual stocks.

THE RUGGIERO/BARNA SEASONAL INDEX

The Ruggiero/Barna Seasonal Index was developed by myself and Michael Barna. The calculations for this index are shown in Table 2.2.

I would like to make one point about the Ruggiero/Barna Seasonal Index: It is calculated rolling forward. This means that all resulting trades are not based on hindsight. Past data are used only to calculate the seasonal index for tomorrow's trading. This allows development of a more realistic historical backtest on a seasonal trading strategy.

Besides the Ruggiero/Barna Seasonal Index, you can use the raw average returns, the percent up or down, and correlation analysis to develop trading strategies. The Ruggiero/Barna index can be calculated either by using the complete data set or by using an *N*-year window.

STATIC AND DYNAMIC SEASONAL TRADING

A seasonal trade can be calculated using the complete day set, some point in the past, or a rolling window of data. This is true for day-of-week,

TABLE 2.2   CALCULATING THE RUGGIERO/BARNA SEASONAL INDEX.

1. Develop your seasonal and update it as you walk forward in the data.
2. For each trading day of the year, record the next *N*-day returns and what percentage of time the market moved up (positive returns) and down (negative returns).
3. Multiply this 5-day return by the proper percentage.
4. Scale the numbers calculated in step 3 between −1 and 1 over the whole trading year. This is the output value of the Ruggiero/Barna Seasonal Index.

day-of-month, and day-of-year seasonals. The question is: Which method is the best? The answer depends on the commodity being analyzed. For example, in markets with fixed fundamentals, the more data used and the longer they are used, the greater the reliability of the seasonal. If we were analyzing corn, we would want to go back, using as much data as possible. On the other hand, if we were doing seasonal research on the bond market, we would not want to use any day before January 1, 1986, because, prior to 1986, the dynamics of the bond market were different.

Another important issue in calculating seasonality is basing results on in-sample trades versus walk forward testing. For example, if we say a given seasonal is 80 percent accurate over the past 15 years, based on the results of the seasonal trades over the past 15 years, that is an in-sample result. If we use one day in the past 15 years to calculate a seasonal and then only take trades in the future using a buy and sell date calculated on past data, and roll the window forward every day, this is walk forward testing. More realistic results may be possible. For example, in 1985, you might not have had a seasonal bias on a given day, but, years later, that day of the year is included in a given walk forward seasonal pattern. Suppose you calculate the seasonal walking forward using only data from 1970 to 1985. You trade in 1986 and then move the window up every year or so. In 1987, you would use data including 1986 to calculate the seasonal, and you could produce a realistic seasonal model that can be used to trade.

JUDGING THE RELIABILITY OF A SEASONAL PATTERN

One of the main criticisms of seasonal trading is that it is only curve fitting and is not based on any real fundamental influence in the market. This problem is more pronounced in trading by day of year because, often, only 10 to 20 cases are available for calculating a seasonal pattern. Because of this issue, it is important to be able to judge whether a seasonal pattern will hold up in the future. Most will not. There is no sure way to know, but reliable seasonals do have similar characteristics. First, the returns of the seasonal pattern must be significantly above the average-day bias over the same period; that is, if the seasonal pattern is based on the S&P500, we might want $200.00 a day on the long side but $100.00 could be acceptable on the short side because the S&P500 has an upward bias. Second, one trade should not account for too large a percentage of the profits.

In a seasonal pattern, a statistically significant percentage of the returns should follow the direction of the bias. For example, in a bullish seasonal, the goal is to analyze the percentage of the time when the market rises during the holding period.

In evaluating the percentage bias, the number of cases is a very important link to the significance of the seasonal pattern. For example, on a day-of-week pattern with hundreds of trades, 57 percent or 58 percent is acceptable. On a day-of-year pattern with only 10 cases, we would want to see 80 percent or better.

Another important issue arises when evaluating a seasonal: Does the seasonal bias make sense? For example, suppose corn falls after the danger of crop damage from drought passes, or T-Bonds fall because of a quarterly refunding. If the seasonal pattern makes sense, it is more likely to work in the future.

COUNTERSEASONAL TRADING

Seasonal trades do not always work. The question is: How can you tell whether a seasonal is going to fail and what should you do when it does? Seasonal trading fails when more important fundamental forces drive a market. In 1995, the S&P500 did not have a correction in September or October because of good fundamentals and falling interest rates. The strength of the market foreshadowed the power moves of the S&P500 during late 1995 and early 1996. In another example of a seasonal failing, corn continued to rise during July 1995, because of the drought damage in the Midwest. There are several ways to see whether a seasonal pattern is working. For example, you can give a seasonal pattern 4 days to work. Or, you can use Pearson's correlation to measure the difference between the actual price movements and the seasonal. This is a very useful measure in developing mechanical seasonal trading systems.

CONDITIONAL SEASONAL TRADING

In conditional seasonal trading, you filter the cases you use in developing your seasonal patterns. For example, you could develop a trading day-of-month seasonal and only include cases when T-Bonds are above their

26-day moving average. Another example of conditional seasonal trading would be developing a day-of-year seasonal for corn but only using years after crop damage in calculating the seasonal. This sounds like a curve fit, but this method has worked well for Moore Research over the years.

OTHER MEASUREMENTS FOR SEASONALITY

The most used measure of seasonality is based on price, but seasonal effects also exist for both volatility and trend. For example, we can measure the average True Range/Close over the next N days based on day of week, month, or year. This measure will give us an idea of future volatility, which is useful for option trading as well as for setting protective stops.

Another useful way to use seasonality is to measure future trends. This can be done using any trend level indicator—for example, ADX or Random Walk Index (RWI). Another good measure is using a simple difference of ADX over the next N days relative to a trading day of month or year. This will tell us historically whether the seasonal effect will cause a trend to get stronger or weaker. This type of information can be used to filter trend-following systems.

Seasonal patterns can also be used to forecast future price movements. An example of this would be to take the current price as a base, and then add to it the future change predicted by the seasonal. Finally, you would apply a correction factor based on the difference of the actual price change over the last few forecasts and the seasonal forecast.

Having discussed the issues involved in seasonal trading, let's now study some examples of using seasonality for trading in several different markets.

What are effects of day of week in several different markets? We will start with the S&P500.

The day-of-week bias in the S&P500 is revealed by measuring the difference between the close and open on a given day of the week during the period from 1/3/83 to 4/12/96, using backadjusted continuous contracts. The results by day of week are shown in Table 2.3. Note that buy and hold during this period is 367.60 points.

Table 2.3 shows that you can outperform buy and hold simply by buying on Mondays and Wednesdays. We can also see that Fridays have a significant downward bias.

TABLE 2.3   DAY OF WEEK AND S&P500.

Day of Week	Net Change (Points)	Average Change (Points)	Percent of Buy and Hold
Monday	282.69	.43	77.1%
Tuesday	8.45	.01	2.2
Wednesday	168.60	.25	45.8
Thursday	42.35	.06	6.6
Friday	−117.26	−.18	−31.9

Other markets—for example, T-Bonds—also have strong day-of-week effects. During the period from 1/1/86 to 4/12/86, the T-Bond market closed .07 point higher than the open on Tuesdays and −.02 point lower on Thursdays. The day-of-week effect on the other days of the week was not statistically significant. The downward bias on Thursdays is caused by the fact that most traders do not want to be long T-Bonds before a major report, and many major reports, such as the monthly unemployment count, are released on Friday mornings just after the open. For this reason, many traders sell bonds on Thursdays. This downward bias is also significant because T-Bonds have had an upward bias over the past ten years.

Besides the financial markets, other markets are influenced by strong day-of-week effects. For example, since 1986, Thursday has been the most bullish day to trade silver. Because silver can be used as a measure of economic strength, it would make sense that silver should have an upward bias on days when T-Bonds have a downward bias.

Even some of the soft commodities have a day-of-week bias; for example, coffee is most bullish on an open-to-close bias on Thursdays, and it has been slightly bearish on Mondays since January 1, 1980. Believe it or not, in the period from 1/1/80 to 4/12/96, if we do not deduct slippage and commissions, coffee has risen by $76,211.25 per contract by buying at the Thursday open and exiting on the close.

BEST LONG AND SHORT DAYS OF WEEK IN MONTH

The day-of-week effect is not the same for every month; in fact, different days of the week can become bullish or bearish, depending on the month of the year. Let's now examine how the month affects the day-of-week analysis on an open-to-close basis. We analyzed several commodities, starting at various dates and ending on April 12, 1996. We did not deduct slippage and commission because we wanted to judge the bias of each market based on a given day of the week in a particular month. Table 2.4 shows our results.

Now that we have shown the effects of simple day-of-week analysis, let's consider some examples of conditional day-of-week analysis, to learn how conditional day-of-week analysis works.

One type of conditional day-of-week analysis reviews a market by day of week and measures what the market has done over the past five days. To illustrate, we will analyze the S&P500 in the period from 4/21/82 to 4/23/96, using a continuous backadjusted contract.

Let a 1 mean that a market finishes higher than it opens; −1 means a lower amount, and a zero (0) means we do not care. Using this simple system, with $50.00 deducted for slippage and commissions, we have found some impressive results:

DOW	D1	D2	D3	D4	D5	Position	Net Profit	Average Trade	Win%
Monday	−1	−1	0	0	0	Long	$25,125.00	$405.24	68%
Friday	−1	0	0	0	0	Short	61,470.00	193.91	54

In another type of conditional day-of-week analysis, we would use intermarket analysis in order to filter the day of the week. For example, let's take only Mondays when T-Bonds are above their 26-day moving average. This simple pattern has averaged $249.45 per trade since April 21, 1982,

TABLE 2.4   DAY OF WEEK IN MONTH EFFECTS.

Commodity	Start	Position	Day of Week	Month	Win%	Average Trade	Net Profit
Coffee	1/1/80	Long	Thursday	Sept.	61%	$221.09	$15,255.00
Coffee	1/1/80	Short	Friday	June	70	278.97	19,248.75
T-Bonds	1/1/86	Long	Tuesday	May	66	289.29	10,125.00
T-Bonds	1/1/86	Short	Friday	Mar.	57	290.60	13,658.00
S&P500	1/3/83	Long	Thursday	July	69	427.73	23,525.00
S&P500	1/3/83	Long	Monday	Dec.	65	536.82	29,525.00
S&P500	1/3/83	Short	Thursday	Dec.	63	374.54	20,225.00

with $50.00 deducted for slippage and commissions. This is only a taste of the work you can do using day-of-week analysis.

TRADING DAY-OF-MONTH ANALYSIS

The concept of analyzing the markets based on the trading day of the month was originally developed by Larry Williams, who found that, in many markets, the trading day-of-month effect is so strong that the results are comparable to commercial trading systems.

Let's analyze several different markets on the basis of entering a position on the next open after a given trading day of the month, and exiting on the open a given number of days later. We performed this analysis on the S&P500, T-Bonds, coffee, and crude oil. The results of this analysis are presented without an allowance for slippage and commissions because we wanted to test the bias of each market. Our results from the start date to April 12, 1996 are shown in Table 2.5.

These results are only a sample of the power available through trading day-of-month analysis. Many different markets have an upward or downward bias 60 percent (or more) of the time, based on a trading day of the month plus a given holding period. Another fact we learned from our analysis is that the end-of-month effects in the S&P500 and T-Bonds are magnified when a month has more than 21 trading days; for example, the 22/23 trading day of the month produces great results but too few trades to be reliable.

TABLE 2.5   SEASONAL EFFECT BY TRADING DAY OF MONTH.

Commodity	Start	Position	Trading Day of Month	Hold	Net Profit	Win%	Average Trade
S&P500	4/21/82	Long	17	5	$140,850.00	68%	$1,354.33
S&P500	4/21/82	Short	2	2	47,775.00	55	459.38
T-Bonds	1/1/86	Long	15	8	66,625.00	63	550.00
T-Bonds	1/1/86	Long	15	5	5,306.25	65	441.00
T-Bonds	1/1/86	Short	3	4	27,875.00	56	230.37
Coffee	1/1/80	Long	10	3	71,362.50	64	432.50
Coffee	1/1/80	Short	14	7	70,826.25	62	429.25
Crude	4/21/82	Long	15	7	26,310.00	61	185.28

DAY-OF-YEAR SEASONALITY

Now that we have discussed day of week and month, let's turn to day-of-year analysis. Day-of-year seasonality requires more comprehensive analysis in order to judge the reliability of a given pattern, because many patterns will have only 20 or fewer occurrences.

In addition, many of the seasonal patterns change over time. Figure 2.1 shows both average five-day returns and the percentage of the time the market rose for the S&P500 futures during the period around the crash of 1987, based on a seasonal calculated using data starting on April 21, 1982. The seasonal for October 7, 1987, shows an average gain of 2.10 points and a percentage up of 100 percent. If we had been trading seasonality back in 1987, we would have been long, not short, during this time. Even a seasonal using data starting in 1960 would have yielded a long position in early October 1987.

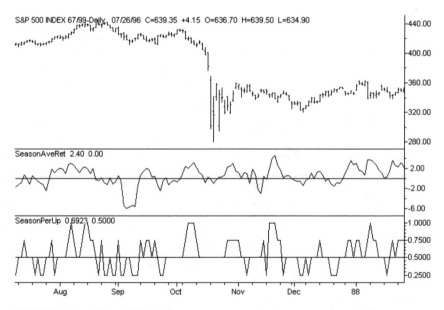

FIGURE 2.1   The S&P500 futures average 5-day returns, and the percentage of the time the market rose over a 5-day period by trading day of year, for the period around the crash of 1987. The data used represent the complete history of the S&P500 futures contract up to 1986.

This revelation should not make you think seasonality does not work, but it should point out that, when evaluating a seasonal, you need to calculate and evaluate in a walk forward manner. Many seasonals are reliable. For example, let's look at the beginning-of-year rally. On January 26, 1988, our seasonal, starting with data on April 21, 1982, shows an average five-day return of 3.14 points and a market rising 75 percent of the time. In 1996, the same seasonal showed an average return of 3.61 points and still a 75 percent accuracy. In 1996, this seasonal made over $7,000.00 in only 5 days.

One of the best ways to judge the reliability of a seasonal pattern is to look over the average returns and the percentage of accuracy over the years. Seasonals that remain constant over the years are more reliable.

USING SEASONALITY IN MECHANICAL TRADING SYSTEMS

Let's now test several methods for evaluating a seasonal mechanically. We will begin by using the S&P500 cash, starting in 1960. We will then wait until we have 2,500 days' data to take a seasonal trade. In our simple experiment, we will view the S&P500 only from the long side. Our goal is to find low-risk buy points for the S&P500. We found in our research that a seasonal pattern must be at least 70 percent reliable. For the S&P500, using a holding period of 8 days and a seasonal return of .03 percent or greater produced the best results for that period. The .03 percent represents about 2 points, based on an S&P500 with a value of $600.00. Finally, we took the seasonal trades only when the S&P500 was below its six-day simple moving average. These rules produced the results shown in Table 2.6.

The table shows that these seasonal trades offer above-average returns for the S&P500. Based on these seasonal patterns, the market rises during the next 8 days almost 70 percent of the time. One of the most important elements in getting these results is the fact that we collect 2,500 days' seasonal information before taking a trade. Having this much data improves the reliability of the seasonal. These seasonal patterns were found using the Universal Seasonal, TradeStation™ and SuperCharts™ and have adjusted themselves over the years. How have these seasonal patterns performed lately? Very well. They have not had a losing trade since October 1992.

TABLE 2.6   S&P500 SEASONAL SYSTEM BASED ON AVERAGE RETURNS OVER .03%.

First trade	3/24/71
Ending date	6/28/96
Buy and hold	571.01
Total points made	270.39
Days in market	1,368
Buy and hold	47.4%
In market	21.67%
Drawdown	−28.90
Win percentage	69%

The Ruggiero/Barna Seasonal Index combines both average returns and percentage of accuracy into a standardized indicator. When we ran this indicator across the same data, we found that the Ruggiero/Barna Seasonal Index can outperform the market based on seasonality. Once again, we waited 2,500 days before taking our first trade. Our data period is the same length as the one used in the previous example, and it started on January 4, 1960. We used a holding period of 5 days and a trigger of −.20 on the Ruggiero/Barna Seasonal Index. We took the seasonal trades only when the S&P500 was below its 10-day moving average. The results using these parameters are shown in Table 2.7.

Table 2.7 shows that, without taking a short position, the Ruggiero/Barna Seasonal Index can outperform buy and hold by over 30 percent

TABLE 2.7   SEASONAL S&P500 SYSTEM RESULTS BASED ON RUGGIERO/BARNA SEASONAL INDEX.

First trade	2/19/71
Ending date	6/28/96
Buy and hold	573.89
Total points made	761.75
Days in market	2,576
Buy and hold	132.73%
In market	40.6%
Drawdown	−44.68
Win percentage	68%

while being in the market about 40 percent of the time. Because the S&P500 has an upward bias, a −.20 value could still represent a market with positive returns over that holding period.

Using all of the data in calculating a seasonal is not always the best solution. My research has shown that this decision depends on the commodity being analyzed. In corn, or other commodities with fixed fundamentals, the more data the better. In commodities like T-Bonds, a moving window will work better. Let's now use a moving window to develop patterns in the T-Bond market. To calculate our seasonal, we used data starting on September 28, 1979. We developed the seasonal by using a walk forward method with various window sizes, holding periods, and trigger levels. We tested seasonality only on the long side, in order to simplify our analysis. We collected 2,000 days' seasonal data before generating our first trade. We found that the best window size was a rolling window of 8 years, with a 6-day holding period and a trigger level above −.20 to generate a buy signal. We filtered our trades by requiring a 6-period momentum to be negative to take a long trade. Our first trade was taken on September 20, 1988. Our data ran to June 28, 1996. The results for these parameters over about 7.75 years of trading, without slippage and commissions, are shown in Table 2.8.

COUNTERSEASONAL TRADING

Many times, the market does not follow its seasonal patterns. Being able to detect an aberration and use it for knowing when to exit a trade, or even for trading against the seasonal, can give you a big advantage. Let's examine 5-day average returns in the T-Bond market, and the correlation between the seasonal returns and the current actual returns. We will use a 15-day Pearson's correlation in our correlation analysis. Figure 2.2

TABLE 2.8   T-BOND RESULTS BASED ON THE RUGGIERO/BARNA SEASONAL INDEX.

Net profit	$57,593.75
Win%	71
Average trade	$282.32
Maximum drawdown	−$7,656.25

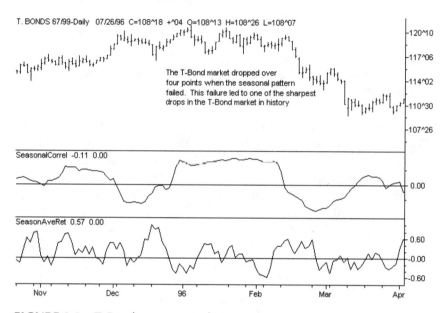

T. BONDS 67/99-Daily 07/26/96 C=108^18 +^04 O=108^13 H=108^26 L=108^07

The T-Bond market dropped over
four points when the seasonal pattern
failed. This failure led to one of the sharpest
drops in the T-Bond market in history

120^10
117^06
114^02
110^30
107^26

SeasonalCorrel -0.11 0.00
0.00

SeasonAveRet 0.57 0.00
0.60
-0.00
-0.60

Nov   Dec   96   Feb   Mar   Apr

FIGURE 2.2   T-Bonds average 5-day return versus trading day of year,
and the correlation of actual market conditions to this seasonal. The
failure of the seasonal rallies in February 1996 led to one of the sharpest
drops in the T-Bond market's history.

shows both 5-day average returns and their correlation to the actual price
action for November 1995 to April 1996.

As shown in Figure 2.2, T-Bonds have positive historical 5-day returns
from late February to mid-March. After that, T-Bonds have near-
zero/negative returns until the end of March, in anticipation of the federal income tax day (April 15). In 1996, during this seasonal strength,
the market decorrelated from its seasonal normal and dropped over 4 full
points in the next 5 days—an example of how a seasonal failure can lead
to explosive moves. This move accelerated during the seasonal flat-to-
lower period during the month of March.

Seasonal trades can be filtered by entering only seasonal trades when
the correlation between the seasonal and the current market conditions is
above a given level or is higher than some number of days ago. This logic
would have protected against several bad seasonal trades in the T-Bond
market in 1996.

In markets that have stronger seasonal influences, such as the corn market, taking the trade in the opposite direction to the seasonal pattern when the seasonal pattern fails can produce great results. Let's test one of the classic seasonal patterns. We will sell corn on the first trading day after June 20 and exit this position on November 1. This seasonal trade has produced using cash corn prices dating back to June 2, 1969: the equivalent of $28,487.50 on a single future contract, which represents an average of $1,095.67 per year and 65 percent profitable trades. The problem with this system is that, during several years (e.g., 1974, 1980, 1993, and 1995), we would have suffered large losses. Let's now see what would happen if we go long on the corn market once we know the seasonal has failed. We go long corn after July 21 if our trade is not profitable. If we take a long position, we will not exit to the first trading day of the following year. Using this method—going long the first trading day after July 21 if the short trade is not profitable—produced $38,537.50 on a single contract. The winning percentage did drop to 58 percent overall. The drawdown as well as the largest losing trade did improve. Using this seasonal failure method increased the net profit and cut the drawdown on the classic seasonal for shorting corn.

This is just one example of how using counterseasonal trading can be a powerful tool for traders. Research in counterseasonal trading is one of the most interesting and profitable areas in seasonal research.

Seasonal patterns do not relate only to price; they can also relate to volatility. We calculate seasonal volatility by finding the next 5-day average (true range/price) × 100 for every given trade day of the year. This measure predicts volatility based on seasonality. The calculation has several uses. The first is for trading options. If volatility is going lower on a seasonal basis, you will want to sell premium. Another use for this information is in setting stops based on historical average true range. If seasonal volatility increases, you will want to widen your stops.

Figure 2.3 shows the average 5-day seasonal volatility for T-Bonds from December 1995 to June 1996. T-Bond volatility has a peak in early January and falls in early February, before it rises again. During the first three quarters of March, T-Bond volatility drops, reaching a low during the last week of March. Based on seasonality, there is high volatility during mid-May and June.

The final type of seasonal analysis is the seasonal trend. Seasonal trend analysis works as follows. For each trading day of the year, we returned

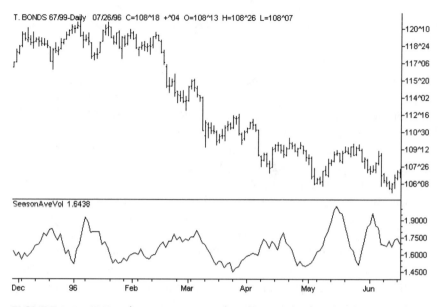

FIGURE 2.3 T-Bonds versus seasonal average volatility for the period December 1995 to June 1996.

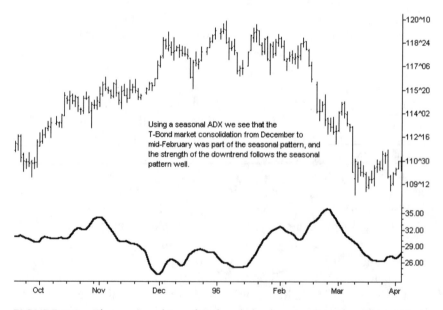

Using a seasonal ADX we see that the T-Bond market consolidation from December to mid-February was part of the seasonal pattern, and the strength of the downtrend follows the seasonal pattern well.

FIGURE 2.4 The seasonal trend index, based on trading day of year for T-Bonds. The downtrend in the T-Bond market during February 1996 was part of the seasonal trend tendency.

the average ADX value *N* days into the future. This indicator is a very good tool to add as a filter for trend-following systems. Figure 2.4 shows a price chart of T-Bonds and a 5-period lookahead of a 10-period ADX seasonal. Note that T-Bonds do not trend seasonally in early December and do not begin to trend again until February. As T-Bonds moved in a trading range during late 1995 and early 1996, the ADX seasonal was low or falling. When the trend seasonal started to rise, T-Bonds started to trend to the downside.

This chapter has given you a brief look at the power of seasonal trading. In later chapters, we will combine some of these ideas with other forms of analysis in order to predict future market direction.

3
Long-Term Patterns and Market Timing for Interest Rates and Stocks

---

This chapter will show you how to use fundamental data to predict long-term trends in both interest rates and stock prices.

This type of long-term analysis is very important for people who switch mutual funds, as well as anyone with a variable rate loan. It is also important for short-term traders because many systems are based on buying pullbacks in the long-term uptrends of both stocks and bonds, which started during the early 1980s. When these bull markets end, these systems will stop working—with disastrous results.

INFLATION AND INTEREST RATES

It is commonly known that interest rates are positively correlated to inflation. As inflation rises, so do interest rates. In general, this relationship is true, but it is not constant. We will examine this relationship using 3-month T-Bill yields and yields on the longest government bond. We will compare these yields to the 1-year inflation rate, calculated by taking a 12-month percentage change in the Consumer Price Index (CPI). These data, as well as the other fundamental data used in this chapter, were supplied by Pinnacle Data Corporation and are part of their index database.

To study the relationship between T-Bill yields and inflation, we researched monthly data going back to 1943. Most major increases in short-term rates occur when the inflation rate is a *negative real rate*—that is, it is greater than the T-Bill yield. It last happened in 1993, just before the start of a severe bear market in bonds. In general, rising premiums on T-Bills lead to lower rates, and falling premiums lead to higher rates. We studied many different ways of comparing inflation to interest rates and have found that one of the best methods is to use a ratio of interest rates to inflation. During the past 53 years, on average, T-Bill yields have been about twice the average inflation rate.

The relationship between long-term interest rates and inflation is not as reliable as the one between short-term interest rates and inflation. In general, the spread between inflation and long-term interest rates is between 300 and 400 basis points. Currently, it is about 380 basis points or 3.80 points as of early April 1996. The ratio between long-term interest rates and inflation is currently about 250 percent; for example, a 3 percent inflation rate would relate to a 7.5 percent long-term bond. This relationship has varied over the years. Long-term rates were kept artificially low during the mid-1970s. On January 31, 1975, long-term rates were at 5.05 percent, which was only about half of the actual inflation rate. Another example occurred during the early 1960s, when inflation was under 2 percent and long-term bond rates were about 4 percent. This was only a 2.00 point difference, but the ratio of long-term interest rates to inflation has recently ranged from 220 percent to 260 percent. This type of premium is common during long periods of economic growth with low inflation. This concept is very important because it means that a 1 percent increase in inflation can produce a 2.5 percent increase in long-term interest rates.

In May 1996, the Treasury Department discussed issuing a bond that yields a fixed number of basis points over the rate of inflation. This would be a smart move because it would reduce the cost of borrowing over the next few years. During the early 1990s, the Treasury moved its own borrowing to the short end of the yield curve just before short-term rates dropped to a low of 3 percent. When it looked as though short-term rates were going to start to rise, the Treasury suggested the issuing of an inflation-based bond.

This type of bond would save the Treasury money during periods of long-term growth and moderate inflation. During these periods, the premium between interest rates and inflation can be expected to remain over 200 percent. For example, suppose the inflation rate rises to 4.0 percent from its current 2.8 percent. On an inflation bond purchased at a 400-basis-point premium, the yield would rise from 6.8 percent to 8.0 percent. Our research has shown that during moderate increases in inflation, long-term rates can retain over a 200 percent premium to inflation. In 1996, the ratio was 243 percent. Based on my model of long-term yields to inflation, the long-term bond yield would increase from 6.8 percent to 9.72 percent. Under these conditions, this new inflation bond, issued in January 1997, would save the government 1.72 percent in interest per year.

PREDICTING INTEREST RATES USING INFLATION

Let's now use the interaction between inflation and short-term interest rates to develop a long-term 3-month T-Bill yield model. Inflation became a better measure of interest rates after 1971, when the U.S. government allowed the price of gold to float and dropped the gold standard to back the U.S. Dollar. Table 3.1 shows how inflation can be used to model short-term interest rates.

This is a very robust model for short-term interest rates since the United States abandoned the gold standard in 1971. The results from January 1, 1971, to April 1, 1996, are shown in Table 3.2.

Even more amazing, the average correct signal lasts 24 months and the average wrong signal lasts only 2 months. This model has not produced a losing signal since January 31, 1986.

This is a good model of how inflation affects short-term interest rates. Let's now apply the same general model to longer-term interest rates. The

TABLE 3.1   INFLATION BASED SHORT-TERM NOTE MODEL.

Ratio=1−(Inflation/Yield)

InflatYieldOsc=Ratio−Average(Ratio,20)

If Ratio<.2 or InflatYieldOsc<0 and Yield>Yield 3 months ago, then 90-day interest rates will rise.

If Ratio>.3 or InflatYieldOsc>.5 and Yield<Yield 3 months ago, then 90-day interest rates will fall.

TABLE 3.2   RESULTS OF INFLATION AND SHORT-TERM INTEREST RATES.

Net basis points	32.17
Rise in basis points	16.34
Fall in basis points	15.83
Average trade	2.34
Largest loser	-.79
Trades	14
Percent correct	86%

effect of inflation on longer-term rates is not as strong as it is on shorter-term rates. Using the same general model with different trigger levels, we can predict longer-term rates using inflation, but not as well as shorter-term rates. The results as well as our new model, for the period from 1/1/71 to 4/1/96, are shown in Table 3.3.

FUNDAMENTAL ECONOMIC DATA FOR PREDICTING INTEREST RATES

Given this interaction between interest rates and inflation, how many other fundamental factors affect both long- and short-term rates? Using data

TABLE 3.3   RESULTS OF INFLATION AND LONG-TERM RATES.

Ratio=1−(Inflation/Yield)

InflatYieldOsc=Ratio−Average(Ratio,20)

If Ratio<.25 or InflatYieldOsc<0 and Yield>Yield 4 months ago then long-term interest rates will rise.

If Ratio>.35 or InflatYieldOsc>.45 and Yield<Yield 4 months ago then long-term interest rates will fall.

Results Summary:

Net basis points	20.55
Rise in basis points	10.88
Fall in basis pointsl	9.67
Largest error	-.64
Forecasts	17
Percent correct	71%

supplied by Pinnacle Data Corporation, let's see how various fundamental factors can be used to predict interest rates. We will use money supply, consumer confidence, and unemployment data to build our models.

We start by showing how changes in the money supply affect interest rates. We use three standard measures of money supply:

M1 = money stored as cash and in checking accounts.

M2 = M1 plus money stored in time deposits, such as CDs.

M3 = M1 and M2 plus assets and liabilities of financial institutions, which can be easily converted into spendable forms.

In general, the greater the amount of money in the system, the more the economy will grow. This growth translates into higher interest rates.

Let's now develop a simple model using the monthly change in M2. When M2 is in an uptrend and rates have begun to increase, then rates will continue to increase. If M2 is in a downtrend and rates have begun to fall, then rates will continue to drop. Using the same period as earlier—January 1971 to April 1, 1996—we can develop a short-term interest rate model based on M2. Our rules are as follows:

1. If M2Chg > M2Chg [6] and 90-day Yields > 90-day Yields 11 months ago, then 90 days interest rates will rise.

2. If M2Chg < M2Chg [6] and 90-day Yields < 90-day Yields 11 months ago, then 90 days interest rates will fall.

The results of this simple system since 1971 are shown in Table 3.4.

TABLE 3.4   RESULTS OF MONEY SUPPLY AND 90-DAY INTEREST RATES.

Net basis points	26.67
Rise in basis points	14.19
Fall in basis points	12.48
Average trade	1.91
Largest loser	−1.13
Forecasts	14
Percent correct	79%

This model has produced about 100 basis points per year for the past 26 years. The average trade is about 23 months. The last signal this system gave was in October 1995, when it predicted a drop in short-term interest rates.

Money supply is highly predictive of short-term interest rates but not as predictive of long-term interest rates. Using the same basic model with different parameters did not produce results as good as those when predicting short-term rates. Current M2Chg was compared with the reading 16 bars before, and current yields were compared with those 3 months before. The model did a fair job of predicting long-term rates. For example, it produced 17.44 points since 1970 and was 65 percent accurate on 26 trades. The draw down was only −1.64 points, and the average trade was .67 points. These are good results but not as good as for the prediction of shorter-term rates.

With this background in money supply and inflation, we can now discuss how some other measures of economic activity can be used to predict interest rates. Let's start by using consumer sentiment to predict short-term rates. Our model is based on the fact that if consumers are positive, then growth will increase and, consequently, interest rates will rise.

Our model compares consumer sentiment and T-Bill yields between a given number of bars. The rules are:

1. If CSenti > CSenti [12] and CSenti > CSenti [11] and Yields > Yields [4], then rates will rise.
2. If CSenti < CSenti [12] and CSenti < CSenti [11] and Yields < Yields [4], then rates will fall.

Table 3.5 shows us the results of this model during the period from 4/30/56 to 4/1/96.

Using consumer sentiment to predict short-term interest rates, the average winning position is 20 months and the average losing position is 12 months. The model predicted that rates would start to fall on May 31, 1995, when 3-month rates were at 5.72 percent. As of March 31, 1996, this position is profitable by .73 points.

Let's now look at how unemployment information—specifically, the average duration of someone's unemployment—can help to predict

**TABLE 3.5   CONSUMER SENTIMENT
AND SHORT-TERM RATES.**

Net basis points	34.19
Rise in basis points	18.56
Fall in basis points	15.63
Average move	1.37
Largest loser	−1.34
Trades	25
Percent correct	84%

short-term interest rates. The theory is that the longer someone is without a job, the slower the economy will be, and interest rates will drop in order to stimulate the economy.

Our simple model is based on unemployment duration as a factor in predicting 90-day T-Bill rates. The rules are:

1. If NoJobDur < NoJobDur [3] and Yields > Yields [6], then interest rates will rise.

2. If NoJobDur > NoJobDur [3] and Yields < Yields [6], then interest rates will fall.

For the period from 4/30/52 to 3/30/96, this simple model produced the results shown in Table 3.6.

This model does not work as well as some of our other models, but it does show that the unemployment duration is predictive of short-term interest rates.

**TABLE 3.6   RESULTS OF UNEMPLOYMENT
DURATION AND SHORT-TERM RATES.**

Net basis points	26.63
Rise in basis points	14.80
Fall in basis points	11.83
Average move	.86
Largest loser	−2.14
Forecasts	31
Percent correct	58%

How can we use unemployment claims to predict short-term interest rates? Our system for timing short-term rates is based on unemployment claims. The rules are:

1. If Claims < Claims [11] and Claims > Claims [14], then interest rates will rise.
2. If Claims > Claims [11] and Claims < Claims [14], then interest rates will fall.

This simple model was tested on T-Bill yields in the period from 1/31/56 to 3/31/96 and produced the results shown in Table 3.7.

This simple model does a great job of predicting short-term interest rates. Its last trade was predicting a drop in rates on July 31, 1995. On long-term interest rates, the same model produces 18.20 points and wins 67 percent of its trades, with an average trade profit of .61 point. It is profitable on both long and short moves. Even though this model did not perform as well as it did on short-term rates, it still shows that unemployment claims are predictive of interest rates.

Our research showed that, when using fundamental-type data, it was easier to predict short-term (rather than long-term) interest rates on a weekly or monthly basis. I think the reason for this is that short-term interest rates are based on current economic activity, and longer-term rates are also affected by the perceived effects of future activity.

TABLE 3.7   RESULTS OF UNEMPLOYMENT CLAIMS AND SHORT-TERM RATES.

Net basis points	37.12
Rise in basis points	19.90
Fall in basis points	17.22
Average move	1.43
Largest loser	−1.37
Forecasts	26
Percent correct	77%

A FUNDAMENTAL STOCK MARKET TIMING MODEL

We have seen how fundamental data can predict interest rates. Let's now see how we can use it to predict the Dow Jones Industrials Average (DJIA).

We need a model that combines the prime rate, the Federal Reserve (Fed) discount rate, and long bond yields. Our model is inspired by Martin Zweig's book, *Winning on Wall Street.* Zweig discusses how a cut in the prime rate is bullish for stocks as long as the prime rate is below a given level.

Another important factor is the Fed discount rate. When the last move in the Fed discount rate is a cut, that is very bullish for stocks. During the past 50 years, there have been several false moves in the prime rate. The number of false moves drops to almost zero when the change in the prime is in the direction of the last Fed move in the discount rate.

The prime rate and discount rate have a strong effect on stock prices, but so do long-term interest rates. Often, the market will lower rates before the Fed or the banks make a move. For example, during most of 1995, the stock market rallied because of a drop in long-term interest rates. This drop occurred months before the Fed cut rates, which led to a drop

TABLE 3.8   RESULTS OF A FUNDAMENTAL MARKET TIMING MODEL.

If Prime < 12, Prime Rate is cut, and last Fed discount move was lower, then buy at close.

If Prime Rate is raised, then go flat.

If Long Bond Yield sets a 42-week low, then buy at close.

Results Summary:	
Net points	4,141.17 + 1,367.63 open = 5,508.80
Trades	21 + open trade
Win%	90 + open
Average trade	197.20
Maximum drawdown	−193.71
Profit factor	66.89
Weeks in market	1,319
Percent buy and hold	100.3%
Percent of time in market	49.99%

in the prime rate. An ideal interest-rate stock-timing model would combine all three of these factors. We developed a model that used all of these concepts but only traded the market on the long side. This model was tested for the period from 8/11/44 to 4/12/96, using weekly data. During this time, the DJIA rose about 5,490 points in about 2,640 weeks, or a little over 2 points per week. The rules for our model and the results for our test period are shown in Table 3.8.

This long-term time model is an incredible tool for asset allocation. It performed as well as buy and hold while being exposed to the market only 50 percent of the time.

The models in this chapter are just a starting point for using fundamental data to predict both interest rates and stock market timing. Many more relationships can be discovered using this type of fundamental data. The data can give you a long-term view of future market direction and can be used as a filter in developing trading systems.

4

Trading Using
Technical Analysis

Technical analysis, as the term applies to trading, studies the use of price
data or chart patterns to make trading decisions. This chapter explains
why many people unjustly criticize traditional forms of technical analysis. It then describes some profitable ways to use technical analysis to develop mechanical trading strategies.

WHY IS TECHNICAL ANALYSIS UNJUSTLY CRITICIZED?

Many of the people who say that technical analysis does not work are
either fundamentalists or skeptics who believe that the markets are random and cannot be predicted. They point to the fact that the published
rules in many introductory books on technical analysis are not profitable
when backtested. This is true; but these simple rules are not the indicators used by professional traders. When used correctly, technical analysis can make money for traders. Let's take a close look at some examples
of the misuse of computer-based technical analysis.

Moving Averages

As a first example, consider a simple moving-average crossover system.
This system works as follows:

1. Calculate a short-term moving average.
2. Calculate a longer-term moving average.
3. When the short-term moving average crosses above the long-term moving average, then buy.
4. When the short-term moving average crosses below the longer-term moving average, then sell.

Moving-average crossover systems work well in trending markets but should not be used when the markets are not trending. Critics of technical analysis will apply a moving-average crossover system to all market conditions and will optimize the lengths of the moving average to find the most profitable set of parameters. Anyone who does this will lose money because many studies, over the years, have shown that the most profitable moving-average lengths over the past 10 years are most likely to lose money over the next 3 to 5 years. Let's look at an example. We optimized the moving averages for the D-Mark for the period from 2/13/75 to 12/31/89. We then tested them for the period from 1/1/90 to 5/31/96. The performance of the best three pairs of moving averages from 2/13/75 to 12/31/89, as well as their performance since 1990, are shown in Table 4.1. (A deduction of $50.00 has been made for slippage and commissions.)

The most profitable moving-average pairs during the earlier period lost money during later periods. If we had selected our optimized parameters based on a robust pair of parameters—one in which small changes in parameters produced little change in performance—we would have

TABLE 4.1   MONEY AVERAGES THEN AND NOW.

Len1	Len2	Net Profit	Average Trade	Win%	Drawdown
		Results from 2/13/75 to 12/31/89			
6	10	$90,137.50	$495.26	43%	−$7,187.50
10	20	89,125.00	521.21	49	−7,475.00
10	22	87,750.00	555.00	49	−8,962.50
		Results Since 1990			
6	10	−1,012.50	−5.53	37	−21,425.00
10	20	−13,300.00	−147.78	37	−22,750.00
10	22	−29,875.00	−373.44	38	−37,125.00

found that moving-average systems are profitable in many markets. We also can improve our results if we trade these systems only when a given market is trending. When used correctly, moving-average crossover systems are valuable trading tools.

Oscillators

The classic oscillators are stochastic and a price-based oscillator that was developed by Welles Wilder (RSI). If we use the simple rules that are often published for both of these types of oscillators, we will lose money. These rules are as follows:

1. Buy when the oscillator crosses above 30 from below 30.
2. Sell when it crosses below 70 from above 70.

Why do these rules lose money? First, most people use a fixed-length stochastic or RSI. George Lane, who popularized stochastics, adjusts the period used in these indicators to half of the current dominant cycle. Second, the standard rules will enter a trade about one-third of a cycle too late. If the cycle is long (30 days or more), being a few days late will still produce profitable signals. If the cycle is only 10 days, then the market rises for 5 days and falls for 5 days. In this case, being 2 days late on both the entry and the exit means that, even in a perfect world, the trader is on the right side of the market for only one day. This is why the rules do not work. George Lane uses divergence between an oscillator and price and generates most of his trading signals via a cycle-tuned indicator. (The concept of divergence is discussed later in this chapter.)

Key Reversal Days

Another classic pattern that will not backtest well when misused involves *key reversal days*. These are days on which the market sets a new low and then closes higher than yesterday's close. We then generate a buy signal at yesterday's high on a stop. If the market sets a new high and closes below close, we sell at yesterday's low on a stop. The problem is that key reversal should be used only to trigger a signal once the market is set up for a given move. For example, if the market is overbought and we get a bearish key reversal, that would be a good sell signal. If we look at key reversals and take them regardless of current market conditions, we will lose money. When they are used properly, they can be valuable tools.

The classic chart patterns—head and shoulders, triangle, and so on—are used by many discretionary traders. The problem is, we cannot test how profitable these patterns are without developing mechanical definitions. The key is to develop mechanical methods for detecting the patterns. Trying to detect market patterns in a mechanical way is the best way to use technical analysis, because we can see how well each method of analysis works. We also can tell when each method works best and can develop mechanical definitions for these specific conditions.

Let's now take a look at several technical methods that can be used to produce very profitable trading systems. These methods are often the core logic behind the best commercial systems on the market.

PROFITABLE METHODS BASED ON TECHNICAL ANALYSIS

Gap Analysis

Gap-based patterns are among the most powerful of all trading patterns. These patterns are produced based on breaking news or changes in market conditions that occurred overnight. The news may turn out to be not as important as originally thought, or it may be proven to be wrong. When this happens, the gap closes. If prices continue in the direction of the gap, then the news was real and a major move in the direction of the gap could be beginning. Gap patterns are represented in Figure 4.1.

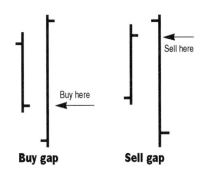

FIGURE 4.1   A standard gap buy-and-sell pattern.

We would buy when the market gaps down below the low on the open and then crosses above yesterday's close. We would sell when the market opens above yesterday's high and crosses below yesterday's close. We can also have a second set of buy-and-sell signals. If the market gaps up and rallies at some percentage of yesterday's range above the open, then we should buy. If the market gaps down at some percentage of yesterday's range and then continues to fall, then we should sell. Most gap patterns are based on the OOPS pattern developed by Larry Williams: Sell at yesterday's high on up gaps, and buy at yesterday's low on down gaps. Williams also developed the strategy of buying or selling in the direction of the gap if the market continues to move in that direction. Gaps are a good tool for day trading or short-term trading (1 to 3 days). Let's look at some examples of using gaps for developing trading models.

To trade the S&P500, we analyze runaway gaps. We perform our analysis using daily bars and accessing the next open in TradeStation, using a Dynamic Link Library (DLL) written by Ruggiero Associates. Our rules, written in EasyLanguage, are shown in Table 4.2.

This simple system buys on a stop order and then exits on the close without holding any overnight positions. We tested this system on the S&P500 in the period from 4/21/82 to 5/31/96, allowing $50.00 for slippage and commissions and a breakout equal to .40. The results are shown in Table 4.3.

Runaway gaps produce good results on the short side and substandard results on the long side. What happens if we apply a very simple filter for both up and down gaps? We will require the S&P500 to close lower than 5 days ago. Our results over the same period, with $50.00 deducted for slippage and commissions, are shown in Table 4.4.

TABLE 4.2   RUNAWAY GAPS.

```
Inputs: Breakout(.3);
If NextOpen>High then buy at NextOpen+Brakeout*Average(TrueRange,3) stop;
If NextOpen<Low then sell at NextOpen+Brakeout*Average(TrueRange,3) stop;
ExitLong at close;
ExitShort at close;
```

TABLE 4.3   RESULTS OF RUNAWAY GAPS.

Net profit	$80,150.00
Profit long	$17,650.00
Profit short	$62,500.00
Trades	384
Average trade	$208.72
Win%	55
Drawdown	$14,750.00

This simple filter improves the performance of runaway gaps in the S&P500. This is only one example; there are many other filters that might work as well. The point is, runaway gaps do work. What happens when a gap fills based on the OOPS pattern? We will sell when we open higher than yesterday's high on a stop at the high. We will buy when we gap lower than yesterday's low on a stop at yesterday's low. We will exit on the close. We tested this system on the S&P500 during the period from 4/21/82 to 6/28/96. These results are shown in Table 4.5.

Note that filling gaps works much better on the long side. Using a money management stop can help this system. If we use a simple $600.00 money management stop, it greatly improves our results, as shown in Table 4.6.

Our results show that, when developing a system based on filling a gap, most of the problems involve large losing trades. Using a simple money management stop, we are able to greatly improve the profitability of the OOPS pattern so that it works as well as most high-priced systems costing thousands of dollars.

TABLE 4.4   RESULTS OF RUNAWAY GAPS WITH SIMPLE FILTER.

Net profit	$86,150.00
Profit long	$23,650.00
Profit short	$62,500.00
Trades	237
Average trade	$363.50
Win%	59
Drawdown	−$8,925.00

TABLE 4.5   RESULTS OF FILLING THE GAP.

Net profit	$73,075.00
Profit long	$58,750.00
Profit short	$14,325.00
Trades	588
Average trade	$124.28
Win%	56
Drawdown	−$19,275.00

Gap patterns work in markets with a high daily range, for example, the S&P500, coffee, and T-Bonds.

Breakout Systems

Breakout systems are among the best methods of technical analysis. There are two major classes of breakout systems: (1) channel breakout and (2) volatility breakout. These systems work very well in trending markets and have been used by most of the top traders in the world. Let's first discuss the channel breakout system, which works as follows:

1. Buy at the Highest (High, 20) + 1 point stop.
2. Sell at the Lowest (Low, 20) − 1 point stop.

In this form, the system is just a modification of Donchian's Weekly Rule: Buy at four-week highs and sell at four-week lows. The system has been discussed in countless publications. It works because it does

TABLE 4.6   RESULTS OF FILLING THE GAP WITH A MONEY MANAGEMENT STOP.

Net profit	$145,950.00
Profit long	$84,450.00
Profit short	$61,500.00
Trades	588
Average trade	$248.21
Win%	53
Drawdown	−$8,150.00

TABLE 4.7 RESULTS OF CLASSICAL CHANNEL BREAKOUT.

Market	Start Date	Net Profit	Open Trade	Win%	Average Trade	Drawdown	Profit Factor
D-Mark	1/2/80	$ 56,663.75	$3,286.25	50%	$544.84	−$22,075.00	1.57
Heating oil	1/2/80	21,903.91	5,333.58	44	182.53	−19,772.67	1.23
Lumber	1/2/80	27,763.52	5,087.68	31	222.11	−49,514.67	1.17
Swiss Franc	1/1/80	71,666.25	5,148.75	50	639.88	−12,858.75	1.59
10-year note	1/3/83	52,116.00	5,030.00	47	606.00	−7,116.00	1.84
T-Bonds	1/1/80	59,614.00	8,499.00	39	527.56	−18,990.00	1.44
Crude oil	1/3/84	59,898.00	−91.00	49	777.90	−8,061.00	2.61
Coffee	1/1/80	101,650.63	2,568.38	36	813.21	−29,121.00	1.52

something that is hard to do—buy at high prices and sell at low prices. In trading, it pays to do the hard thing. Most people can't, and most people lose money.

We tested the simple channel breakout system on several different markets (allowing $50.00 for slippage and commissions) and our results from start date to May 17, 1996, using continuous backadjusted contracts, were as shown in Table 4.7.

These results show that this simple system is profitable in each market used in our tests. If we had traded one lot of each commodity listed from the start date until May 18, 1996, we would have averaged over $28,000.00 a year since 1980, and, as of May 17, 1996, we would have had a combined open equity of over $33,000.00 on all eight commodities. When trading a basket of commodities, as in this example, the total drawdown of the portfolio is less than the maximum drawdown produced by the individual commodities, because of the effects of diversification. The concept of trading a basket of commodities with a channel breakout system is the heart of the Turtle trading system, but our system still needs money management rules, filters, and more advanced exit methods that we will discuss in later chapters.

The volatility breakout system, made famous by Larry Williams, works by buying or selling when the market breaks above or below its open or previous close by a given percentage of the previous day's range. Let's look at an example—a purchase at a given percentage above today's open. The rules are:

1. Buy at opening price+.6 × Average (True Range, 3) stop.

2. Sell at opening price−.6 × Average (True Range, 3) stop.

This simple system buys when the market breaks 60 percent of the average true range above today's open, and it sells when the market breaks 60 percent of the 3-day average true range below today's open. Let's see how this simple system works on the T-Bond markets. We tested this system from September 27, 1979, to May 31, 1996. The results, after deducting $50.00 for slippage and commissions, are shown in Table 4.8.

This system had an equity curve profit similar to the channel breakout on the D-Mark. It worked very well until September 1994, and then went into a drawdown until the end of 1995. From January 1, 1996, to May 31, 1996, this system made over $10,000.00 on one contract.

Different technical methods work well in different types of markets. We call these types *modes*. Developing indicators and systems to identify modes is one of the most powerful uses of technical analysis. Let's now discuss trending and the countertrend mode, as well as something called the breakout mode.

Market Modes

The most important market mode involves identifying when a market is trending and will continue to trend or knowing whether a market will consolidate. One of the best tools for detecting the strength of a trend is an indicator called Average Directional Movement (ADX), originally developed by Welles Wilder. Based on my research, the rules for using a

**TABLE 4.8   RESULTS OF VOLITITY
BREAKOUT SYSTEM FOR T-BONDS.**

Net profit	$163,868.75
Net profit long	$114,856.25
Net profit short	$49,012.50
Trades	1,282
Win%	43
Average trade	$127.82
Drawdown	−$22,256.25

TABLE 4.9 RULES FOR TREND MODE.

1. If ADX crosses above 25, then the market is trending.
2. If ADX crosses below 20, then the market is consolidating.
3. If ADX crosses below 45 from above, then the market is consolidating.
4. If ADX rises from below 10 on 3 out of 4 days, then the market will start to trend.
5. If a trend is based on rule 4, it remains in effect until the 5-day difference in ADX is less than 0.

14-day ADX to detect a trend and consolidation mode are as shown in Table 4.9.

These rules are a modified version of the classic rules for using ADX, which simply say that the market is trending when ADX is above 25. My rules handle two conditions: (1) the exhaustion of a trend, and (2) the early detection of a trend.

Figure 4.2 shows the T-Bonds market and a trend indicator described above for the period from 1/1/96 to 5/31/96. You can see a trend end, based on an exhaustion of the trend, when ADX crosses from above to below 45 during late March and continues downward through the end of May 1996. The market started to trend on February 26, 1996, and dropped 3 points in less than 6 weeks.

How do we use this trend mode indicator in a trading system? We start by using the modified channel breakout system. We have not optimized the parameter and will use a 17-day breakout to enter a trade and a 10-day breakout to exit a trade. We tested this system on T-Bonds, from 9/28/79 to 5/31/96. The results for both the simple system and a system filtered with our trend mode detector filter are shown in Table 4.10. (A deduction of $50.00 was made for slippage and commissions.)

This simple trend filter works very well at filtering breakouts. The original results were not remarkably profitable, but by entering a breakout only when we are in a trend mode, we improved profit, cut drawdown, and almost tripled the average trade.

We used T-Bonds data to develop the levels of ADX for our indicator, so they are not optimal for all markets and time frames. Still, the levels selected for the example are a good starting point, and the values can be

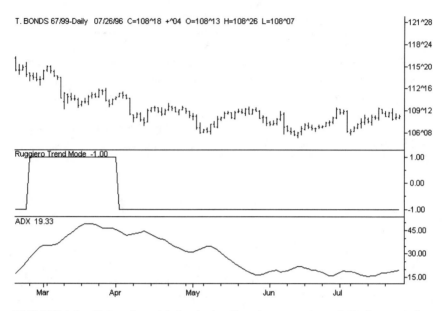

FIGURE 4.2   T-Bonds, with both the Ruggiero trend mode index and the ADX.

**TABLE 4.10   MODIFIED CHANNEL
BREAKOUT WITH AND WITHOUT OUR
TREND FILTERS SHOWN IN TABLE 4.9.**

Net profit	$46,562.50
Trades	180
Average trade	$258.68
Win%	40
Drawdown	−$21,012.50
Results with Trend Filter:	
Net profit	$66,125.00
Trades	85
Average trade	$777.94
Win%	47
Drawdown	−$8,275.00

optimized by combining this indicator with a channel breakout system and then optimizing those results.

During an interview with market wizard Linda Raschke, she discussed something she called a "breakout mode"—a period of low volatility followed by a period in which the market is in equilibrium. When the market enters the period of equilibrium, there is often an explosive move.

Let's develop a breakout mode indicator, which can serve as a good filter for a channel or volatility breakout system.

The market is in equilibrium when technical indicators are confused, so we begin by building a *confusion indicator.*

First, we study simple market momentum. We use three different momenta, with durations of 5 periods, 10 periods, and 20 periods, respectively. When these three momentums do not all have the same sign, we can say they are in confusion. Second, we look at the classic overbought and oversold indicators: stochastic and RSI. We will use both a 9-period and a 14-period SlowK. This is the slow unsmoothed stochastic value. For us to be in a breakout mode, the values of the two periods must be between 40 and 60.

Third, we look at volatility because the market often makes large moves after a period of low volatility. To judge periods of low volatility, we develop a *volatility trend indicator.* As coded in TradeStation's Easy-Language, this indicator works as follows:

```
Value1 = Volatility(10);
If value1 = Highest (value1, 20), then value2 = 1;
If value1 = Lowest (value1, 20), then value2 = −1;
Plot1 (value2, "Volbreak"),
```

When this indicator is at −1, the volatility is low enough to sustain a breakout. Our final indicator will be the efficiency with which the market moves. Our indicator, coded using the EasyLanguage Quick Editor, is as follows:

```
(Close − Close[Len])/summation(abs(Close − Close[1])),Len)
```

Let's use a period length (Len) of 10. In this case, our efficiency indicator signals a breakout mode when its value is ± .20.

Now we combine these indicators to develop a breakout mode index. Our indicator will simply sum how many of these conditions are true and then take the average of this simple sum over a given number of days. The longer the average of this indicator stays at or above 2, the stronger the resulting move will be. Let's use the modified channel breakout we discussed earlier, and then compare the resulting system using this filter. We will buy or sell at a 17-day high or low and will exit on a 10-day high or low. Let's take a look at this system for the D-Mark futures.

We tested this simple system on the D-Mark in the period from 2/13/75 to 5/31/96, allowing $50.00 for slippage and commissions. The results are shown in Table 4.11.

We can modify this system so that we will take the trade only when our breakout mode indicator signals a breakout mode. The system will enter trades only when the breakout mode indicator is greater than or equal to 2. (We tested moving averages between 4 and 30 in order to determine our breakout mode indicator.) We found that this filter helps the overall performance of the system over the whole optimization range. Table 4.12 lists several of the combinations tested, to give an idea of how this filter performed.

The table shows the power of our breakout mode indicator. We reduced drawdown, and the winning percentage, in most cases, has risen to over 60 percent. This simple test shows the potential of a breakout mode index, but how low is the level of adverse movement when a breakout mode filter is introduced into the system? We will test a breakout mode index length of 30 for our average, and then add a simple money management stop. We range the stop from $200 to $1,000, in steps of 50. Over this complete range of parameters, the stop either reduces the drawdown and

**TABLE 4.11   MODIFIED CHANNEL BREAKOUT
SYSTEM FOR D-MARK FUTURES.**

Net profit	$74,587.50
Net profit long	$39,325.00
Net profit short	$35,262.50
Trades	204
Win%	48
Average trade	$365.63
Drawdown	−$15,800.00

TABLE 4.12   MODIFIED CHANNEL BREAKOUT WITH
DIFFERENT LENGTH BREAKOUT MODE FILTERS.

Breakout Index Len	Net Profit	Trades	Win%	Drawdown
10	$85,537.50	125	54%	−$10,000.00
16	73,887.50	91	63	−5,437.50
18	57,637.50	75	60	−6,937.50
20	52,912.50	72	60	−6,937.50
26	58,075.00	57	65	−5,462.50
28	57,600.00	50	66	−4,800.00
30	53,012.50	46	67	−4,050.00

reduces the profit slightly (small stop) or improves profits and drawdown (larger stop). For example, using a $250.00 stop, we made $40,950.00 on 60 trades with only a −$2,962.50 drawdown. If we had used a $1,000.00 stop, we would have made $55,000.00 on 46 trades, winning 67 percent of them, with only a −$3,225.00 drawdown. These results show the potential of this breakout mode filter.

Momentum Precedes Price

One of the most valuable concepts in trading is: Momentum precedes price. This concept is one of the major themes in Linda Raschke's trading methods. Figure 4.3 shows the Yen from January 1995 to July 1995. This was the last major top in the Yen. The subgraph shows an oscillator constructed by taking the difference between a 3-day and a 10-day simple moving average. Figure 4.3 shows that the momentum makes a lower high while prices are still making higher highs. Once the top is made, prices fall about 8.00 full points, or $10,000.00 within the next 5 weeks.

How can the concept of momentum preceding price be used to develop a trading system? A simple momentum-precedes-price system, coded in TradeStation's EasyLanguage, is shown in Table 4.13.

The rules in Table 4.13 say to buy when the oscillator sets a new high, and sell when the oscillator sets a new low. This is mandated because momentum precedes price and a new high or low in an oscillator should be followed by a new high or low in price. We filtered the oscillator so that we would buy only when the oscillator is above zero and sell only when

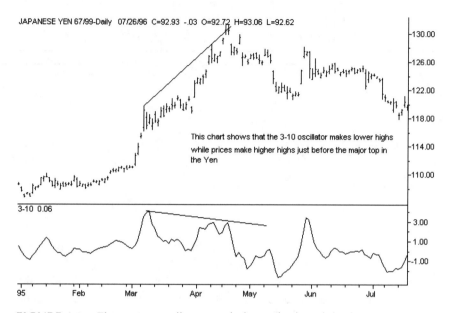

JAPANESE YEN 67/99-Daily 07/26/96 C=92.93 -.03 O=92.72 H=93.06 L=92.62

This chart shows that the 3-10 oscillator makes lower highs while prices make higher highs just before the major top in the Yen

3-10 0.06

FIGURE 4.3 The 3–10 oscillator made lower highs while the Yen made higher highs during early 1995, just before the major top in the Yen.

the oscillator is below zero. This prevents buying into a bear market and selling in a bull market.

We then optimized this system on the Yen, using a range of 20 to 40, in steps of 2, for LookBack, and a range of 2 to 20, in steps of 2, for StopLen. Over these ranges, we found many very profitable combinations; for example, 56 of 110 tests produced more than $100,000.00 in

TABLE 4.13   MOMENTUM FIRST SYSTEM.

Inputs: LookBack(32),StopLen(12);
Vars: Osc(0);
Osc = Average(Close,3)–Average(Close,10);
If Osc = Highest(Osc,LookBack) and Osc > 0 then buy at open;
If Osc = Lowest(Osc,LookBack) and Osc < 0 then sell at open;
ExitShort at Highest(High,StopLen) Stop;
ExitLong at Lowest(Low,StopLen) Stop;

**TABLE 4.14   MOMENTUM FIRST
RESULTS ON THE YEN.**

Net profit	$135,550.00
Profit long	$78,812.50
Profit short	$56,737.50
Trades	192
Win%	43
Average trade	$705.99
Drawdown	−$11,437.50

net profit over the period from 8/2/76 to 6/28/96. Using a LookBack ranging from 30 to 34 and a StopLen ranging from 10 to 14, a cluster of combinations produced between $125,000.00 and $137,000.00. We selected a LookBack of 32 and a StopLen of 12 as the parameters to use when trading the Yen. Our results during the period from 8/2/76 to 6/28/96 are shown in Table 4.14.

The results in Table 4.14 show that the concept of momentum preceding prices can produce a profitable trading system.

In this chapter, we have shown that the classic rules for various technical indicators, although often published in books, do not really work and are not used by professional traders. For example, George Lane does not use a fixed-length stochastic; he tunes it by using the current dominant cycle. This method substantially improves performance. Other profitable and reliable methods used by professional traders include gaps, channel breakout systems, and momentum precedes price.

We also showed how markets have many different modes that can be detected by combining several different technical indicators into a composite indicator. As composites, the indicators are more predictive than when used by themselves. They can improve existing trading systems or be used to build new ones.

5
The Commitment of Traders Report

Have you ever wished you knew what position great traders like John Henry and Paul Tutor Jones currently had open? With this information, you would, in effect, have access to all of the research they paid millions of dollars for, and you would be able to piggyback their trades.

This information is available to you, a few days after the great traders have made their moves, in a report called the *commitment of traders* (COT) report, published by the Commodity Futures Trading Commission (CFTC). The COT report tells how many contracts large professional traders are currently long or short.

WHAT IS THE COMMITMENT OF TRADERS REPORT?

The COT report gives the actual numbers for the three major groups of traders: (1) commercial, (2) noncommercial, and (3) small traders. Commercial traders are hedgers who are trading a given commodity because they have a business that produces it or they need it as an ingredient or material in a product. For instance, Eastman Kodak, which depends on silver, may hedge against a rise in silver prices. Noncommercial traders, such as commodity funds, are large speculators. Small traders—small hedgers and speculators—are in a class called nonreportable.

The COT report was first published during the 1970s and was halted during 1982. From 1983 to November 1990, the report was released monthly. It was then published twice a month until October 1992, when the current biweekly reporting schedule was adopted.

The COT report is calculated after the market closes each Tuesday. Because of auditing restraints, two weekly reports are issued on alternating Fridays. These electronically issued reports indicate traders' positions for the most recent week. At publication, the data are 3 days old.

HOW DO COMMERCIAL TRADERS WORK?

You may be skeptical about the value of this information, considering that it is 3 days old (and during earlier years of this data series, was even 2 weeks old). The information is still valuable because it tells how large commercial traders work. They manage their positions by using a process called accumulation and distribution. Because of the size of their positions, most commercial traders are countertrend traders. They buy as prices fall and then begin to sell into the rally. Because of this process, the COT data could lead the market by 2 weeks or more.

Let's study some examples of this process. Figure 5.1 shows the S&P500 and the net long commercials during the stock market bottom of November 1994. The commercials began to build their position as the market fell, and the market did not begin to turn up until they had built their position.

Another example was the large correction in the T-Bonds market, once the commercials had built their short position in late 1995 and early 1996. As shown in Figure 5.2, they began to cover their short positions as the market collapsed. This is additional evidence of how the commercials are really countertrend traders.

USING THE COT DATA TO DEVELOP TRADING SYSTEMS

Let's now talk about how to analyze the COT data. The COT report supplies the number of contracts each group is long or short, as well as the number of traders in each group. It also publishes the number of spreads put on by each group, and the net change and percent of open interest each group holds.

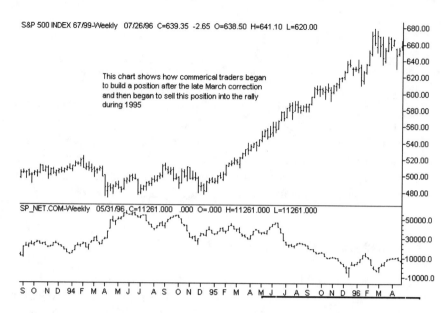

FIGURE 5.1 The S&P500 weekly versus the net commercial traders. Note how the commercials built positions in early 1995, while the S&P500 was bottoming. They began to liquidate as the S&P500 rallied.

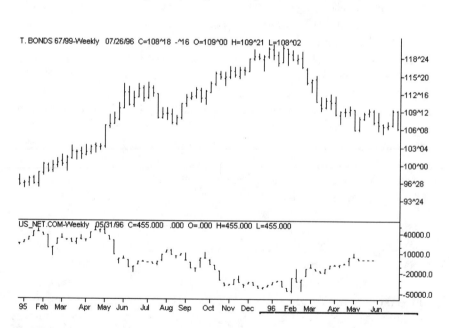

FIGURE 5.2 Commercials began to liquidate their T-Bonds position as bonds rallied during late 1995 and early 1996.

The first step in using these data is to calculate the net long position for each group. This is done by subtracting the number of long contracts from the number of short contracts. When there are more longs than shorts, the number is positive. When there are more shorts than longs, the number is negative. The absolute levels of the net long commercials are not important. What is important is how these levels compare to the historical normals; for example, in markets like silver, the commercials have never been net long.

The COT data are predictive because the large traders have a lot of money and their inside connections give them an edge over the public. If you were to use the positions of the small traders, the results would be the opposite, because these traders are normally wrong.

Steven Briese's newsletter, *Bullish Review,* uses an index based on COT data to give trading recommendations. This index is an oscillator based on the net long positions for a given trading group. We calculate this oscillator as follows:

COT Index = 100 × (Current Net − Lowest (Net, N))/(Highest (Net, N) − Lowest (Net, N))

N is the LookBack and can vary between 1.5 and 4 years.

This indicator is scaled between 0 and 100. When calculating this indicator using the commercials, 0 is the most bearish and 100 is the most bullish. We generate a buy signal when this index is above 90, and a sell signal when it is below 10.

When we calculate this indicator using small traders' data, lower values are more bullish and higher values are more bearish. Compared to the indicator calculated using commercials, this is an opposite result because small traders often buy tops and sell bottoms.

The COT report is a valuable indicator in many markets—T-Bonds, the S&P500, the agricultural markets such as corn and soybeans, and markets such as gold and crude oil. On the other hand, the COT report does not do well in markets such as currencies because, in these markets, futures represent only a small percentage of the complete market.

How can the COT report be used to develop mechanical trading systems?

We tested the classic rules for the COT index in several markets and found that they produced unimpressive results. This is not to say that the COT data are not predictive. Combining the COT index calculations, using both commercials and small traders, produces some very impressive results, and we developed a basic model for using the COT weekly data in this way. The rules are:

1. If (COT Index Commercials)[Lag1] > Ctrigger and (COT Index Small) < Strigger, then buy at open.
2. If (COT Index Commercials)[Lag1] < Ctrigger and (COT Index Small) > Strigger, then buy at open.

Ctrigger is the level of the trigger used to generate buy or sell signals based on the commercials' version of the COT index. Strigger is the level for generating buy and sell signals using the small traders' version of the COT index. The higher the index is when calculated using the commercials and the lower it is when using the small traders, the more bullish it is. The lower the index is when calculated using the commercials and the higher it is when using the small traders, the more bearish these data are for that market. Lag1 is the delay in weeks for the values used in our model. Because the COT index calculated using commercials leads the market at turning points, the COT data are more predictive if we lag the index calculated using commercial traders. We tested this model on T-Bonds, using 30 for Ctrigger, 50 for Strigger, and 1 for Lag1. Our test used data for the period from 1/1/84 to 5/31/96. After deducting $50.00 for slippage and commissions, the results were as shown in Table 5.1.

This basic model also worked on other commodities. We tested this model on coffee for the period from 9/7/84 to 5/31/96, and used 55 for Ctrigger, 35 for Strigger, and 3 for Lag1. Again deducting $50.00 for slippage and commissions, the results were as shown in Table 5.2.

TABLE 5.1 RESULTS FOR COT T-BOND SYSTEM.

Net profit	$110,412.50
Trades	28
Win%	75
Average trade	$3,932.50
Drawdown	−$13,156.25
Profit factor	7.45

**TABLE 5.2   RESULTS FOR COT
COFFEE SYSTEM.**

Net profit	$100,983.75
Trades	24
Win%	75
Average trade	$4,207.66
Drawdown	−$43,530.00
Profit factor	5.88

The high winning percentage, average trade amount, and profit factor confirm that these results are predictive. The drawdown is very high but it still shows that the COT data are predictive for coffee.

These two examples are only a start in how to use the COT data as a filter for developing high-accuracy trading systems. The goal of this chapter has been to provide the basic tools for using the COT report when developing more advanced trading systems.

Part Two

STATISTICALLY BASED MARKET PREDICTION

6

A Trader's Guide to Statistical Analysis

A trader does not have to be a statistical genius, but he or she should have a basic understanding of statistics that are descriptive of various properties of the data being analyzed. This chapter gives an overview of some of the most important statistical concepts that traders should understand. These concepts are as follows:

1. Mean, median, and mode.
2. Standard deviation.
3. Types of distributions and their properties.
4. How mean and standard deviation interact.
5. Hypothesis testing.
6. Mean or variance with two or more distributions.
7. Linear correlation.

A trader who has a general idea of these concepts can use statistics to develop trading systems as well as to test patterns and relationships. Let's now discuss each of these concepts in more detail.

MEAN, MEDIAN, AND MODE

The mean is another term for the average. The median of a sample is the middle value, based on order of magnitude. For example, in the number sequence 1,2,3,4,5,6,7,8,9, the median is 5 because it is surrounded by four higher values and four lower values. The mode is the most frequently occurring element.

To clarify the definitions of mean, median, and mode, let's look at two different cases:

1. 1,2,3,4,5,6,7,8,9,10.
2. 1,2,3,4,5,100,150,200,300.

In the first case, the mean is 5.5 and the median is either 5 or 6. Hence, in this case, the mean and the median are similar. In the second case, the median would still be 5, but the mean would be 85. In what is called a normal distribution, the mean and the median are similar. When the distribution is not normal, the mean and the median can be different.

TYPES OF DISTRIBUTIONS AND THEIR PROPERTIES

Most standard statistical methods are based on what is called a normal or gaussian distribution. This is the standard bell curve, which is represented in the symmetrical chart shown in Figure 6.1.

A distribution can have several different properties. The first is skewness. The skewness of a distribution is the degree of its asymmetry around the mean. Positive skewness indicates a distribution with an asymmetric tail extending more toward positive values. Negative skewness indicates a distribution with an asymmetric tail extending more toward negative values. Next, we observe the kurtosis of the distribution. Kurtosis characterizes the relative peakedness or flatness of a distribution, compared to the normal distribution. A positive kurtosis indicates a relatively peaked distribution. A negative kurtosis indicates a relatively flat distribution.

When we look at the distribution of financial data, we see some interesting things. First, financial data have a distribution that is leptokurtotic: large moves occur more than they should for a normal distribution. This property of being leptokurtotic is very important. The fact that large

Normal Distribution

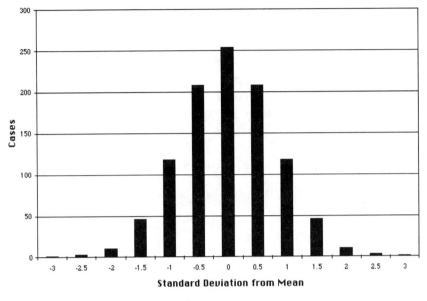

FIGURE 6.1   An example of a normal distribution.

moves occur more than they should is why trend-following systems work. Figure 6.2 shows the distribution of 5-day returns for the D-Mark from 2/13/75 to 7/1/96.

Dr. Benoit Mandelbrot, one of the patriarchs of chaos theory, suggested in 1964 that the capital markets follow a family of distributions he called "stable Paretian." Stable Paretian distributions have higher peaks at the

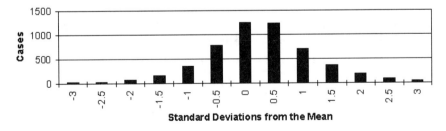

FIGURE 6.2   The distribution of 5-day returns for the D-Mark.

mean and fat tails, and they are characterized by a tendency to trend as well as to be cyclical. They also have discontinuous changes, and they can be adjusted for skewness. They are different from simple leptokurtotic gaussian distributions in that they have an infinite or undefined variance. These types of distributions are now called "fractal distributions." Because financial markets do not follow a gaussian distribution, using standard statistics can give us only an imperfect estimate, but that estimate is good enough to give us an edge.

THE CONCEPT OF VARIANCE AND STANDARD DEVIATION

The variance and standard deviation of a data set are very important. The variance is the average deviation of the data set from its mean. The variance is calculated as follows:

$$V = \frac{1}{N} \sum_{i=1}^{N} (D_i - M)^2$$

where N is the number of elements, M is the same mean, and D is the current value. The standard deviation is simply the square root of the variance. The standard deviation has some very interesting trading applications and is used in many different indicators. A Bollinger band, for example, is simply a price band drawn two standard deviations away from the mean.

HOW GAUSSIAN DISTRIBUTION, MEAN, AND STANDARD DEVIATION INTERRELATE

The interaction between the mean and the standard deviation has many trading applications. First, there is a basic relationship between the mean of a data set and the standard deviation. This relationship states that, for a normal or standard distribution, 68 percent of the data is contained within one standard deviation and 95 percent of the data is within two standard deviations. Almost all of the data is contained within three standard deviations. For a normal distribution, this number is 99.5 percent.

STATISTICAL TESTS' VALUE TO TRADING SYSTEM DEVELOPERS

Many statistical testing methods are valuable for analyzing a market or for developing and testing a trading system, and you should learn how to use some of these methods. Most of the statistical methods used in market analysis will tell (1) whether the distributions of two data sets are different or (2) whether the means of the populations are different. An understanding of what each method is trying to prove is necessary because, when using statistical methods, you need to formulate both a hypothesis and its inverse, called the null hypothesis.

Hypothesis testing works as follows. We formulate a statistical method so that the null hypothesis is used in the formulation. For example, if we had a trading system with an average trade of $200.00 and wanted to prove statistically that our average trade was greater than 0, we would formulate our statistical measure to assume a zero average trade. We would then calculate our statistical measure and use that value to decide whether to accept or reject the null hypothesis. If we reject the null hypothesis, we show the original hypothesis to be true. This decision is based on a gaussian distribution of the statistical values for a given test. The relevant charts and values are available in every textbook on statistics. If we are two standard deviations from the mean value of a statistic based on a standard distribution, then we can reject the null hypothesis at the 95 percent confidence level.

To fully understand how to formulate a statistical test, let's take a closer look at some of the tests we could use. We will start with something called the Z test, which is calculated as follows:

$$Z = \frac{M - D}{\sqrt{V / N}}$$

where:

M is the mean of the sample,

D is the value based on the null hypothesis,

V is the variance and its root is the standard deviation of the sample, and

N is the number of cases.

Let's now see how we would use this in a trading application. Say we want to know whether an S&P500 trading system had greater than a $250.00 average trade. When we collect the system's results, we find that the average trade was $275.00 with a standard deviation of $30.00, and there were 100 trades. We use the Z test to see whether this is true. Our first step is to formulate our hypothesis. Because our average trade is $275.00, our null hypothesis can be that our average trade is $250.00 because $275.00 is greater than $250.00. We would then state as our hypothesis: The average trade is greater than $250.00.

Our Z calculation is as follows:

$$Z = \frac{275 - 250}{\sqrt{900/100}}$$

$$Z = \frac{25}{30/10}$$

$$Z = 8.33$$

Based on a normal distribution, 1 percent of the scores will have a Z value greater than 2.33. Because 8.33 is greater than 2.33, we can conclude that our average trade was greater than $250.00.

Another valuable statistical measure is called the "Chi-square test." This test is used to judge whether the hypothesis results are valid for a small sample and is often used to test hypotheses based on discrete outcomes. The formula for Chi-square is as follows:

$$\chi^2 = \sum_{i=1}^{n} \frac{(O_i - E_i)}{E_i}$$

where O_i is the observed frequency in the ith class and E_i is the expected frequency in the ith class.

Let's look at an example of how we would use this. Suppose we have a pattern, in that the market rises 134 times out of 200 cases. We would like to know whether this is statistically significant. Because 134 cases out of 200 is greater than 50 percent or 100 cases, which is our expected frequency based on a random population, Chi-square will tell us whether our pattern is predictive of rises in the market. In this case, we would calculate Chi-square as follows:

$$\text{Chi - square } \left(\chi^2 \right) = \frac{\left(134 - 100 \right)^2}{100} = \frac{1,156}{100} = 11.56$$

In our simple case, the Chi-square value is 11.56. For a two-tail Chi-square test, the 99.9 percent confidence level is above 10.83. We can now conclude that, for our sample, our results are predictive.

Another test, called student t, is often used. This test can indicate whether two distributions have the same mean or variances. The formula is as follows:

$$\text{Student } t = \frac{\overline{X}_{one} - \overline{X}_{two}}{s_D},$$

$$\text{where } s_D = \sqrt{\frac{\sum_{one}(X_i - \overline{X}_{one})^2 + \sum_{two}(X_i - \overline{X}_{two})^2}{N_1 + N_2 - 2}\left(\frac{1}{N_1} + \frac{1}{N_2}\right)}$$

s_D is the standard error of the difference of the means. Each sum is over the points in one sample, the first or second. Likewise, each mean refers to one sample or the other, and N_1 and N_2 are the numbers of points in the first and second samples, respectively. $N_1 + N_2 - 2$ would be our degrees of freedom.

Once we calculate t, we need to get the critical values for t based on the degrees of freedom and a standard distribution.

CORRELATION ANALYSIS

One of the most powerful tools for developing and testing trading indicators and systems is a statistical measure called Pearson's correlation, a measure of the correlation between two data series. A 1 is a perfect positive relationship and a -1 would be a perfect negative relationship. The formula for Pearson's correlation r is as follows:

$$r = \frac{\sum_i (x_i - \bar{x})(y_i - \bar{y})}{\sqrt{\sum_i (x_i - \bar{x})^2}\sqrt{\sum_i (y_i - \bar{y})^2}}$$

where (X_i, Y_i), $i = 1, \ldots, N$ is the pair of quantities whose correlation we want to estimate, and $\bar{x}$ and $\bar{y}$ are the means of the X_i's and Y_i's, respectively.

Pearson's correlation is useful in many trading applications, for example, in evaluating the current strength of different intermarket relationships. Pearson's correlation can also be used to evaluate inputs for neural networks or other machine learning methods.

These examples are only a few of the many trading-based applications for simple correlation analysis. We will be using correlation analysis many times in later chapters of the book.

This chapter has given an overview of some simple statistical methods that are valuable to traders. Other valuable methods are in use, but these were chosen for discussion because we will use them in later chapters.

7
Cycle-Based Trading

Cycles are recurring patterns in a given market. The area of cycles has been intensely researched for almost 100 years. In fact, there are organizations dedicated to the study of cycles. Cycle-based trading has become a hot topic because of the software now available for analyzing financial data and for developing trading systems. Because of this software, we can now see how a market is really composed of a series of different cycles that together form its general trading patterns. We can also see that the markets are not stationary. This means that the cycles in a market change over time. Change occurs because the movements of a market are not composed solely of a series of cycles. Fundamental forces, as well as noise, combine to produce the price chart.

Cycle-based trading uses only the cycle and the noise part of the signal. There are many tools that can be used for cycle analysis. The best known are the mechanical cycle tools that are laid over a chart. An example is the Stan Ehrlich cycle finder, a mechanical tool that is overlaid on a chart to detect the current dominant cycle.

Among the several numerical methods for finding cycles, the most well known is Fourier analysis. Fourier analysis is not a good tool for finding cycles in financial data because it requires a long, stationary series of data—that is, the cycle content of the data does not change. The best numerical method for finding cycles in financial data is the maximum entrophy method (MEM), an autoregressive method that fits an equation by minimizing error. The original MEM method for extracting cycles from data was discovered by J. P. Burg in 1967. Burg wrote a thesis on MEM, which was applied to oil exploration in the 1960s. The method was used to analyze the returning spectra from sound waves sent into rock to detect oil. There are several products that use the MEM algorithm. The first cycle-based product was MESA, by John Ehlers. It is now available as a stand-alone Windows™ product as well as an add-in for TradeStation. Another powerful product is TradeCycles™, codeveloped by Ruggiero Associates and Scientific Consultant Services. There are other products, such as Cycle Finder by Walter Bresser, but they do not offer the ability to backtest results. If you cannot use a tool to backtest your results, then, in my opinion, you should be very careful trying to trade it.

Using MEM to develop trading applications requires some understanding of how MEM works. The MEM algorithm was not originally designed for financial data, so the first thing that must be done to make MEM work on financial data is detrend it. There are many ways to detrend data. We used the difference between two Butterworth filters, one with a period of 6 and the other with a period of 20. (A Butterworth filter is a fancy type of moving average.) Once the data has been detrended and normalized, the MEM algorithm can be applied. The MEM algorithm will develop a polynomial equation based on a series of linear predictors. MEM can be used to forecast future values by recursively using the identified prediction coefficients. Because we need to preprocess our data, we are really predicting our detrended values and not the real price. MEM also gives us the power of the spectra at each frequency. Using this information, we can develop cycle-based forecasts and use MEM for trading. MEM requires us to select (1) how much data are used in developing our polynomial and (2) the number of coefficients used. The amount of data will be referred to as window size, and the number of coefficients, as poles. These numbers are very important. The larger the window size, the better the sharpness of the spectra, but the spectra will also then contain false peaks at different frequencies because of noise in the data. The number of poles also affects the sharpness of the spectra. The spectra are less defined and smoother when fewer poles are used. TradeCycles allows adjustment of both of these parameters, as well as others, because different applications of MEM require different optimal parameters.

THE NATURE OF CYCLES

Let's start our discussion by probing the nature of cycles. A cycle has three major components: (1) frequency, (2) phase, and (3) amplitude. Frequency is a measure of the angular rate of change in a cycle. For example, a 10-day cycle has a frequency of 0.10 cycle per day. The formula for frequency is:

$$\text{Frequency} = 1/\text{Cycle length}$$

The phase is an angular measure of where you are in a cycle. If you had a 20-day cycle and were 5 days into the cycle, you would be at 90 degrees: a complete cycle is 360 degrees, and you are 25 percent into the cycle.

The last major characteristic of a primitive cycle is amplitude. Amplitude is the power of a cycle and is independent of frequency and phase.

All three of these features make up a simple cycle. Let's now use them to plot a simple sine wave in Omega TradeStation, using the following formula:

$$\text{Value1} = (\text{Sine} ((360 \times \text{Current Bar})/\text{Period})*\text{Amplitude}) + \text{Offset};$$

Using a period of 30, an amplitude of 20, and an offset of 600, these parameters produce the curve shown in Figure 7.1, which looks a little like the S&P500 and shows how phase interacts with a simple sine wave.

Note in Figure 7.1 that, by using the TradeCycles phase indicator, tops occur at 180 degrees and bottoms occur at 0 degrees.

A simple sine wave is not very interesting, but by adding and subtracting harmonics we can produce a pattern that looks a little like an Elliott Wave. Our formula is as follows:

$$\begin{aligned}
\text{Elliott Wave} = {} & \text{Sine}(\text{Period} \times 360) \times \text{Amplitude} \\
& -.5 \times \text{Sine}(2 \times \text{Period} \times 360) \times \text{Amplitude} \\
& + \tfrac{1}{3} \times \text{Sine}(3 \times \text{Period} \times 360) \times \text{Amplitude}
\end{aligned}$$

This simple curve resembles as Elliott Wave pattern using a period of 30 and an amplitude of 20 (see Figure 7.2).

The figure is an example of how chart patterns are actually made up of combinations of cycles. Let's use our sine wave to test the relationship

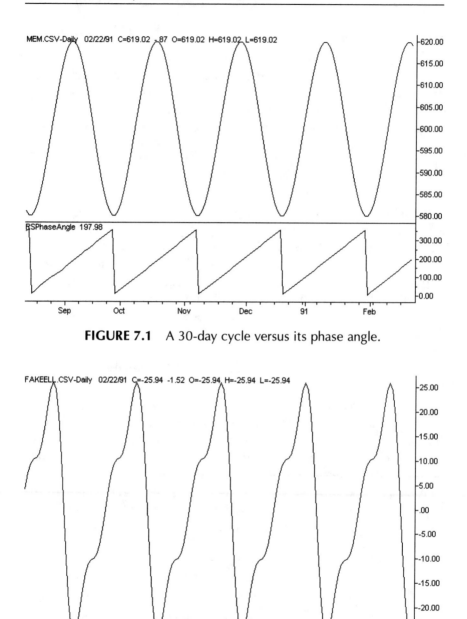

FIGURE 7.1 A 30-day cycle versus its phase angle.

FIGURE 7.2 An example of a fake Elliott Wave composed of sine waves.

between cycles and a simple moving average. We can start with a simple half-cycle moving average. The lag in a half-cycle moving average is 90 degrees. Figure 7.3 shows a sine wave curve, a half-period moving average, and a full-period moving average. The full-period moving average is always zero because it has as many values below zero as above zero.

If we buy when the half-period moving average crosses below the full-period moving average, and sell when it crosses above it, we have the perfect system. We will buy every bottom and sell every top. These rules are the opposite of the classic moving-average system.

Let's now build a simulated Elliott Wave with a period of 30 and an amplitude of 20. If we trade the classic moving-average crossover system, we see that a 2-period and a 15-period moving average produce the best results (about 16.90 points per cycle). This system bought just as our fake wave three took out our fake wave one to the upside, and it sold about one-third of the way down on the short side. On the other hand, if we use the reverse rules and a 15-period and 30-period moving average, we then make over 53.00 points per cycle. This system would buy at the bottom

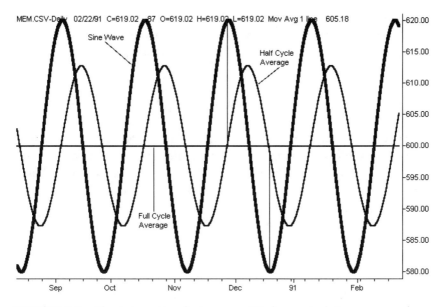

FIGURE 7.3 The interaction between a 30-day period sine wave and both a full-period and half-period moving average.

and sell about one-third before the top, or about at the point where wave five begins. These results show that, in a pure cycle-based simulated market, the classic moving-average system would lose money. In real life, moving-average systems only make money when a market moves into a trend mode or because of shifting in cycles that causes changes in the phase of the moving averages to price. We cannot predict these shifts in phase. Unless a market trends, a system based on moving-average optimization cannot be expected to make money into the future.

Let's now look at another classic indicator, the RSI, which expresses the relative strength of the momentum in a given market. Once again, we use our simulated Elliott Wave, based on a 30-day dominant cycle. We have found that combining a 16-day RSI with the classic 30 and 70 levels produces good results, showing that RSI is really a cycle-based indicator. Using a simulated market over 5 complete cycles, we produced over 59.00 points per cycle and the signals produced bought 1 day after the bottom sold and 3 days after the top.

Another classic system that actually works well in cycle mode and will continue to work in trend mode is a consecutive close system. Channel breakout also would work, but you would want to use a 2-day high or low to maximize the profit based on our simulated Elliott Wave. If you use a 1-day high, your trades would be whipsawed in waves two and four, as they would be in a real market, because the channel length is too short.

CYCLE-BASED TRADING IN THE REAL WORLD

Let's now talk about using the MEM algorithm to trade cycles in the real world. The MEM algorithm requires tuning of many technical parameters. MESA 1996 adjusts these parameters for you. TradeCycles adjusts many of these parameters too, but it also lets you set the window and the number of poles. Real financial data are noisy, so it is important to know the power of the dominant cycle. We call the power, relative to the power of the rest of the spectra, the signal-to-noise ratio. The higher the signal-to-noise ratio, the more reliable the cycle. In TradeCycles, we calculate this ratio by determining the scaled amplitude of the dominant cycle and dividing it by the average strength of all frequencies. The level of the signal-to-noise ratio tells us a lot about the markets. Many times, the signal-to-noise ratio is lower when a market is in breakout mode. (We discussed this mode in Chapter 4.) When using MEM for cycle-based trading applications, the higher the signal-to-noise ratio, the more reliable the trading results. If we are using MEM for trend-based trading, then the signal-to-noise ratio relationship is less clear. This is currently one of my main areas of research.

USING CYCLES TO DETECT WHEN A MARKET IS TRENDING

Let's start our discussion of cycle-based trading by investigating how to tell when a market is in a trend. We begin by studying the dominant cycle and signal-to-noise ratio for the Yen during the period from 3/20/96 to 7/26/96. Figure 7.4 shows how the dominant cycle increases at the start of a major trend.

We will start by studying the spectral intensity of a market over different time frames, beginning with an uptrend followed by a major top. Figure 7.5 shows the spectra for the D-Mark on October 23, 1995, the

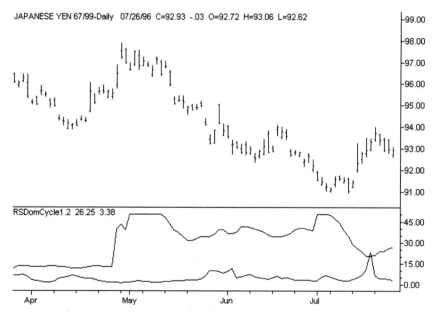

FIGURE 7.4 The dominant cycle, signal-to-noise ratio, and price for the Yen, for April to July 1996.

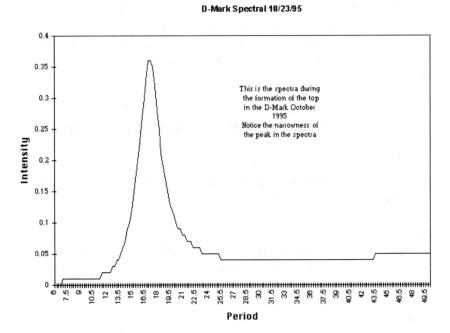

FIGURE 7.5 The spectra during the formation of the top in the D-Mark during October 1995.

date of the most recent top in the D-Mark. At this point, the current dominant cycle was 17.25 days. Looking at the spectra, we can see a narrow peak at 17.25 days. A narrow peak is common in a trading range market.

Let's now look at the D-Mark during the start of the major downtrend—specifically, let's look at the spectra for January 4, 1996. The dominant cycle increased to 23.25, and the width of the area of the spectra around the dominant cycle increased. (See Figure 7.6.)

Widening of the spectra and a move to longer periods are common in a trending market. Knowing now how the spectra changes when a market is trending, let's attempt to develop indicators that signal when a market has started to trend. Recalling the discussion of how a moving-average period relates to a simple sine wave, you know that, for a perfect sine wave, the curve will stay above or below a full-period moving average for half of a cycle. If in real market conditions it stays above the full-cycle moving average for longer than a half-cycle, we can say the market

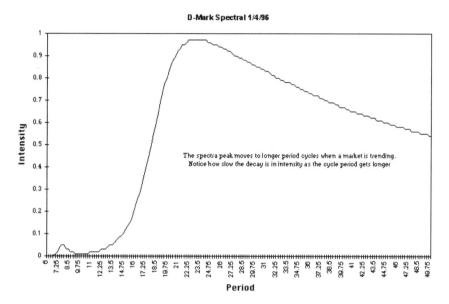

FIGURE 7.6   The spectra for the D-Mark on January 4, 1996, and how the spectra widen when the market trends.

is trending. This simple concept gets into many trends very late and only catches big trends. If we could anticipate whether prices will remain above or below the moving average for more than a half-cycle, we would have a good trend indicator. Let's now build such an indicator.

A trend occurs when (1) a market stays above or below a full-cycle moving average for more than a quarter-cycle, and (2) a 2-day difference of the oscillator created by subtracting price from the moving average has the same sign as the value 2 days before. These rules work well for identifying a trend early enough to trade. When a market starts to trend, it should not retrace against the trend more than the lowest low of the last 50 percent of the dominant cycle bars for uptrends nor the highest high of the last 50 percent of the dominant cycle bars for downtrends. Using TradeCycles and TradeStation's EasyLanguage, we find the code of this simple trend ShowMe. A ShowMe puts a dot above or below a bar which meets a given criteria. The coding is reproduced in Table 7.1.

This ShowMe is good at detecting trends early enough to be able to trade them. Let's look at how this ShowMe detected trends in the D-Mark

TABLE 7.1   CYCLE BASED TREND INDICATOR.

Vars: DCycle(0),Osc(0)TrFlag(0);

DCycle=RSMemCycle1.2(C,6,50,30,12,0);

Osc=Close-Average(Close,DCycles);

TrFlag=0;

If MRO(sign(Osc)<>sign(Osc[1]),.25*value1,1)=-1 and sign(Osc-Osc[2])= sign(Osc[2]-Osc[4]) then TrFlag=1;

If Osc<0 and High=Highest(High,.5*Dcycle) then TrFlag=0;

If Osc>0 and Low=Lowest(Low,.5*Cycle) then TrFlag=0;

If TrFlag=1 then Plot1(High,"CycleTrend");

over the period from 12/1/94 to 5/1/95. Note in Figure 7.7 that the market has a major uptrend that is detected near the bottom in December 1994, as shown by the dots at the top of the bars.

How can the phase between the price data and the current dominant cycle be used to detect when a market is trending or is in cycle mode? If we assume that we have a perfect 30-day cycle, the phase should change 360/30, or 12 degrees per day. The more this rate of change of phase differs from the ideal, the less the market is acting as if it is in cycle mode. Using this theory, let's develop a cycle and trend mode indicator based on phase. We will compare the ideal rate of change with the actual rate of change calculated using our price data. When the rate of change of the phase is the same when using real data as when using theoretical data the market is in a perfect cycle mode. When the rate of change is less than 1 by some threshold, then the market is trending. If it is greater than 1 by some threshold, the market is consolidating. When we are within + − our threshold of 1, then the market is in cycle mode. Because real data are noisy, we smooth this ratio by using a quarter-cycle moving average. Let's take a look at how this indicator worked for the D-Mark during the period from 1/1/96 to 7/1/96 (see Figure 7.8).

During this period, the D-Mark started to trend several times. We can tell it was trending because the RSPhaseMode indicator described above was significantly below 1. When this indicator stays at about 1, the market is moving in cycle mode. If it is significantly above 1, the market is consolidating. When we use this indicator, we normally use below 0.67 for trending and above 1.33 for the consolidation mode. If this indicator is between these levels, we can say the market is in cycle mode.

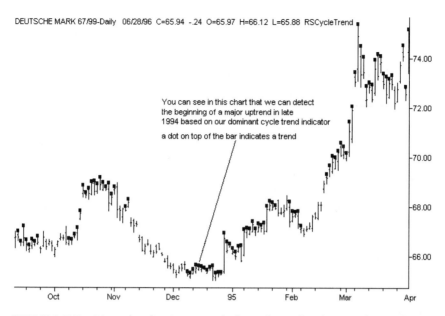

FIGURE 7.7 How the dominant cycle-based trend indicator shows the major uptrend in the D-Mark that started in December 1994.

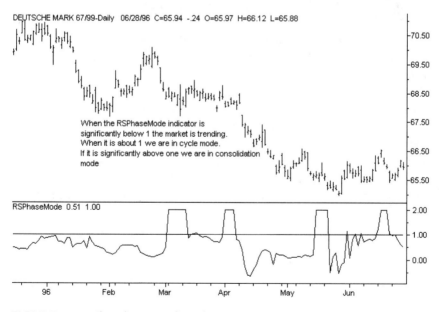

FIGURE 7.8 The phase mode indicator points to a trending market when it is much below 1, a cycle market when it is near 1, and a consolidation mode market when it is much above 1.

ADAPTIVE CHANNEL BREAKOUT

Let's now look at another method for using cycle analysis to confirm not only whether the market is trending but also its direction. This method, called *adaptive channel breakout,* defines an uptrend as occurring when the market makes the highest high of the past dominant cycle bars. The trend is then up, and you should buy on a stop. When the market makes the lowest low of the past dominant cycle bars, you should sell on a stop. This definition of both trend and direction is so good that it can be traded as a stand-alone system. My research in the area of developing trading systems using MEM has shown that the size of the window used to calculate MEM and the number of poles used in the calculations have an effect on how MEM performs for different applications. We have optimized the number of poles using a fixed window size of 30 and have found that when using MEM in a trend-following application, fewer poles produce more reliable performance, because the output from both the dominant cycle and the MEM predictions is smoother. For example, using a window size of 30, we found that having 6 poles produces the best results on daily data for currencies for our adaptive channel breakout system. The results for the D-Mark, Yen, and Swiss Franc for the period from 1/1/80 to 6/22/96 are shown in Table 7.2. (A deduction of $50.00 was made for slippage and commissions.)

These results across the three most popular currencies show the power of this method. It can be used to trade a basket of commodities by optimizing window size and poles over the complete basket and selecting the most robust pair of parameters. We will learn later that this concept can be made even more adaptive by optimizing the window size and poles in line, based on the current performance of each set of parameters over recent history. This concept is called *optimal adaptive channel breakout.*

TABLE 7.2   RESULTS OF ADAPTIVE CHANNEL BREAKOUT.

	D-Mark	Yen	Swiss Franc
Net profit	$99,237.50	$161,937.50	$131,325.00
Trades	94	95	105
Win%	49	47	44
Average trade	$1,055.72	$1,704.61	$1,250.71
Drawdown	−$11,312.50	−$8,775.00	−$12,412.00

USING PREDICTIONS FROM MEM FOR TRADING

Predictions from MEM can be used to develop trading strategies. These predictions are good for predicting turning points but not for predicting magnitude. The MEM prediction works only when the market is in a cycle mode. Let's now look at an example of how to use the prediction from MEM. We will learn later in this book, when we develop systems based on any autoregressive method or even on neural networks, that it is easier to develop models on weekly data than on daily data. Once you can get a prediction method to work well on weekly data, you can then move to daily data and then intraday data. Our basic model is shown in Table 7.3.

We tested this model on weekly D-Mark data from 1/1/80 to 6/22/96 and deducted $50.00 for slippage and commissions. Based on our testing, we decided that, in normal conditions, our MEM prediction should look ahead only 4 bars. Our optimal window size was 24 bars, and we used 12 poles for both the MEM cycle calculation and the predictions. Table 7.4 shows how our simple model, using these parameters, performed over our analysis period.

The results show that this simple model is predictive. We can improve the results if we trade the model only when the market is in a cycle mode. For example, from May 22, 1992, to September 18, 1992, the system traded six times and lost about $2,000.00 overall. The D-Mark was in a major uptrend, rising almost 8.00 full points in this short period of time. During this type of period, the method will perform badly. This is a good example for your own use of MEM to develop trading systems and filters for when a market is in a cycle mode.

The predictions from MEM can also be used in intermarket analysis. We can use the classic intermarket relationships discussed in Chapter 1, and then filter our trades by requiring that the prediction from MEM

TABLE 7.3   SYSTEM USING MEM PREDICTIONS.

If MEMPred>MEMPred[2] and MEMPred[4]>MEMPred[2] then buy at open;

If BarsSinceEntry>Dominate Cycle*.25 then exitlong at open;

If MEMPred<MEMPred[2] and MEMPred[4]<MEMPred[2] then sell open;

If BarsSinceEntry>Dominate Cycle*.25 then exitshort open;

TABLE 7.4 MEM PREDICTION RESULTS WEEKLY D-MARK.

Net profit	$75,562.50
Trades	255
Win%	49
Average trade	$296.32
Drawdown	−$10,787.50

must confirm the system. Let's look at an example of this concept. Suppose we are trading the S&P500 using T-Bonds. If bonds are in an uptrend and the S&P500 is in a downtrend, we would then buy the S&P500. If T-Bonds are in a downtrend and the S&P500 is in an uptrend, we would then sell the S&P500. We showed in Chapter 1 that this type of model works very well. We could filter this model by requiring the MEM prediction to be positive for both markets to buy the S&P500, and negative for both markets to sell the S&P500. This type of filter can help solve the problem of an intermarket change of direction just as the signal is generated. Table 7.5 shows this concept, coded in TradeStation's Easy-Language and using TradeCycles. Note that the S&P500 is in Data1 and T-Bond futures are in Data2.

We tested this system from April 21, 1982 to June 28, 1996. We optimized the moving-average lengths for both TrLen and InterLen, using the range of 10 to 30 in steps of 2. We used a window size of 30, 6 poles, and a lookahead of 6. On average, we realized a higher winning percentage and

TABLE 7.5 INTERMARKET BASED CYCLE ANALYSIS SYSTEM.

```
Inputs: LK1(6),LK2(6),TrLen(20),InterLen(30),Win(30),Poles(6);
Vars: TrOsc(0),InterOsc(0),TrPred(0),InterPred(0);
TrPred=RSMemPred(Close of Data1,Win,Poles,LK1);
InterPred=RSMemPred(Close of Data2,Win,Poles,LK2);
TrOsc=Close of Data1−Average(Close of Data1,TrLen);
InterOsc=Close of Data−Average(Close of Data2,InterLen);
If InterPred>0 and TrPred>0 and TrOsc<0 and InterOsc>0 then buy at open;
If InterPred<0 and TrPred<0 and TrOsc>0 and InterOsc<0 then sell at open;
```

fewer trades than when using divergence without the MEM prediction filter. We did not optimize the other parameters. They were selected based on other research that recommended a window size of 30 and 6 poles for many trading applications. We found that using 20 for the TrLen and 30 for InterLen produced reliable and stable results. Our results over our test period are shown in Table 7.6. (A deduction of $50.00 was made for slippage and commissions.)

Table 7.6 shows that this system produced better overall results than even the best intermarket divergence system for the S&P500. The concept of confirming intermarket relationships using MEM predictions does have value and is an important area of future research.

One fact is little discussed: Predictions from MEM change when different parameters are used. One method for improving performance when using MEM would be to combine different predictions made with different parameters. A consensus or even an average method is a possible choice. A lot of computer power would be required, but the performance would improve.

This chapter has shown how cycles can be used to create a trading system, or can become part of a trading system, or can even be inputted into a neural network or genetic algorithm. These issues are addressed further in Chapter 18, but I will give you one example now. If you look at the rate of change of a dominant cycle, it will give you an idea of whether the predicted turning points would be too early, or late, or on time. When the

TABLE 7.6   RESULTS OF INTERMARKET CYCLE BASED SYSTEM S&P500 USING T-BONDS AS THE INTERMARKET.

Net profit	$326,775.00
Profit long	$269,100.00
Profit short	$57,675.00
Trades	54
Win%	80
Win% long	93
Win% short	67
Average trade	$6,051.39
Drawdown	−$27,600.00
Profit factor	8.02

dominant cycles are getting longer, the turning points you predict would be too early. When the cycles are getting shorter, the turning points would be too late.

This chapter is a starting point for future work on using spectral analysis to develop trading systems. This area of research should be one of the most important technologies in developing the next generation of trading systems.

8

Combining Statistics and Intermarket Analysis

In Chapter 1, we discussed many different intermarket relationships that are valuable for developing trading systems. If you actually have programmed some of the examples in Chapter 1, you have learned that these systems work very well during some periods, but do have long periods of drawdown.

Our research over the past few years has shown that analysis of intermarket relationships, based on current correlations between the intermarket and the market you are trading, is a very valuable tool in developing trading strategies.

USING CORRELATION TO FILTER INTERMARKET PATTERNS

Let's now show how Pearson's correlation can be used to improve classic intermarket relationships. In Chapter 1, we showed that you can trade crude oil using the Dollar index (see Table 1.3). You go long when the dollar is below its 40-day moving average, and you go short when it is above that average. This relationship has been steady over the years, but it did have problems during 1991 and 1992. During those years, this model *lost* $3,920.00 and recorded its maximum drawdown.

By using Pearson's correlation as a filter for this simple intermarket relationship, we are able to improve our model's performance. We will still enter and exit our trades using a 40-day moving average of the Dollar, but we now also require a 40-day correlation between the Dollar and crude oil to be less than −.5.

Using this new filter, we more than doubled our average trade and cut our drawdown in half. Our first trade was on March 17, 1986, and our results, after deducting $50.00 for slippage and commissions, are as shown in Table 8.1.

This model did not make as much as the original one, but the average trade, drawdown, and profit factor all improved. In addition, the model, using the correlation filter, made $1,800.00 during 1991 and 1992, when the original model suffered its largest drawdown. Use of the filter reduced the number of trades from 167 to 55, and increased the profit factor from 2.07 to 3.07.

Let's look at another example of using correlation analysis to develop intermarket trading models. We will use the relationship between T-Bonds and UTY, which was discussed in Chapter 1. Our model was based on prices relative to a moving average. We used an 8-day period for T-Bonds and a 24-day period for UTY. We took trades when T-Bonds and UTY diverged. If UTY was rising and T-Bonds were falling, we bought T-Bonds. If UTY was falling and T-Bonds were rising, we sold T-Bonds. For the period from 6/1/87 to 6/18/96, this model produced a little over $98,000.00, with 64 percent winning trades and about a −$9,500.00 drawdown. Can filtering our trades, using the correlation between UTY and T-Bonds, help even a system that performed this well? If we filter our signals, we require a 12-day correlation between UTY and T-Bond to be greater than .50. Our results for the period from 6/1/87 to 7/26/96 are shown in Table 8.2.

TABLE 8.1   RESULTS OF TRULONG CRUDE OIL USING THE DOLLAR INDEX AND CORRELATION.

Net profit	$39,499.00
Profit long	$34,319.00
Profit short	$5,180.00
Win%	49
Average trade	$718.16
Drawdown	−$5,930.00

**TABLE 8.2   RESULTS USING UTY TO TRADE
T-BOND WITH CORRELATION AS A FILTER.**

Net profit	$108,037.50
Trades	68
Win%	75
Average trade	$1,588.79
Maximum drawdown	−$6,593.75
Profit factor	5.28

The use of correlation as a filter improved almost every part of this system's performance. Net profit increased and drawdown dropped by about 30 percent. We also won 75 percent of our trades.

Let's now apply a simple intermarket pattern filter to the use of day-of-week analysis. We will buy the S&P500 on Monday's open when T-Bonds are above their 26-day moving average, and we will exit this position on the close. This pattern has performed well from 1982 to date. Table 8.3 shows the results from 4/21/82 to 7/26/96, with $50.00 deducted for slippage and commissions.

The results of our buy-on-Monday pattern are good, but we can improve them by using correlation. We first use a simple correlation between T-Bonds and the S&P500. Because we base this pattern on the relationship between T-Bonds and the S&P500, we want to filter out trades when the link between the S&P500 and T-Bonds is weaker than normal. We therefore take trades only when the 20-day correlation between T-Bonds and the S&P500 is greater than .40. This filter improves the performance of our original pattern. Table 8.4 shows our results

**TABLE 8.3   RESULTS OF BUY MONDAY
WHEN T-BONDS ARE IN AN UPTREND.**

Net profit	$89,100.00
Trades	417
Average trade	$213.67
Win%	55
Profit factor	1.57
Drawdown	−$18,975.00

TABLE 8.4   RESULTS OF BUY MONDAY WHEN
T-BONDS ARE IN AN UPTREND AND S&P500
AND T-BONDS ARE STRONGLY LINKED.

Net profit	$88,200.00
Trades	268
Average trade	$329.10
Win%	58
Profit factor	2.01
Drawdown	-$7,775.00

for the period from 4/21/82 to 7/26/96, allowing $50.00 for slippage and commission.

Filtering the trades by using correlation not only improves our average trade by 54 percent, but also improves our percentage of wins, drawdown, profit factor, and win/loss ratio. We were able to filter out about 160 trades that averaged about $6.00 each. We could have used higher thresholds for our trigger, but that tactic would have filtered out too many trades. For example, using an 8-day correlation and a .90 trigger yielded over $500.00 per trade but produced only 36 trades in 13 years.

Let's start again with our buy-on-Monday strategy when T-Bonds are above their 26-day moving-average pattern and we have an additional filter. We now buy at the open on a Monday only when T-Bonds are above their 26-day moving average and when T-Bonds closed higher than they opened on Friday.

The new requirement, that T-Bonds had to close higher than they opened on Friday, improved the performance of our original pattern. The results are shown in Table 8.5.

TABLE 8.5   RESULTS OF MONDAY RISK
WITH T-BONDS HEAVY AND UP FRIDAY.

Net profit	$75,825.00
Trades	244
Average trade	$310.76
Win%	57
Profit factor	1.86
Drawdown	-$13,800.00

PREDICTIVE CORRELATION

A correlation between two markets does not always mean that the current movement in one market can be used to predict the movement in the other. To address this issue, I have developed a concept called *predictive correlation*. The idea behind predictive correlation requires taking a correlation between an indicator *N* periods ago and a change in a given market over the last *N* periods. For example, on daily data, we can take a correlation between T-Bonds[5]–T-Bonds[10] and the S&P500–S&P500[5]. This correlation will tell us how predictive a simple momentum of T-Bonds has been over the length of the correlation. The predictive correlation curve is much different from the curve generated by standard correlation, but it does seem that they both trend in the same direction. The power of predictive correlation is that we can correlate an indicator or intermarket market relationship to future price movements in the market we are trying to trade. This allows us to use relationships and indicators in rules, and to trade these rules only when these indicators are currently predictive. Let's now add predictive correlation to our modified S&P500 pattern.

We use Close[1] of T-Bonds–Open[1] of T-Bonds as our independent variable, and Close–Open of the S&P500 as our dependent variable. We go long on Mondays only when a 35-day predictive correlation is above 0. The amazing results, from 4/21/82 to 7/26/96, are shown in Table 8.6.

This system produced over $600.00 per trade, after deducting $50.00 for slippage and commissions. We won 66 percent of our trades and had a profit factor of 3.75. These numbers are much better than any of the variations that did not use predictive correlation, and they should prove the power of predictive correlation.

**TABLE 8.6   RESULTS OF ADDING
PREDICTIVE CORRELATION.**

Net profit	$55,050.00
Trades	88
Average trade	$625.57
Win%	66
Profit factor	3.75
Drawdown	–$4,400.00

USING THE CRB AND PREDICTIVE CORRELATION
TO PREDICT GOLD

In Chapter 1, we discussed many of the classic methods for expressing intermarket relationships. One of the most powerful methods is a ratio between the intermarket and the commodity being traded. I will now show you how to combine the ratio between the CRB and gold with predictive correlation to develop a very profitable and reliable system for trading gold.

The Commodity Research Bureau index (the CRB) is a basket of 21 commodities.* This index has been traded as a futures contract since mid-1986. It has had an inverse correlation to T-Bond prices and it has been positively correlated to gold during its history.

On the basis of this relationship, I decided to use the ratio between the CRB and gold to develop a trading system for gold. When this ratio is moving up, the CRB is outperforming gold, and gold should catch up.

Another fact about gold was revealed in my research. Often, when the CRB starts moving, gold will first move in the opposite direction and test support, before moving in the direction of the CRB.

On the basis of my understanding of the gold market, I am proposing a system that (1) uses a moving-average crossover of the ratio between the CRB and gold to generate its signals and (2) enters the market on a limit order set at the level of an *N*-day exponential moving average. This concept was tested on backadjusted contracts over the period from 11/18/86 to 7/26/96. The system is based on a sound premise. If inflation increases, so will the price of gold. Still, it performed badly and made only $4,000.00 in profit over the test period. The reason the system did so badly is that it had large drawdown during periods when the CRB and gold decoupled. We can filter these periods out by using correlation analysis. Let's now add the predictive correlation between the ratio of the CRB/gold 5 days ago and the past 5-day change in gold. This simple gold model, coded in TradeStation's EasyLanguage with parameters selected based on my research, is shown in Table 8.7.

This simple model has performed very well in the gold market over the past decade. We tested the model using continuous backadjusted contracts for the period from 11/18/86 to 7/26/96, and deducted $50.00 for slippage and commissions. The results are shown in Table 8.8.

---

* The CRB was reformulated in December 1995.

TABLE 8.7   GOLD/CRB RATIO SYSTEM.

Vars: IntRatio(0),IntOsc(0),Correl(0);
Vars: Ind(0),Dep(0);
IntRatio=Close of data2/Close;
Ind=IntRatio[5];
Dep=Close-CLose[5];
Correl=RACorrel(Ind,Dep,24);
IntOsc=Average(IntRatio,12)-Average(IntRatio,30);
If IntOsc>0 and Correl>.6 then buy at XAverage(Close,80) Limit;
If IntOsc<0 and Correl>.6 then sell at XAverage(Close,80) Limit;

RACorrel is a user function developed by Ruggiero Associates. It calculates the standard Pearson's correlation found in any statistics textbook.

The model made over $48,000.00 during this period, and the system was profitable on both the long and short sides. Another important point: The entry method (buy on a limit set at the 80-day exponential moving average of the close) increased the average trade by over $500.00 when compared to the method of entering at the next open when the signal first occurs.

The system does have some problems, however. For example, the average winning trade lasted 45 days but the average losing trade lasted 144 days. We can help solve this problem by developing better exits for the model. Even with this problem, the model is fundamentally sound and could be the core for a system for trading gold futures or gold mutual funds.

TABLE 8.8   GOLD/CRB RATIO SYSTEM RESULTS.

Net profit	$48,794.70
Trades	35
Wins	27
Losses	8
Win%	77
Average trade	$1,394.13
Drawdown	-$11,250.00
Win/loss ratio	1.56
Profit factor	5.26

INTERMARKET ANALYSIS AND PREDICTING THE EXISTENCE OF A TREND

Intermarket analysis is another powerful tool for predicting when a market will trend. My research has shown that many markets will trend when well-known intermarket linkages are strong—for example, the link between the S&P500 and T-Bonds. I have found that the S&P500 trends when the 50-day correlation between the S&P500 and T-Bonds is high.

Let's look at some examples of how intermarket linkage relates to a market's trending. Figure 8.1 shows that the 50-day correlation between the S&P500 and T-Bonds started to fall in mid-July of 1995, at just about the time when the S&P500 moved into a trading range. The correlation bottomed in early September and then rose rapidly. During this rapid rise and a stabilization at higher levels, the S&P500 rose 57.55 points in about 70 trading days without recording more than two consecutive days on which the market closed lower than it opened.

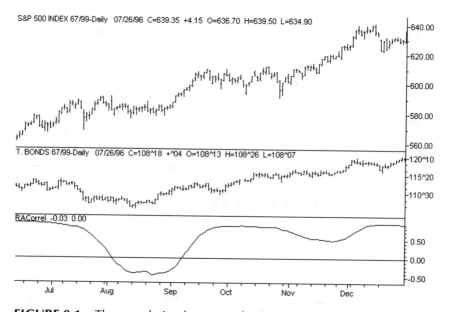

FIGURE 8.1   The correlation between the S&P500 and T-Bonds can predict when a market will trend. In 1995, as correlation rose, the S&P500 exploded and rose 57.55 points in only about 70 trending days.

This link between correlation and trend also occurs during major downtrends. An example, the last important stock market correction, in February 1994, is shown in Figure 8.2.

One of the few downtrends in the S&P500 occurred during the period from 1993 to 1995. During this short time, the S&P500 dropped almost 40.00 points during just a 45-day trading period. When trading the S&P500, correlation analysis can tell you when the trend is really your friend.

This relationship between trend and intermarket linkage does not exist solely for the S&P500 using T-Bonds. Gold almost never trends without a strong link to the CRB index. Using a 50-day correlation between gold and the CRB, I have found that almost every major up or down move in gold started when the correlation between the CRB and gold was above .40 and rising, or was stable above .6. The only major trend in gold that this relationship missed was the rally in gold that started in June 1992.

Let's review an example of how the CRB can be used to predict trends in gold. One of the last explosive rallies in the gold market was in early

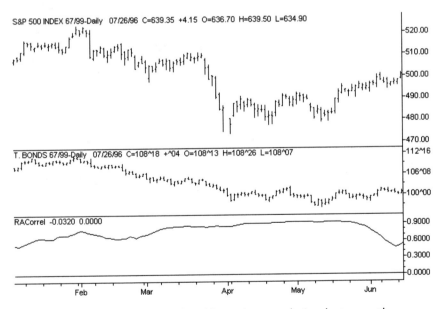

FIGURE 8.2 Another example of how the correlation between the S&P500 and T-Bonds predicts trends. The last major stock market correlation occurred in February 1994.

November of 1989. The correlation between the CRB and gold started to increase in mid-October and rose steadily until November 27, 1989. During this time, the gold market rallied over $50.00 per ounce. The correlation broke above .50 on November 7, 1989, and did not drop below .50 until December 21, 1989. During this time, gold rallied $26.70 per ounce in only 31 trading days. (See Figure 8.3.)

On the basis of my research, the gold market will almost never have a major move until the 50-day correlation between gold and the CRB rises above .50. This means that the great bull market that many believe will happen soon in gold will most likely not start until the 50-day correlation between the CRB and gold rises above .50 while the CRB is in a major uptrend. Without the intermarket link between the CRB and gold, most breakouts to the upside will fail within several trading days.

In early 1996, gold had a breakout to $420.00 per ounce, and many experts predicted that gold would go to $450.00 per ounce within a few months. Using correlation analysis, we could see that this breakout would

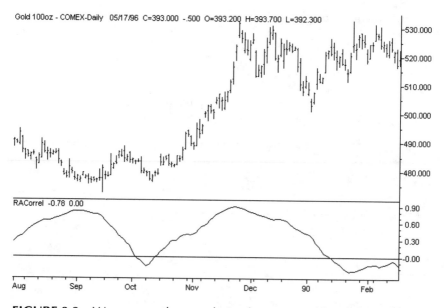

FIGURE 8.3 We can use the correlation between gold and the CRB to predict when gold will trend. The correlation broke above .50 on January 7, 1989, and gold rallied $26.70 per ounce in only 31 days.

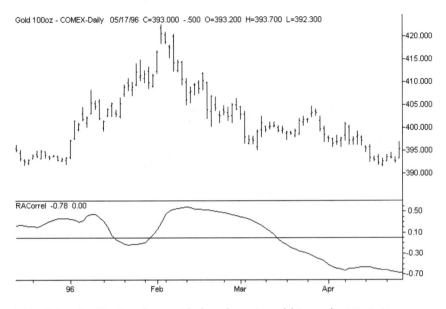

Gold 100oz - COMEX-Daily 05/17/96 C=393.000 -.500 O=393.200 H=393.700 L=392.300

RACorrel -0.78 0.00

FIGURE 8.4   During the upside breakout in gold in early 1996, it decoupled from the CRB and then failed.

fail and that the correlation from $420.00 down to $400.00 would be a very strong trending move. Figure 8.4 shows that the breakout during early 1996 occurred as the gold decoupled from the CRB. The move was not a long-term move that would produce a rally of $50.00 or more. When gold collapsed in early February 1996, it had a 50-day correlation with the CRB of greater than .50. Once gold started its collapse, it dropped 24.00 points in one month. After that, the correlation between gold and the CRB dropped, and gold once again moved into a trading range.

The correlation between intermarkets is a valuable tool for developing trading systems and can even be a tool for discretionary traders. We will learn later that it is even useful as an input for a neural network. Correlation analysis and predictive correlation, combined with intermarket analysis, can be used to develop trading systems as well as to improve existing ones. Later in the book, we will use this type of analysis to develop systems based on advanced technologies such as neural networks.

9

Using Statistical Analysis to Develop Intelligent Exits

When most traders develop mechanical trading systems, they spend 90 percent of their time developing the entry signals. The exit signals are usually less complex and are tested only in combination with the entries. Unfortunately, this process does not develop optimal exits for a given system and market. This chapter discusses how to develop properly designed exit signals, using various statistical methods.

THE DIFFERENCE BETWEEN DEVELOPING ENTRIES AND EXITS

The underlying logic between developing entry and exit signals is different. When developing entry signals, we are trying to find a set of conditions that statistically produces a good risk–reward ratio when taking a position in a given direction. To judge how predictive an entry rule is, I use the set of primitive exits shown in Table 9.1.

Test your entry rules using different values of N for each of the primitive exits defined above. This will allow you to evaluate how well a given entry rule works in predicting future market direction. It is easy to understand the logic needed to develop and test entry rules. The problem with developing exit rules is that the logic is not as easy to define because

TABLE 9.1   ENTRY RULE TESTS.

1. Exit after holding a position for *N* bars.
2. Exit on an *N* bar low for longs or an *N* bar high for shorts.
3. Exit after *N* consecutive bars in which the trades moves against you.
4. Exit at a target profit of *N*.

N is a series of values used in the above rules to test the entry method.

there are many reasons to exit a trade. The exit development process requires mixing money management and technical information about a system for a given market. For example, you can exit a losing trade using a $500.00 stop, or you can exit a long position when the market reaches a 5-bar low. You should exit a trade when the assumptions that caused you to enter the trade are proven wrong. Let's suppose you entered a long trade because the price bounced off a support line. You should then exit the trade if the price closes below that support level. You might also exit a trade if you have no opinion about the future direction of the market you are currently trading.

Now that you have a better understanding of the logic used in developing exits, I can show you how to develop your own intelligent exits.

DEVELOPING DOLLAR-BASED STOPS

One of the most frequently used methods for exiting a trade is triggered when the market moves some given level against investors. These types of exits, called "stops," are used in two ways:

1. If a trade is losing money, exit at a given loss level to protect the trading capital.
2. If a trade is winning, use money-level stops. Exit the trade after reaching a minimum profit level and retracing a given percentage of the maximum profit during that trade. This is called a "trailing stop."

Scatter charts can be used to develop intelligent Dollar-based stops for a given system. In Chapter 4, we showed a simple channel breakout

TABLE 9.2   CODE TO GENERATE MAXIMUM ADVERSE MOVEMENT SPREADSHEET.

```
Input: Length(10);
Vars: Direct(0);
Buy Highest(High,Length)+1 point Stop;
Sell Lowest(Low,Length)-1 point Stop;
Direct=MarketPosition;
If CurrentBar=1 then
Print(file("d:\book\chap9\dmadver.txt"),"EntryDate",",","MarketPosition",",","
MaxPositionLoss",",","PositionProfit");
If Direct<>Direct[1] then begin
Print(file("d:\book\chap9\dmadver.txt"),EntryDate(1),",",MarketPosition(1),",",
MaxPositionLoss(1),",",PositionProfit(1));
end;
```

system that used a 20-day high or low to set the breakout. The system was profitable over many different commodities. Let's look at how this system performed on the D-Mark and how we can use intelligent exits to improve the system.

The original system on the D-Mark, shown in Table 4.8, made a little over $56,000.00 and had a drawdown of over −$22,000.00 from 1/1/80 to 5/17/96. Let's develop an intelligent money management stop for this system.

We start by collecting the maximum adverse movement and final profit for each trade. The code (in TradeStation's EasyLanguage) for collecting this information in an ASCII file is shown in Table 9.2.

This code first saves the current market position for each bar in the variable "Direct." When the market position changes from one bar to the next, we have just closed out a position. We then output the following to an ASCII file: entry date, market position, and maximum position loss, which we refer to as maximum adverse movement.

USING SCATTER CHARTS OF ADVERSE MOVEMENT TO DEVELOP STOPS

Figure 9.1 shows a scatter plot of maximum adverse movement on the X axis and final trade profit on the Y axis. Only three trades that had a

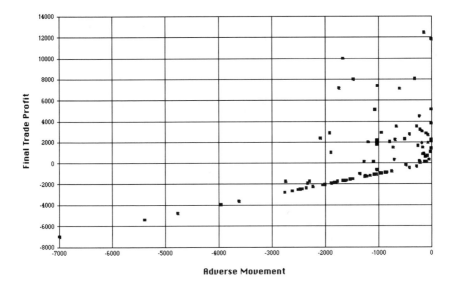

FIGURE 9.1   Adverse movement versus final trading profit.

maximum adverse movement of more than −$1,800.00 also made more than $2,000.00 when the trade was closed. During the trade history, 29 trades finished with a profit of more than $1,500.00. There were 25 trades with a maximum adverse movement of more than −$1,800.00.

On the basis of our analysis using the scatter chart, we can set a protective stop of −$1,800.00. This stop level is based on the fact that only three winning trades had adverse movement of −$1,800.00 or more. We used this −$1,800.00 level and then added $50.00 for commissions. The protective stop produced the results shown in Table 9.3.

Drawdown was reduced by over 50 percent. Net profit increased slightly and the winning percentage decreased by only 1 percent!

**TABLE 9.3   SYSTEM RESULTS
USING NEW STOPS.**

Net profit	$72,462.50
Percent profitable	49%
Average winner	$2,964.42
Average loser	−$1,512.61
Maximum drawdown	−$10,087.50

You might ask: Why not just use the optimizer in TradeStation to set the stops? Analyzing scatter charts will produce better results, for several reasons. First, we want to improve overall system performance, not just net profit or drawdown. The TradeStation optimizer can optimize on only one factor. This can cause a major problem because protective stops always lower the winning percentage of a system. The optimal stop based on profit or drawdown could reduce the winning percentage by 30 to 70 percent. For many trend-following systems, such as our D-Mark example, the winning percentage could drop from 40 or 50 percent down to 25 percent or less. Second, and more important, when stops are developed based on the distribution of trades, they are more robust and should continue to work into the future. When stops are developed based on optimization, it is possible that a few isolated events could have produced the improvements. Because these improvements are not based on the distribution of trades, they might not be as robust.

We also can analyze current trading profits versus final trading profits on a bar-by-bar basis. TradeStation's EasyLanguage code for creating these statistics in an ASCII file, for any bar in a trade, is shown in Table 9.4.

This code generates the trades and saves the current market position and the bars since entry. We save the open position profit for bar N. We

TABLE 9.4   CODE TO OUTPUT ADVERSE MOVEMENT OF BAR N.

```
Input: Length(10),BarNo(5);
Vars: MarkPos(0),TradeLen(0),OpProf(0);
Buy Highest(High,Length)+1 point Stop;
Sell Lowest(Low,Length)-1 point Stop;
MarkPos=MarketPosition;
TradeLen=BarsSinceEntry;
if BarsSinceEntry=BarNo then OpProf=OpenPositionProfit;
if CurrentBar=1 then
Print(file("d:\book\chap9\chap9B.txt"),"EntryDate",",",","MarketPosition",",",","
CurrentProfit",",",","PositionProfit");
if MarkPos<>MarkPos[1] and TradeLen[1]>=BarNo then begin
Print(file("d:\book\chap9\chap9B.txt"),EntryDate(1),",",MarketPosition(1),",",Op
Prof,",",PositionProfit(1));
end;
```

then check to see whether the position in the market has changed and whether the trade has lasted N or more bars. If so, we output the entry date, Position, P/L at bar N, and final profit. We can then chart these results using a scatter chart by plotting profit on bar N on the X axis and final trade profit on the Y axis.

Let's analyze our simple system on the D-Mark for bar 5 of our trade. Figure 9.2 shows a scatter chart of adverse movement on day 5 versus final trade profit.

Only 3 trades that were losing more than $500.00 during day 5 are profitable. Only 5 trades closed profitably that were not profitable by day 5. Based on this analysis, we can use either a $500.00 stop on day 5 or a breakeven stop on day 5. The results for both possibilities are given in Table 9.5.

Table 9.5 shows that using a breakeven stop on day 5 cuts the drawdown by over 50 percent from the original system and cuts the average losing trade from −$1,899.50 to −$961.72. Because we can use a breakeven or a $500.00 stop on day 5, we have greatly reduced the risk

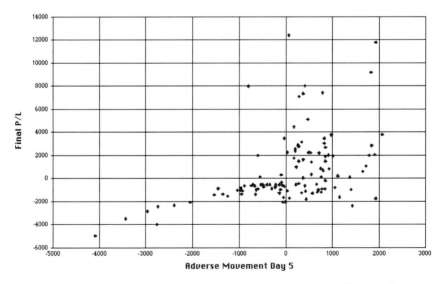

FIGURE 9.2 Adverse movement on day 5 versus final trading profit and loss.

TABLE 9.5 RESULT BASED ON ADVERSE MOVEMENT
ON DAY 5 OF THE TRADE.

	$500.00 Stop	Breakeven
Net profit	$72,475.50	$70,562.50
Percent profitable	45%	38%
Average winner	$3,042.00	$3,072.92
Average loser	-$1,284.27	-$961.72
Average trade	$647.10	$551.27
Maximum drawdown	-$11,312.50	-$9,637.50

attached to using the $1,800.00 stop we discussed earlier. Using this type of analysis, we can set an ideal stop or even a trailing stop for the complete life of the average trade. The analysis can be repeated for at least the number of bars in the average winning trade or average losing trade, whichever is greater. Our D-Mark trader would run this analysis from bar 1 to bar 60 because an average winning trade lasted 60 days and an average losing trade lasted only 19 days.

With the filter, trades that would have been stopped out on previous bars can be excluded from analysis. This method offers the possibility of developing both protective stops and trailing stops, based on the statistics of the system and market we are trading. Using the bar-by-bar analysis method, it is possible to exit trades using much smaller stops, or even to exit at a profit trades that would normally have been exited at a loss. Suppose we have a system in which trades that had an open position profit of more than $200.00 on bar 20 average a final profit of $1,000.00, and trades that had an open position profit of less than $200.00 produce an average loss of $200.00 per trade. We could use a profit floor of $200.00 for bar 20 and improve our system's performance. This is only the beginning of the uses of bar-by-bar analysis to develop stops for a mechanical trading system.

Using a scatter chart to develop intelligent exits is a valuable method for creating stops, but it does have some drawbacks. Primarily, it is very time-consuming and must be run for each system and commodity being traded. Using TradeStation, let's try to develop self-adjusting exits based on this technology.

ADAPTIVE STOPS

To develop a simple adaptive example, we start with an S&P500 pattern we have discussed in Chapter 1 and Chapter 8. This pattern buys on Mondays when T-Bonds futures are above their 26-day moving average. This pattern made a little over $89,000.00 from April 21, 1982, to July 27, 1996, with a drawdown of about −$19,000.00. We will now develop an adaptive stop for this pattern. On every bar, we will find and keep track of the adverse movement on winning trades only. We will then calculate both the average and the standard deviation. We will place our stop at one standard deviation from the mean below the open.

To develop an adaptive intelligent exit, we simulate taking trades without stops and we collect the adverse movement information. If we use TradeStation to manage the trades once we begin to use the stops, we then have a different statistical profile. For this reason, we must simulate the trades without stops and then apply the information to rules that actually take these trades in TradeStation. We also must make sure that we have enough information before applying it to our system. In our example, we waited and collected 30 winning trades. Until then, we used a 2-point ($1,000.00) stop. The TradeStation code for this system and stop is shown in Table 9.6.

The results for this system for the period from 4/21/82 to 7/26/96, with $50.00 deducted for slippage and commissions, are shown in Table 9.7.

We have improved our net profit and still cut our drawdown in half. We have also won about the same percentage of our trades (55%), and cut our largest losing trade from −$9,425.00 to only −$1,925.00.

This simple example shows the power of developing a system using adaptive intelligent exits. This example made it easy to show how to collect the adverse movement information and simulate the trades. You can apply this type of technology to any system, as long as you can write code to simulate the trades and collect the statistics.

This chapter has introduced the concepts of developing statistically based intelligent exits. This technology can also be used to develop exits based on the potential profit and risk for your trade. Other technologies, such as neural networks and machine induction, which are discussed later in this book, can also be used to develop intelligent exit methods.

TABLE 9.6   S&P500 MONDAY SYSTEM WITH ADAPTIVE STOPS.

```
Vars: WinNo(0),AveWin(0),StopLev(2);
Vars: stdwin(0),Count(0);
{ If we had signal to buy Monday and it was a winning trade store adverse
movement}
if (DayOfWeek(Date)=5 and Close of Data2>Average(Close of Data2,26))[1] and
close>Open then begin AdvWin[WinNo]=Open-Low;
WinNo=WinNo+1;
end;

{ Calculate the Average Adverse movement}
if WinNo>30 then begin
For Count=0 to WinNo begin
AveWin=AveWin+AdvWin[Count];
end;

AveWin=AveWin/WinNo+1;
{ Calculate the Standard Deviation}
for Count=0 to WinNo begin
stdwin=(AdvWin[Count]-AveWin)*(AdvWin[Count]-AveWin)+stdwin;
end;

stdwin=SquareRoot(stdwin/(WinNo+1));
end;

if DayOfWeek(Date)=5 and Close of Data2>Average(Close of Data2,26) then
buy at open;
exitlong at close;
{ Use Adaptive Exit After 30 Trades and 2 point exit before}
{ Using one Standard Deviation from the mean will only stop out 5% of the
trades based on a normal distribution}
if WinNo>30 then exitlong ("Adaptive") at NextOpen-AveWin-stdwin stop
else exitlong ("Adaptive2") at NextOpen-2.00 stop;
```

**TABLE 9.7   RESULTS OF BUY MONDAY
WITH ADAPTIVE STOPS.**

Net profit	$92,950.00
Win%	55
Average trade	$224.52
Drawdown	−$9,175.00
Profit factor	1.62

We also learned how to develop a very simple trade simulator and collect the statistics based on these signals. The next chapter addresses the development of these simulators in more detail. What we have learned here will be used later to develop system examples using advanced technologies such as neural networks and genetic algorithms.

10
Using System Feedback to Improve Trading System Performance

A mechanical trading system is really a predictive model of a given market. Many predictive models suffer from the effect of noise or an inadequate understanding of the problem being modeled. In most fields outside of trading, the errors of the last few forecasts are analyzed in order to improve future forecasts. This concept is called *feedback*. Most predictive models output numerical values. A simple trading system has four discrete values: (1) long, (2) exit long, (3) short, and (4) cover.

HOW FEEDBACK CAN HELP MECHANICAL TRADING SYSTEMS

In a mechanical trading system, feedback is valuable in efforts to identify which signals from the system have the highest probability of being profitable. Feedback also helps in selecting which system to trade when multiple systems are trading in the same market. Later in this book, we will discuss how to implement this application using advanced technologies such as machine learning.

HOW TO MEASURE SYSTEM PERFORMANCE
FOR USE AS FEEDBACK

We measure the performance of a system based on its trade history. We can look at the trading results from two different perspectives: (1) on the basis of only closed-out positions, or (2) on a bar-by-bar basis, by recording the opening equity of each position. In this book, we will study only the equity of closed-out positions.

We also can consider how technical and intermarket analysis can be combined with equity analysis to improve system performance. When we analyze which component of a trading system model generated a signal and combine this knowledge with trading performance feedback, we are able to see relationships that are important in modeling the markets but would not otherwise be observed.

METHODS OF VIEWING TRADING PERFORMANCE
FOR USE AS FEEDBACK

The first method of viewing performance is to build an *equity curve,* which is a moving cumulative value of all closed out trades over the evaluation period for a particular system. A modified version of this method is to view not all trades, but only closed-out trades, over a period of N days—usually, the past 100 days.

Another method is to view a trade history, which can be generated in a program like SuperCharts™. The trade history would have a trade on each row and would show the type of signal, entry date and price, exit date and price, trade profit and loss, and current equity. SuperCharts allows exporting this type of history to a spreadsheet.

We can also view closed trade equity versus technical or intermarket relationships. For example, a 100-day change in equity can be plotted on the Y axis, and volatility on the X axis. Figure 10.1 is an example of this type of chart.

Alternatively, current volatility can be plotted versus the next N-day change in equity.

The interrelationships between the trading systems and the market price actions are very complex and are well hidden from simple analysis. When a system is complex and uses many indicators, it becomes

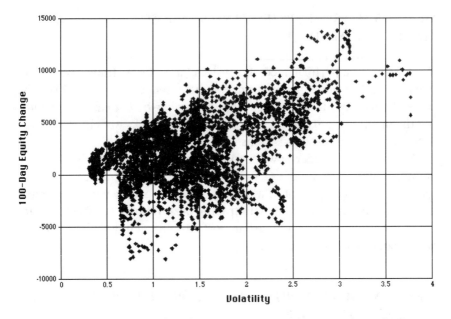

FIGURE 10.1   A 100-day change in equity versus 100-day volatility.

impossible to judge how it will perform in any given market condition. Feedback analysis is a valuable tool for making this impossible job manageable. All mechanical systems have a given trading pattern or "footprint." When we test most trend-following methods over a long enough time period, a common trading pattern emerges. The classic channel breakout system will win 35 to 50 percent of its trades, and the average winner will be much larger than the average loser. The winner will also have more bars in its winning trades than in its losing trades. Another often overlooked fact is that most trading systems are directly or indirectly based on cycles. System performance will change as the different dominant cycles in the market appear, disappear, and shift. We will also see changes in the trading results as changes occur in the composite of multiple cycles present in the market.

WALK FORWARD EQUITY FEEDBACK

In Chapter 9, we showed how we can simulate a trading system and calculate its adverse excursion on a system. We can then use this information to develop stops for the actual trading system in a walk forward adaptive manner. The same idea can be used to adapt system parameters and rules based on a moving window of equity.

Let's look at an example of how this approach can improve system performance. We will use a 20-bar channel breakout, as in Chapter 4, and will apply this analysis to the D-Mark.

Channel breakout systems can be helpful using equity feedback because there are dependencies for trades. For example, if the last trade on the buy side was winning, the chances of the next trade on the buy side, winnings are increased. Let's now develop code for TradeStation, which can track a simulated equity curve for both the long and the short sides. We need to simulate these trades because once we change the trades based on our analysis, we have, in effect, changed the system. If we want to develop statistics on our original system and use them to modify a new system, we need to simulate the trade. The code for simulating both the long and short sides for a channel breakout system is shown in Table 10.1.

These two simple user functions—TrendChanShort and TrendChan-Long—keep track of the equity on the long side and the short side, respectively. They work well, but in order to simplify this example, we avoid handling several special cases. First case is that, if you are using backadjusted contacts, we do not handle cases in which prices of a commodity go negative. Another unaddressed issue is when both a long and a short signal are generated on the same day. These issues are not a problem with commodities like the currency, the S&P500, and T-Bonds, but they are a problem with crude oil because this market often moves in a tight range. The code for handling these issues exists but is beyond the scope of this book.

Let's now use these routines in the channel breakout trading system. We ran this system on the D-Mark, using data from 1/1/80 to 5/17/96. Using equity analysis, we found a pattern that worked well on the D-Mark: Take only short trades when the system has been profitable on the long side but has been losing money on the short side. Using the same logic, we take only long trades when the system is making money on the short side and losing on the long side. We also wait 10 trades before applying equity analysis. The code for our feedback channel breakout system is shown in Table 10.2.

We tested this code on the D-Mark data from the period 1/1/80 to 5/17/96. Our results are shown in Table 10.3, along with the results for the original system.

TABLE 10.1 CODE TO SIMULATE EQUITY
ON LONG TRADES ONLY.

```
Inputs: ChanLen(Numeric);
Vars: BuyLev(0),SellLev(0),BuyEntry(0),SellEntry(0),Position(0);
Vars: Returns(0);
if CurrentBar=1 then Returns=0;
BuyLev=Highest(High,ChanLen)[1];
SellLev=Lowest(Low,ChanLen)[1];
If High>BuyLev and position<>1 then begin
BuyEntry=MaxList(BuyLev,Open);
Position=1;
end;
If Low<SellLev and position<>-1 then begin
SellEntry=MinList(SellLev,Open);
Position=-1;
end;
if Position=1 and Position[1]=-1 then Returns=Returns+(SellEntry-BuyEntry);
TrendChanLong=Returns;

{ Code to simulate equity on short trades only}
Inputs: ChanLen(Numeric);
Vars: BuyLev(0),SellLev(0),BuyEntry(0),SellEntry(0),Position(0);
Vars: Returns(0);
if CurrentBar=1 then Returns=0;
BuyLev=Highest(High,ChanLen)[1];
SellLev=Lowest(Low,ChanLen)[1];
If High>BuyLev and position<>1 then begin
BuyEntry=MaxList(BuyLev,Open);
Position=1;
end;
If Low<SellLev and position<>-1 then begin
SellEntry=MinList(SellLev,Open);
Position=-1;
end;
if Position=-1 and Position[1]=1 then Returns=Returns+(SellEntry-BuyEntry);
TrendChanShort=Returns
```

TABLE 10.2   CHANNEL BREAKOUT WITH SIMULATED EQUITY CODE.

```
Input: SLen(180),LLen(120);
Vars: LongEqu(0),ShortEqu(0),TBars(0);
ShortEqu=TrendChanShort(20,0);
LongEqu=TrendChanLong(20,0);
If TotalTrades<10 then begin
Buy Highest(High,20)+1 point Stop;
Sell Lowest(Low,20)-1 point Stop;
end;
If ShortEqu-ShortEqu[SLen]<0 and LongEqu-LongEqu[LLen]>0 then Sell
Lowest(Low,20) -1 point Stop;
ExitShort at Highest(High,20)+1 point stop;
If LongEqu-LongEqu[LLen]<0 and ShortEqu-ShortEqu[SLen]>0 then Buy
Highest(High,20) -1 point Stop;
ExitLong at Lowest(High,20)+1 point stop;
```

By using this method of equity feedback to filter our trades, we reduced both the number of trades and the drawdown by almost half. We made 11 percent less money but increased our average trades by 84 percent.

Our second example, a 20-day channel breakout system applied to the D-Mark, used a moving-average crossover of equity as a filter for both long and short trades. We take only long trades when a faster period moving average of long equity is greater than a slower period one. We take only short trades when a faster period moving average of equity on the

TABLE 10.3   CHANNEL BREAKOUT ON D-MARK WITH AND WITHOUT EQUITY ANALYSIS.

	Original System	Equity Feedback Demo 1
Net profit	$56,663.75	$50,945.00
Trades	104	50
Win%	50	54
Average trade	$544.84	$1,018.90
Drawdown	-$22,075.00	-$12,245.00
Profit factor	1.57	2.53

TABLE 10.4   CODE FOR MOVING AVERAGE OF EQUITY FILTER WITH CHANNEL BREAKOUT SYSTEM.

```
Input: SLen(130),LLen(150);
Vars: LongEqu(0),ShortEqu(0),TBars(0);
ShortEqu=TrendChanShort(20,0);
LongEqu=TrendChanLong(20,0);
If TotalTrades<10 then begin
Buy Highest(High,20) + 1 point Stop;
Sell Lowest(Low,20) - 1 point Stop;
end;
If Average(ShortEqu,SLen)>Average(ShortEqu,LLen) then Sell Lowest(Low,20) - 1 point Stop;
ExitShort at Highest(High,20)+1 point stop;
If Average(LongEqu,SLen)>Average(LongEqu,LLen) then Buy Highest(High,20) - 1 point Stop;
ExitLong at Lowest(High,20)+1 point stop;
```

short side is above a slower period one. The code for this system is shown in Table 10.4.

On the basis of our analysis, we found that using a 130-day average of equity minus a 150-day average produced good results. It might be surprising to know that these two moving averages produce good results when they are so close together. We were surprised, but almost all of the top sets of parameters had moving-average lengths very close together. Using lengths this close reduced our analysis to a mechanical way of saying that the last trade was profitable, and we did not have a quick 1- or 2-day whipsaw. The results based on these parameters, over the same period used earlier, are shown in Table 10.5.

TABLE 10.5   RESULTS OF CHANNEL BREAKOUT WITH EQUITY FILTER.

Net profit	$57,886.25
Trades	69
Win%	52
Average trade	$838.93
Drawdown	-$10,335.00
Profit factor	2.11

Using this moving average filter, we cut the drawdown by over 200 percent and filtered out a little more than one-third of the trades. We did this while slightly increasing net profit.

HOW TO USE FEEDBACK TO DEVELOP ADAPTIVE SYSTEMS OR SWITCH BETWEEN SYSTEMS

Equity curve analysis is a powerful tool for improving the performance of trading systems. The examples presented are only a sample of what can be done using this technology. In another application, this technology can be used to switch between different trading systems. Suppose we had a channel breakout system, a system based on intermarket analysis, and a countertrending type of system. We could simulate the equity curves for each of these systems, and then, based on our analysis, select the one that currently has the highest probability of producing the best trade. When developing these types of models, we can combine technical or fundamental factors with our equity curve analysis to further improve performance.

Another application of this technology is to adjust parameters for a given system in a walk forward manner. This can be done by simulating the equity curve of many different sets of parameters for the same system and then, based on our analysis, selecting the best one to currently trade.

WHY DO THESE METHODS WORK?

For a channel breakout system to work well, two conditions must be true:

1. The market must be trending.
2. The performance of a channel breakout system is linked to a relationship between the period used in breakout and the dominant cycle.

If the cycle length becomes longer, then the channel breakout system will get whipsawed during Elliott Waves two and four. ADX can be used to see whether the market is trending. The problem is that the interaction between the dominant cycle and how much the market is trending is complex and has a major effect on the performance of a channel break-out system. Modeling this interaction would require developing complex rules that will make the system less robust. Equity curve analysis can be used to solve this problem because the equity curve contains information about this interaction that can be used to improve the system without a lot of complex analysis.

The concept of system feedback is a powerful trading tool that can improve profit, drawdown, and the winning percentage for most trading strategies. Trading a system without at least being aware of the equity curve is like driving a car at night without lights—possible, but dangerous.

11

An Overview of
Advanced Technologies

Advanced technologies are methods based on machine learning or on analysis of data and development of models or formulas. I have used many different advanced technologies in developing market timing systems. These technologies include neural networks, machine induction methods, and genetic algorithms. This chapter gives a technical overview of each of these methods and introduces chaos theory, statistical pattern recognition, and "fuzzy logic."

THE BASICS OF NEURAL NETWORKS

Neural networks are loosely based on the human brain but are more similar to standard regression analysis than to neurons and synapses. Neural networks are much more powerful than regression analysis and can be programmed for many complex relationships and patterns that standard statistical methods can not. Their effectiveness in pattern recognition makes them ideal for developing trading systems.

Neural networks "learn" by using examples. They are given a set of input data and the correct answers for each case. Using these examples, a neural network will learn to develop a formula or model for solving a given problem.

Let us now discuss how a simple neural network works. Artificial neural networks, like the human brain, are composed of neurons and synapses. Neurons are the processing elements of the brain, and synapses connect them. In our computer-simulated neural networks, neurons, also called nodes, are simply elements that add together input values multiplied by the coefficients assigned to them. We call these coefficients *weights*. After we have added together these values, we take this total and apply a decision function. A decision function translates the total produced by the node into a value used to solve the problem.

For example, a decision function could decide to buy when the sum is greater than 5 and sell when it is less than or equal to 5. Figure 11.1 shows a simple example of a neural network.

The rows of one or more nodes are called layers. The first row of nodes is the input layer, and the last row is the output layer. When only these simple neurons are connected, we call it a two-layer perceptron.

During the early 1960s, Bernard Widrow used two-layer perceptrons to solve many real-world problems—for example, short-range weather forecasts. Widrow even developed a weather forecasting neural network that was able to perform as well as the National Weather Service.

How do we get the value of the weights used to solve a problem? Before a neural network starts learning how to solve a problem, each weight

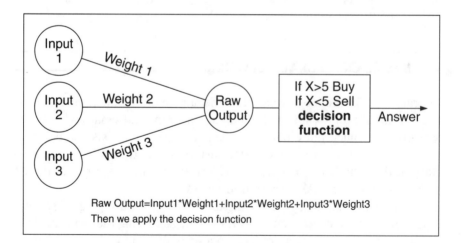

FIGURE 11.1   A simple two-layer perceptron.

is set to a random value. We call this process "initializing the weights." Once we have initialized the weights, we can adjust them during the learning process.

A perceptron neural network learns by repeatedly producing an answer for each case, using the current value of its weights and comparing that value to the correct answer. It then adjusts the weights to try to better learn the complete set of data. We call this process "supervised learning."

With simple two-layer perceptrons, the method or algorithm used to adjust these weights could not solve a very important type of problem.

In 1969, Minsky and Papart, in a book entitled *The Perceptron,* proved that a simple perceptron with two layers could not solve "non-linearly separable problems" such as "Exclusive OR." An example of an Exclusive OR problem is: You can go to the store or to see a movie, but you cannot do both.

This flaw in two-layer perceptron neural networks killed funding for neural network research until the mid-1980s. Many researchers still continued working on neural networks, but, without funding, progress was slow.

In 1974, Dr. Paul Werbos developed a method for using a three-layer neural network to solve nonlinearly separable problems such as Exclusive OR. Rumelhart popularized a similar method and started the neural explosion in the mid-1980s. This method, called "backpropagation," is the most widely used neural network algorithm today.

Let's see how this method differs from two-layer perceptrons.

Figure 11.2 shows a simple backpropagation neural network. The second row of nodes is called the hidden layer. The first and third layers are called the input layer (inputs) and the output layer (outputs), respectively. A backpropagation neural network will have one or more hidden layers. There are two major differences between a backpropagation neural network and a simple two-layer perceptron. The first difference is that the decision functions must now be more complex and nonlinear. The second difference is in how they learn. In general, a backpropagation neural network learns in the same way as the two-layer perceptron. The main difference is that, because of the hidden layer(s), we must use advanced mathematics to calculate the weight adjustments during learning.

The classic backpropagation algorithm learns slowly and could take thousands of passes through the data to learn a given problem. This is

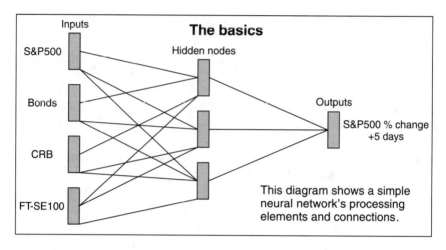

FIGURE 11.2   A simple three-layer neural network.

why each neural network product has its own proprietary version of a backpropagation-like algorithm.

When you develop a solution to a problem using neural networks, you must preprocess your data before showing it to the neural network. Preprocessing is a method of applying to the data transforms that make the relationships more obvious to the neural network. An example of this process would be using the difference between historical prices and the moving average over the past 30 days. The goal is to allow the neural network to easily see the relationships that a human expert would see when solving the problem.

We will be discussing preprocessing and how to use neural networks as part of market timing systems in the next few chapters.

Let's now discuss how you can start using neural networks successfully. The first topic is the place for neural networks in developing market timing solutions. The second is the methodology required to use neural networks successfully in these applications.

Neural networks are not magic. They should be viewed as a tool for developing a new class of powerful leading indicators that can integrate many different forms of analysis. Neural networks work best when used as part of a larger solution.

A neural network can be used to predict an indicator, such as a percent change, N bars into the future; for example, the percent change of the S&P500 5 weeks into the future. The values predicted by the neural network can be used just like any other indicator to build trading systems. Neural networks' predictions don't need to have high correlation with future price action; a correlation of .2 or .3 can produce huge returns.

MACHINE INDUCTION METHODS

Machine induction methods are ways to generate rules from data. There are many different machine induction methods, and each one has its own strengths and weaknesses. The two that I use are called C4.5, which is a descendant of an algorithm called ID3, and rough sets.

C4.5

In the late 1940s, Claude Shannon developed a concept called "information theory," which allows us to measure the information content of data by determining the amount of confusion or "entropy" in the data. Information theory has allowed us to develop a class of learning-by-example algorithms that produce decision trees, which minimize entropy. One of these is C4.5. C4.5 and its predecessor, ID3, were developed by J. Ross Quinlan. Using a decision tree, they both classify objects based on a list of attributes. Decision trees can be expressed in the form of rules. Figure 11.3 shows an example of a decision tree.

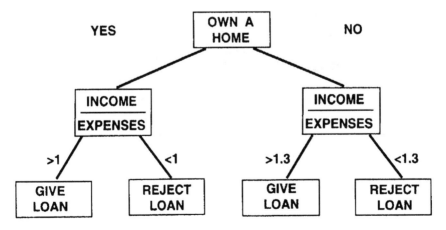

FIGURE 11.3   A simple decision tree.

Let's take a closer look at the binary version of C4.5. It creates a two-way branch at every split in the tree. Attributes are selected for splitting based on the information content of each attribute in terms of classifying the outcome groups. The attributes containing the most information are at the top of the tree. Information content decreases as we move toward the bottom level of the tree, through the "leaves."

For discrete attributes, the values are split between branches so as to maximize information content. Numerical data are broken into bins or ranges. These ranges are developed based on a numeric threshold derived to maximize the information content of the attribute. The output classes or objects must be represented by discrete variables. This requires numerical output classes to be manually split into ranges based on domain expertise.

Both C4.5 and ID3 handle noise by performing significance testing at each node. The attributes must both reduce entropy and pass a significance test in order to split a branch. C4.5 and ID3 use the Chi-square test for significance. Several parameters can be set to help C4.5 develop rule sets that will generalize well. The first parameter is the lower branch limit—the number of data records below which the induction process will terminate the branch and develop a leaf. A good starting point for this parameter is about 2 percent of the number of records in the database. After the decision tree is induced, a process called "pruning" can improve generalization. Noise causes excessive branches to form near the leaves of the tree. Pruning allows us to remove these branches and reduce the effects of noise. There are two types of automatic pruning: (1) error reduction and (2) statistical. Error reduction pruning is based on a complexity/accuracy criterion. Branches that fail the test are pruned.

The statistical pruning algorithm is particularly suited to situations where the noise in the data is caused by not having all the relevant attributes to classify the outcome and by the presence of irrelevant attributes. This is true of the financial markets as well as many other real-world problems.

The statistical pruning algorithm works backward from the leaves to remove all attribute branches of the induced tree that are not statistically significant (using the Chi-square test).

Another type of pruning is based on domain expertise. A domain expert could examine the rules generated and delete any of them that don't make sense in the real-world application. Rules can also be generalized by dropping conditions and then retesting them on unseen data. A domain expert could also specialize a rule by adding a condition to it. When developing machine-induced rules, you don't want to use all the rules that were generated. You only want to use "strong rules"—those with enough supporting cases. For this reason, when using C4.5, you need a product that offers statistical information about each of the leaves on the tree. An example of a product that has this feature is XpertRule™ by Attar Software.

Rough Sets

Rough sets is a mathematical technique for working with the imperfections of real-world data. Rough sets theory, proposed by Pawlak in 1982, can be used to discover dependencies in data while ignoring superfluous data. The product of rough sets theory is a set of equivalence classifications that can handle inconsistent data. Rough sets methodology facilitates data analysis, pattern discovery, and predictive modeling in one step. It does not require additional testing of significance, cross-correlation of variables, or pruning of rules.

Let's now try to understand how rough sets work. We will assume that real-world information is given in the form of an information table. Table 11.1 is an example of an information table.

The rows in this table are called examples. Each example is composed of attributes and a decision variable. In Table 11.1, headache, muscle pain, and temperature are attributes, and flu is the decision variable.

Rough sets theory uses this type of table to develop rules from data. Rough sets theory is an extension of standard set theory, in which the definition of the set is integrated with knowledge.

TABLE 11.1   ROUGH SETS EXAMPLE 1.

Row	Headache	Muscle Pain	Temperature	Flu
1	Yes	Yes	Normal	No
2	Yes	Yes	High	Yes
3	Yes	Yes	Very high	Yes
4	No	Yes	Normal	No
5	No	No	High	No
6	No	No	Very high	Yes

To make this explanation easier to understand, let's review some of the basics of set theory.

Subsets

Subsets are made up of only elements contained in a larger set. A superset is the inverse of that makeup. A proper set is a subset that is not identical to the set it is being compared to. Let's now look at some examples of subsets and supersets.

Let A = {R1,R2,R3,R4,R5,R6,R7,R8,R9}

Let B = {R4,R5,R8}

In this example, B is a subset of A; this is expressed as $B \subset A$. We can also say that A is a superset of B: $A \supset B$.

The union of two sets forms a set containing all of the elements in both sets. For example, let's suppose we have two sets, A and B, as follows:

A = {R1,R2,R3,R4,R5,R6}
B = {R7,R8,R9}

The union of these sets yields the set {R1,R2,R3,R4,R5,R6,R7, R8,R9}. This is expressed as $X = A \cup B$.

Let's now calculate the intersection of the following two sets:

A = {R1,R2,R3,R4,R5,R6,R7}
B = {R2,R4,R6,R8,R10}

These two sets intersect to form the set {R2,R4,R6}. The intersection is expressed as $X = A \cap B$. Another set function is called the cardinality—the size of a given set.

With this overview of set theory, let's now use these basics to see how rough sets work.

The Basics of Rough Sets

The main concept behind rough sets is collections of rows that have the same values for one or more attributes. These sets, called elementary sets, are said to be indiscernible. In the example shown in Table 11.1, the attributes headache and muscle pain can be used to produce two different subsets. These are formed by the rows {R1,R2,R3} and {R4,R6}. These two subsets make up two different elementary sets.

Any union of elementary sets is called a definable set. The concept of indiscernibility relation allows us to define redundant attributes easily. Using Table 11.1, let's define two sets. The first is based on the attributes headache and temperature. The second will add muscle pain and use all three attributes. Using either pair of attributes produces the same elementary sets. These are the sets formed by the single elements {R1},{R2},{R3},{R4},{R5},{R6}. Because these sets of attributes form the same sets, we can say that the attribute muscle pain is redundant: it did not change the definition of the sets by addition or deletion. Sets of attributes with no redundancies are called independents. Sets that contain the same elements as other sets but possess the fewest attributes are called reducts.

In Table 11.2, muscle pain has been removed because it did not add any information.

Let's now develop elementary sets based on the decisions in Table 11.2. An elementary set that is defined based on a decision variable, which in our case would be yes or no, is called a "concept." For Tables 11.1 and 11.2, these are {R1,R4,R5} and {R2,R3,R6}. These are defined by the sets in which the decision (flu) is no for {R1,R4,R5} and yes for {R2,R3,R6}.

What elementary sets can be formed from the attributes headache and temperature together? These are the single-element sets {R1},{R2}, {R3},{R4},{R5},{R6}. Because each of these sets is a subset of one of

TABLE 11.2   ROUGH SETS EXAMPLE 2.

Row	Headache	Temperature	Flu
1	Yes	Normal	No
2	Yes	High	Yes
3	Yes	Very high	Yes
4	No	Normal	No
5	No	High	No
6	No	Very high	Yes

TABLE 11.3   RULES FOR EXAMPLE 2.

(Temperature, normal)=(Flu,No)

(Headache, No) and (Temperature, High)=(Flu,No)

(Headache, Yes) and (Temperature, High)=(Flu,Yes)

(Temperature, Very High)=(Flu,Yes)

our decision-based elementary sets, we can use these relationships to produce the rules shown in Table 11.3.

Let's now add the two examples {R7,R8} shown in Table 11.4.

Having added these two examples, let's redefine our elementary sets of indiscernibility relationships for the attributes headache and temperature. These sets are: {R1},{R2},{R3},{R4},{R5,R7},{R6,R8}. Our elementary sets, based on our decision variable, are:

For Flu = No, {R1,R4,R5,R8}

For Flu = Yes, {R2,R3,R6,R7}.

As shown in Table 11.4, the decision on flu does not depend on the attributes headache and temperature because neither of the elementary sets, {R5,R7} and {R6,R8}, is a subset of any concept. We say that Table 11.4 is inconsistent because the outcomes of {R5} and {R7} are conflicting. For the same attribute values, we have a different outcome.

The heart of rough sets theory is that it can deal with these types of inconsistencies. The method of dealing with them is simple. For each concept X, we define both the greatest definable and least definable sets. The

TABLE 11.4   ROUGH SETS EXAMPLE 3.

Row	Headache	Temperature	Flu
1	Yes	Normal	No
2	Yes	High	Yes
3	Yes	Very high	Yes
4	No	Normal	No
5	No	High	No
6	No	Very high	Yes
7	No	High	Yes
8	No	Very high	No

greatest definable set contains all cases in which we have no conflicts and is called the lower approximation. The least definable sets are ones in which we may have conflicts. They are called the upper approximation.

As in our earlier example, when there are no conflicts, we simply create a series of sets of attributes and a set for each decision variable. If the attribute set is a subset of the decision set, we can translate that relationship into a rule. When there are conflicts, there is no relationship and we need to use a different method. We solve this problem by defining two different boundaries that are collections of sets. These are called the upper and lower approximations. The lower approximation consists of all of the objects that surely belong to the concept. The upper approximation consists of any object that possibly belongs to the concept.

Let's now see how this translates into set theory. Let I = an elementary set of attributes, and X = a concept. The lower approximation is defined as:

$$Lower = \{x \in U : I(x) \subseteq X\}$$

In words, this formula says that the lower approximation is all of the elementary sets that are proper subsets of the concept X. In fact, the U means the universe, which is a fancy way of saying *all*.

The upper approximation is defined as:

$$Upper = \{x \in U : I(x) \cap X \neq 0\}$$

This simply means that the upper approximation is all of the elementary sets that produce a nonempty intersection with one or more concepts.

The boundary region is the difference between the upper and lower approximations.

Rough sets theory implements a concept called vagueness. In fact, this concept causes rough sets to sometimes be confused with fuzzy logic. The rough sets membership function is defined as follows:

$$\mu_x^I = \frac{|X \cap I(x)|}{|I(x)|}$$

This simple formula defines roughness as the cardinality of the intersection of (1) the subset that forms the concept and (2) an elementary set of attributes, divided by the cardinality of the elementary set. As noted earlier, cardinality is just the number of elements. Let's see how this concept would work, using the sets in Table 11.4 in which headache is no and temperature is high, {R5 and R7}. If we want to compare the rough set membership of this set to the decision class Flu = Yes, we apply our formula to the attribute set and the Flu = Yes membership set {R2,R3,R6,R7}. The intersection of these two sets has just one element, R7. Our Headache = No and Temperature = High set has two elements, so the rough set membership for this elementary set of attributes and the Flu = Yes concept is ½ = 0.5.

This roughness calculation is used to determine the precision of rules produced by rough sets. For example, we can convert this into the following possible rule:

If Headache and Temperature = High, Flu = Yes (.50).

Rough sets technology is very valuable in developing market timing systems. First, rough sets do not make any assumption about the distribution of the data. This is important because financial markets are not based on a gaussian distribution. Second, this technology not only handles noise well, but also eliminates irrelevant factors.

GENETIC ALGORITHMS—AN OVERVIEW

Genetic algorithms were invented by John Holland during the mid-1970s to solve hard optimization problems. This method uses natural selection, "survival of the fittest," to solve optimization problems using computer software.

There are three main components to a genetic algorithm:

1. A way of describing the problem in terms of a genetic code, like a DNA chromosome.
2. A way to simulate evolution by creating offspring of the chromosomes, each being slightly different than its parents.
3. A method to evaluate the goodness of each of the offspring.

This process is shown in Table 11.5, which gives an overview of the steps involved in a genetic solution.

TABLE 11.5   STEPS USING GENETIC ALGORITHM.

1. Encode the problem into chromosomes.
2. Using the encoding, develop a fitness function for use in evaluating each chromosome's value in solving a given problem.
3. Initialize a population of chromosomes.
4. Evaluate each chromosome in the population.
5. Create new chromosomes by mating two chromosomes. (This is done by mutating and recombining two parents to form two children. We select parents randomly but biased by their fitness.)
6. Evaluate the new chromosome.
7. Delete a member of the population that is less fit than the new chromosome, and insert the new chromosome into the population.
8. If a stopping number of generations is reached, or time is up, then return the best chromosome(s) or, alternatively, go to step 4.

Genetic algorithms are a simple but powerful tool for finding the best combination of elements to make a good trading system or indicator. We can evolve rules to create artificial traders. The traders can then be used to select input parameters for neural networks, or to develop portfolio and asset class models or composite indexes. Composite indexes are a specially weighted group of assets that can be used to predict other assets or can be traded themselves as a group. Genetic algorithms are also useful for developing rules for integrating multiple system components and indicators. These are only a few of the possibilities. Let's now discuss each component and step of a genetic algorithm in more detail.

DEVELOPING THE CHROMOSOMES

Let's first review some of the biology-based terminology we will use. The initial step in solving a problem using genetic algorithms is to encode the problem into a string of numbers called a "chromosome." These numbers can be binary real numbers or discrete values. Each element on the chromosome is called a "gene." The value of each gene is called an "allele." The position of the gene on the chromosome is called the "locus." The string of numbers created must contain all of the encoded information needed to solve the problem.

As an example of how we can translate a problem to a chromosome, let's suppose we would like to develop trading rules using genetic algorithms. We first need to develop a general form for our rules, for example:

> If **Indicator (Length)** > **Trigger** and **Indicator (Length)**[1] < **Trigger**, then **Place order** to open and exit N days later.

Note: Items in **bold** are being encoded into chromosomes.

We could also have encoded into the chromosomes the > and < operators, as well as the conjunctive operator "AND" used in this rule template.

Let's see how we can encode a rule of this form. We can assign an integer number to each technical indicator we would like to use. For example: RSI = 1, SlowK = 2, and so on. **Trigger** would be a simple real number. **Place order** could be 1 for a buy and −1 for a sell. N is the number of days to hold the position.

Let's see how the following rule could be encoded.

> If **RSI(9)** > **30** and **RSI(9)**[1] < **30**, then **Buy** at open and Exit **5** days later.

The chromosome for the above rule would be: 1,9,30,1,9,30,1,5.

Having explained the encoding of a chromosome, I now discuss how to develop a fitness function.

EVALUATING FITNESS

A fitness function evaluates chromosomes for their ability or fitness for solving a given problem. Let's discuss what would be required to develop a fitness function for the chromosome in the above example. The first step is to pass the values of the chromosome's genes to a function that can use these values to evaluate the rule represented by the chromosome. We will evaluate this rule for each record in our training. We will then collect statistics for the rule and evaluate those statistics using a formula that can return a single value representing how fit the chromosome is for solving the problem at hand. For example, we can collect Net Profit,

Drawdown, and Winning percentage on each rule and then evaluate their fitness using a simple formula:

Fitness = (Net Profit/Drawdown)*Winning percentage

The goal of the genetic algorithm in this case would be to maximize this function.

INITIALIZING THE POPULATION

Next, we need to initialize the population by creating a number of chromosomes using random values for the allele of each gene. Each numerical value for the chromosomes is randomly selected using valid values for each gene. For example, gene one of our example chromosome would contain only integer values. We must also limit these values to integers that have been assigned to a given indicator. Most of the time, these populations contain at least 50 and sometimes hundreds of members.

THE EVOLUTION

Reproduction is the heart of the genetic algorithm. The reproductive process involves two major steps: (1) the selection of a pair of chromosomes to use as parents for the next set of children, and (2) the process of combining these genes into two children. Let's examine each of the steps in more detail.

The first issue in reproduction is parent selection. A popular method of parent selection is the roulette wheel method,* shown in Table 11.6.

We will now have the two parents produce children. Two major operations are involved in mating: (1) crossover and (2) mutation. (Mating is not the only way to produce members for the next generation. Some genetic algorithms will occasionally clone fit members to produce children. This is called "Elitism.")

---

*Using this method, we will select two parents who will mate and produce children.

TABLE 11.6   PARENT SELECTION.

1. Sum the fitness of all the population members, and call that sum X.
2. Generate a random number between 0 and X.
3. Return the first population member whose fitness, when added to the fitness of the preceding population member, is greater than or equal to the random number from step 2.

There are three popular crossover methods or types: (1) one-point (single-point), (2) two-point, and (3) uniform. All of these methods have their own strengths and weaknesses. Let's now take a closer look at how the various crossover methods work.

The One-Point Crossover

The one-point crossover randomly selects two adjacent genes on the chromosome of a parent and severs the link between the pair so as to cut the chromosome into two parts. We do this to both parents. We then create one child using the left-hand side of parent 1 and the right-hand side of parent 2. The second child will be just the reverse. Figure 11.4 shows how a one-point crossover works.

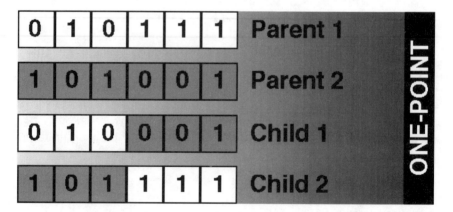

FIGURE 11.4   An example of a one-point crossover.

The Two-Point Crossover

A two-point crossover is similar to the one-point method except that two cuts are made in the parents, and the genes between those cuts are exchanged to produce children. See Figure 11.5 for an example of a two-point crossover.

The Uniform Crossover

In the uniform crossover method, we randomly exchange genes between the two parents, based on some crossover probability. An example of a uniform crossover appears in Figure 11.6.

All three of our examples showed crossovers using binary operators. You might wonder how to perform crossovers when the genes of the chromosomes are real numbers or discrete values. The basics of each of the crossover methods are the same. The difference is that, once we have selected the genes that will be affected by the crossover, we develop other operators to combine them instead of just switching them. For example, when using real-number genes, we can use weighted averages of the two parents to produce a child. We can use one set of weighting for child 1 and another for child 2. For processing discrete values, we can just randomly select one of the other classes.

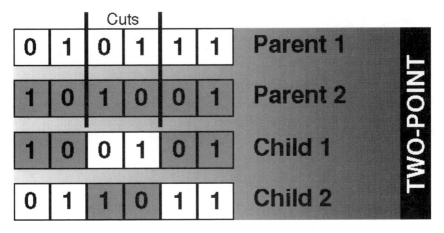

FIGURE 11.5   An example of a two-point crossover.

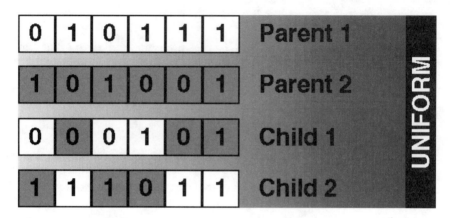

FIGURE 11.6   An example of a uniform crossover.

Mutation

Mutation is a random changing of a gene on a chromosome. Mutations occur with a low probability because, if we mutated all the time, then the evolutionary process would be reduced to a random search.

Figure 11.7 shows an example of a mutation on a binary chromosome.

If we were working with real-number chromosomes, we could add a small random number (ranging from ± 10 percent of the average for that gene) to its value to produce a mutation.

Several concepts are important to genetic algorithms. We will overview these concepts without covering the mathematics behind them.

The first concept we must understand is the concept of similar templates of chromosomes, called schemata. If we are working with binary

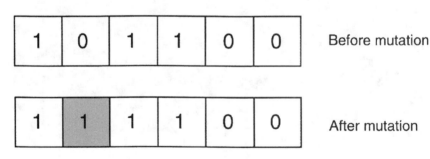

FIGURE 11.7   An example of mutation.

genes, defining schemata requires the symbols 0,1, and *, where 0 and 1 are just binary digits, and * means don't care. Figure 11.8 examines a chromosome and two different schemata.

Schema 1 is a template that requires genes 1,2,3,6 to be 1. Schema 2 requires a 0 in gene 4 and a 1 in gene five. Our sample chromosome fits both schemata, but this is not always the case. Let's say that, in a population of 100 chromosomes, 30 fit schema 1 and 20 fit schema 2. One of the major concepts of genetic algorithms then applies.

Let's suppose that the average fitness of the chromosomes belonging to schema 1 is 0.75, and the average fitness of those in schema 2 is 0.50. The average fitness of the whole population is 0.375. In this case, schema 1 will have an exponentially increased priority in subsequent generations of reproduction, when compared to schema 2.

Schemata also affect crossovers. The longer a schema, the more easily it can get disrupted by crossover. The length of a schema is measured as the length between the innermost and outermost 0 or 1 for a binary chromosome. This distance is called the "defining length." In Figure 11.8, schema 1 has a longer defining length.

Different crossovers also have different properties that affect combining the schemata. For example, some schemata cannot be combined without disrupting them using either a single-point or a two-point crossover. On the other hand, single-point and two-point crossovers are good at not disrupting paired genes used to express a single feature. The uniform crossover method can combine any two schemata that differ by

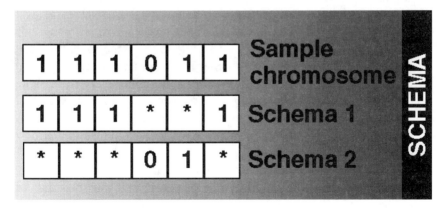

FIGURE 11.8   An example of a schema.

one or more genes, but has a higher probability of disrupting schemata that require paired genes to express a feature. This point must be kept in mind when selecting encoding or crossover methods for solving problems.

UPDATING A POPULATION

After the genetic algorithm has produced one or more children, we apply the fitness function to each child produced, to judge how well the child solves the problem it was designed for. We compare the fitness of the new children to that of the existing population, and delete a randomly selected member whose fitness is less than that of a child we have evaluated. We then add this child to the population. We repeat this process for each child produced, until we reach a stopping number of generation or time.

Genetic algorithms are an exciting technology to use in developing trading-related applications. To use them effectively, it is important to understand the basic theory and to study case material that offers other applications in your domain or in similar domains. You don't need to understand the mathematics behind the theory, just the concepts.

CHAOS THEORY

Chaos theory is an area of analysis that describes complex modes in which not all of the variables or initial conditions are known. One example is weather forecasting; predictions are made using an incomplete series of equations. Chaos theory is not about randomness; it's about how real-world problems require understanding not only the model but also the initial conditions. Even small numerical errors due to round off can lead to a large error in prediction over very short periods of time. When studying these types of problems, standard geometry does not work.

For example, suppose we want to measure the sea shore. If we measure the shore line using a yardstick, we get one distance. If we measured it using a flexible tape measure, we get a longer distance; the length depends on how and with what tools we make the measurement.

Benoit Mandelbrot tried to solve this problem by creating *fractal geometry*. The fractal dimension is a measure of how "squiggly a given line is." This number can take values of 1 or higher—the higher the number, the more the measured length curves. It can also be a fractional number, such as 1.85. The fractal dimension of the data is important because systems with similar fractal dimensions have been found to have similar properties. The market will change modes when the fractal dimension changes. A method called *rescaled range analysis* can give both an indicator that measures whether the market is trending or not (similar to random walk), and the fractal dimension on which the financial data is calculated.

Thanks to Einstein, we know that in particle physics the distance that a random particle covers increases with the square root of the time it has been traveling. In equation form, if we denote by R the distance covered and let T be a time index, we see that:

$$R = \text{constant} \times T^{0.5}$$

Let's begin with a time series of length M. We will first convert this time series of length $N = M - 1$ of logarithmic ratios:

$$N_i = Log \frac{M_{(i+1)}}{M_i} \quad i = 1, 2, 3, \ldots (M-1)$$

We now need to divide our time period of length N into A contiguous subperiods of length n so that $A \times n = N$. We then label each of these subperiods I_a, with $a = 1,2,3....A$. We then label each of these elements I_a as $N_{k,a}$ such that $k = 1,2,3...n$. We then define our mean e by taking the time series of accumulated departures $(X_{k,a})$ from the mean value e in the following form:

$$X_{k,a} = \sum_{i=1}^{k} \left(N_{i,a} - e_a \right)$$

Summing over $i = 1$ to k, where $k = 1, 2, 3, \ldots, n$. The range is defined as the maximum minus the minimum value of X_k for each subperiod I_a:

$$R_{I_a} = Max(X_{k,a}) - Min(X_{k,a})$$

where $1 <= k <= n$. This adjusted range is the distance that the underlying system travels for time index M. We then calculate the standard deviation of the sample for each subperiod I_a.

$$S_{I_a} = \left(\frac{1}{n}\right) \times \sum_{k=1}^{n} \left(N_{k,a} - E_a^2\right)^{.0.50}$$

where $1 \leq k \leq n$. This standard deviation is used to normalize the range R. Hurst generalized Einstein's relation to a time series whose distribution is unknown by dividing the adjusted range by the standard deviation, showing that:

$$\frac{R}{S} = \frac{1}{A} \sum_{a=1}^{A} \frac{R_{I_a}}{S_{I_a}}$$

Now we can calculate H using the relationship

$$\left(\frac{R}{S}\right)_n = \text{Constant } n^H$$

where n is a time index and H is a power called the Hurst exponent, which can lie anywhere between 0 and 1. We can calculate the (R/S) equation for subperiod n and create a moving Hurst exponent. This can now be used like any other indicator to develop trading rules.

This is a simplified version of Peter's published methodology, yet still gives a good estimate of H.* The normal process for calculating H requires you to do a least squares on all $(R/S)_n$. We can skip this step and use the raw H value to develop indicators which are of value in trading systems. This does make H noisier but removes much of the lag. Peters suggests that the Hausdorff dimension can be approximated by the following relationship:

$$DH = 2 - H$$

where DH is the fractal dimension and H is the Hurst exponent.

The Hurst exponent H is of interest to traders since a value of 0.5 is simply a random time series. If H is above 0.5, then the series has a memory; in traders' terms this is called "trending." If H is less than 0.5 the market is an antipersistent time series, one in which less distance is

---

*See Peters, Edgar E. (1994). *Fractal Market Analysis*. (New York: John Wiley & Sons).

covered than in a completely random time series. In trading terms, this is called a "trading range."

We know that the Hurst exponent can be used to tell if the market is trending or if it is in a trading range. The question is: Can changes in the Hurst exponent be used to predict changes in the correlation between markets or in the technical nature of the market?

STATISTICAL PATTERN RECOGNITION

Statistical pattern recognition uses statistical methods to analyze and classify data. Statistical pattern recognition is not just one method; it is a class of methods for analyzing data.

One example of statistical pattern recognition is called case-based reasoning (CBR). CBR compares a library of cases to the current case. It then reports a list of similar cases. This idea is used by traders such as Paul Tutor Jones and even by Moore Research in their monthly publication. This process requires developing an index for the cases, using methods such as C4.5 or various statistical measures. One of the most common methods for developing these indexes is "nearest neighbor matching." Let's see how this matching is done.

If the database depends on numerical data, calculate the mean and the standard deviation of all fields stored in the database. For each record in the database, store how far each field is from the mean for that field in terms of standard deviation. For example, if the mean is 30 with a standard deviation of 3, an attribute with a value of 27 would be −1.0 standard deviation from the mean. Make these calculations for each attribute and case in the database. When a new case is given, develop a similarity score. First, convert the new case in terms of standard deviation from the mean and standard deviation used to build the index. Next, compare each of the attributes in the new case to the standardized index values, and select the cases that are the nearest match. An example of a closeness function is shown in Table 11.7.

Apply this function to each record in the database, and then report the lower scoring cases as the most similar. Use these methods to find similar patterns for automatic pattern recognition.

Similarity analysis can also be done using Pearson's correlation or another type of correlation called "Spearman ranked correlation."

TABLE 11.7 CLOSENESS FUNCTION.

$$\text{Closeness} = \sum \frac{(\text{New case attribute} - \text{Stored case attributes}) \times \text{Weight}}{\text{Total weights}}$$

New case attribute is the normalized value of a given attribute for new cases.

Stored case attribute is the normalized value of a given attribute for the current database case being measured.

Total weights is the sum of all of the weighting factors.

Statistical pattern recognition can also be used to develop subgroups of similar data. For example, we can subclassify data based on some statistical measure and then develop a different trading system for each class.

Statistical pattern recognition is a broad area of advanced methods, and this brief explanation only touches the surface. I showed the nearest neighbor matching method because it is simple and useful in developing analogs of current market conditions to previous years.

FUZZY LOGIC

Fuzzy logic is a powerful technology that allows us to solve problems that require dealing with vague concepts such as tall or short. For example, a person who is 6 feet tall might be considered tall compared to the general population, but short if a member of a basketball team. Another issue is: How would we describe a person who is 5 feet 11 inches, if 6 feet is considered tall? Fuzzy logic can allow us to solve both of these problems.

Fuzzy logic operators are made of three parts: (1) membership function(s), (2) fuzzy rule logic, and (3) defuzzifier(s). The membership function shows how relevant data are to the premise of each rule. Fuzzy rule logic performs the reasoning within fuzzy rules. The defuzzifier maps the fuzzy information back into real-world answers.

Let's see how fuzzy logic works, using a simple height example. We want to develop fuzzy rules that predict a one-year-old male child's height in adulthood, based on the height of his mother and father. The first step in developing a fuzzy logic application is to develop fuzzy membership functions for each variable's attributes. We need to develop fuzzy membership functions for the height attributes of the mother, father, and child. For our example, these attributes are tall, normal, and short. We have defined generic membership functions for these height attributes as follows (SD = standard deviation):

Tall=maximum(0,min(1,(X−Average Height)/(SD of height))).
Short=maximum(0,min(1,(Average Height−X)/(SD of height))).
Normal=maximum(0,(1−(abs(X−Average Height)/(SD of height)))).

When using these membership functions, substitute the following values for average height and standard deviation for the mother, father, and child.

Mother: average height 65 inches, SD 3 inches.

Father: average height 69 inches, SD 4 inches

Child: average height (12 months) 30 inches, SD 2 inches.

Having developed the membership functions, we can now develop our fuzzy rules. These rules and their supporting facts are shown in Table 11.8.

Using the above facts and our fuzzy membership functions for both the mother and father, we calculate the following output values for each membership function:

Mother's height short .66 normal .33 tall 0

Father's height short .5 normal .5 tall 0

TABLE 11.8   RULES FOR CHILD'S HEIGHT.

These two fuzzy rules are in our expert system:

1. If Mother_Short and Father_Short, then Child_Short.
2. If Mother_Short and Father_Normal, then Child_Normal.

We also have the following facts:
Mother is 63 inches tall.
Father is 67 inches tall.

Let's see what happens if we rerun the fuzzy rules using these facts.

1. If Mother_Short (.66) and Father_Short (.5), then
   Child_Short (.5).
2. If Mother_Short (.66) and Father_Normal (.5), then Child_Normal
   (.5).

Using the rules of fuzzy logic, we take the minimum of the values associated with the conditions when they are joined by an "and." If they are joined by an "or," we take the maximum.

As you can see, the child is both short and normal. We will now use something called defuzzification to convert the results of these rules back to a real height. First, find the center point of each of the membership functions that apply to the height of the child. In our case, that is 28 for short, 30 for normal, and 32 for tall. Next, multiply the output from the rules associated with each membership function by these center point values. Divide the result by the sum of the outputs from the membership

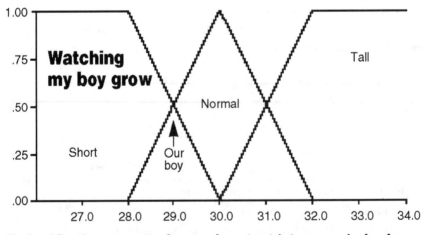

Defuzzification converts fuzzy rule output into numerical values.

FIGURE 11.9   An example of a simple defuzzication function for height.

functions. This will convert the fuzzy output back into a real height for our one-year-old male child:

$$(.5 \times 28 + .5 \times 30 + 0 \times 32)/(.5 + .5) = 29 \text{ inches tall}$$

To see how these membership functions interact for the height of our one-year-old child, look at Figure 11.9.

This chapter has given an overview of different advanced technologies that are valuable to traders. We will use these technologies in many examples in the remaining chapters. Now that we have domain expertise in both analyzing the markets and using many different advanced technologies, we are ready to design state-of-the-art trading applications.

Part Three

MAKING SUBJECTIVE METHODS MECHANICAL

12
How to Make Subjective Methods Mechanical

Ways of making subjective forms of analysis mechanical form one of the hottest areas of research in trading systems development. There are two key reasons for this concentrated activity. First, many people use subjective methods and would like to automate them. Second, and more important, we can finally backtest these methods and figure out which ones are predictive and which are just hype.

Based on both my research and the research of others such as Tom Joseph, I have developed a general methodology for making subjective trading methods mechanical. This chapter gives an overview of the process. The next two chapters will show you how to make Elliott Wave and candlestick recognition mechanical, using Omega TradeStation. Let's now discuss the general methodology I use to make subjective methods mechanical.

The first step is to select the subjective method we wish to make mechanical. After we have selected the method, we need to classify it, based on the following categories:

1. Total visual patterns recognition.
2. Subjective methods definition using fuzzy logic.

3. Human-aided semimechanical methods.

4. Mechanical definable methods.

A subjective form of analysis will belong to one or more of these categories. Let's now get an overview of each one.

TOTALLY VISUAL PATTERNS RECOGNITION

This class of subjective methods includes general chart patterns such as triangles, head and shoulders, and so on. These are the hardest types of subjective methods to make mechanical, and some chart patterns cannot be made totally automated. When designing a mechanical method for this class of pattern, we can develop rules that either will identify a large percentage of that pattern but with many false identifications, or will identify a small percentage of the pattern with a high percentage of accuracy. In most cases, either approach can work, but developing the perfect definition may be impossible.

SUBJECTIVE METHODS DEFINITION USING FUZZY LOGIC

Subjective methods that can be defined using fuzzy logic are much easier than methods that develop a purely visual type of pattern. Candlestick recognition is the best example of this type of subjective method. Candlestick recognition is a combination of fuzzy-logic-based attributes and attributes that can be defined 100 percent mechanically. Once you have developed the fuzzy definitions for the size of the candlesticks, it is very easy to develop codes to identify different candlestick patterns.

HUMAN-AIDED SEMIMECHANICAL METHODS

A human-aided semimechanical method is one in which the analyst is using general rules based on observations and is actually performing the analysis of the chart. There are many classic examples of this method. The first one that comes to mind is divergence between price and an oscillator. This type of pattern is often drawn on a chart by a human, using rules that are understood but may not be easily defined. My work has shown that, in these types of subjective methods, the better approach is to identify only 15 percent to 40 percent of all cases, making sure that each has been defined correctly. The reason is that the eye can identify many different patterns at once.

For example, if we are trying to mechanize divergence between price and an oscillator, we need to define a window of time in which a divergence, once set up, must occur. We also need to define the types of divergence we are looking for. The human eye can pick up many types of divergences, that is, divergences based on swing highs and lows or on the angle between the swing high and the swing low.

Figure 12.1 shows several different types of divergence that can be picked up by the human eye. It also shows how a product called DivergEngine™, by Inside Edge Systems, was able to identify several different divergences during late 1994, using a five-period SlowK. One

FIGURE 12.1   Several different types of divergence can be picked up by the human eye. A product called DivergEngine™ is able to identify simple divergences automatically.

example is a divergence buy signal set up in late September and early October of 1994. (Divergences are shown by circles above the bars in Figure 12.1.) In early November 1994, we had a sell signal divergence. This divergence led to a 30-point drop in the S&P500 in less than one month.

Another type of analysis that falls into this class is the method of drawing trend lines. When a human expert draws a trend line, he or she is connecting a line between lows (or between highs). Important trend lines often involve more than two points. In these cases, an expert's drawn trend line may not touch all three (or more) points. The subjective part of drawing trend lines involves which points to connect and how close is close enough when the points do not touch the trend line. Figure 12.2 shows an example of a hand-drawn major trend line for the S&P500 during the period from July to October 1994. Notice that not all of the lows touch the trend line. After the market gapped below this trend line, it collapsed 20 points in about three weeks.

FIGURE 12.2   An example of an S&P500 trend line, drawn between July and October 1994.

MECHANICALLY DEFINABLE METHODS

Mechanically definable methods allow us to develop a mathematical formula for the patterns we are trying to define. One example of these types of patterns is the swing highs and lows that are used to define pivot-point trades. Another example would be any gap pattern. There are many examples of this class of methods, and any method that can be defined by a statement or formula falls into this class.

MECHANIZING SUBJECTIVE METHODS

Once you have classified the category that your method belongs to, you need to start developing your mechanical rules. You must begin by identifying your pattern or patterns on many different charts—even charts using different markets.

After you have identified your subjective methods on your charts, you are ready to develop attributes that define your patterns—for example, in candlestick charts, the size and color of the candlestick are the key attributes. With the attributes defined, you can develop a mathematical definition or equivalent for each attribute. Definitions may use fuzzy concepts, such as tall or short, or may be based on how different technical indicators act when the pattern exists. Next, you should test each of your attribute definitions for correctness. This step is very important because if these building blocks do not work, you will not be able to develop an accurate definition for your patterns. After you have developed your building blocks, you can combine them to try to detect your pattern. When using your building blocks' attributes to develop your patterns for making your subjective method mechanical, it is usually better to have many different definitions of your pattern, with each one identifying only 10 percent of the cases but with 90 percent correctness.

Making subjective methods mechanical is not easy and should continue to be a hot area of research for the next 5 to 10 years. Given this outline of how to make a subjective method mechanical, I will now show you two examples: (1) Elliott Wave analysis and (2) candlestick charts. These will be shown in the next two chapters, respectively.

13
Building the Wave

Elliott Wave analysis is based on the work of R. N. Elliott during the 1930s. Elliott believed that the movements of the markets follow given patterns and relationships based on human psychology. Elliott Wave analysis is a complex subject and has been discussed in detail in many books and articles. Here, we will not go into it in detail but will provide an overview so that you can understand (1) why I think Elliott Wave analysis is predictive, and (2) how to make it mechanical so that it can be used to predict the markets.

AN OVERVIEW OF ELLIOTT WAVE ANALYSIS

Elliott Wave theory is based on the premise that markets will move in ratios and patterns that reflect human nature. The classic Elliott Wave pattern consists of two different types of waves:

1. A five-wave sequence called an *impulse wave.*
2. A three-wave sequence called a *corrective wave.*

The classic five-wave patterns and the three-wave corrective wave are shown in Figure 13.1. Normally, but not always, the market will move in a corrective wave after a five-wave move in the other direction.

Let's analyze a classic five-wave sequence to the upside. Wave one is usually a weak rally with only a few traders participating. When wave one

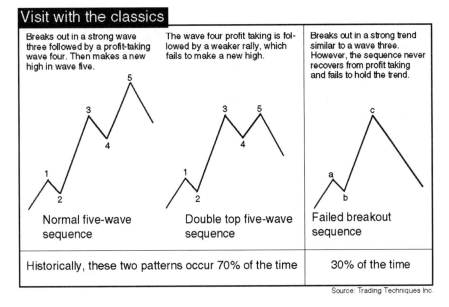

FIGURE 13.1 Three possible five-wave Elliott Wave patterns.

is over, the market sells off, creating wave two. Wave two ends when the market fails to make new lows and retraces at least 50 percent, but less than 100 percent, of wave one. Wave two is often identified on a chart by a double-top or head-and-shoulders pattern. After this correction, the market will begin to rally again—slowly at first, but then accelerating as it takes out the top of wave one. This is the start of wave three. As another sign of wave three, the market will gap in the direction of the trend. Commercial traders begin building their long position when the market fails to make new lows. They continue to build this position during wave three as the market continues to accelerate. One of the Elliott Wave rules is that wave three cannot be the shortest wave and is, in fact, normally at least 1.618 times longer than wave one. This 1.618 number was not selected out of thin air. It is one of the Fibonacci numbers—a numerical sequence that occurs often in nature. In fact, many of the rules of Elliott Wave relate to Fibonacci numbers.

At some point, profit taking will set in and the market will sell off. This is called wave four. There are two types of wave four: (1) simple and (2) complex. The type of wave four to expect is related to the type of wave two that occurred. If wave two was simple, wave four will be complex. If wave two was complex, wave four will be simple. After the wave-four correction, the market rallies and usually makes new highs, but the rally is fueled by small traders and lacks the momentum of a wave-three rally. This lack of momentum, as prices rally to new highs or fall to new lows, creates divergence using classic technical indicators. After the five waves are finished, the market should change trend. This trend change will be either corrective or the start of a new five-wave pattern. The mirror image of this pattern exists for a five-wave move to the downside.

Elliott Wave patterns exist on each time frame, and the waves relate to each other the same way. For example, a five-wave pattern can be found on a monthly, weekly, daily, or intraday chart. You must be in the same wave sequence in each time frame. For example, in a five-wave downward pattern, you would be in a wave four in a monthly or weekly time frame, and in a wave three to the upside on a daily or intraday time frame.

When you study an Elliott Wave pattern closely, you will see that each wave is made up of similar patterns. Many times, in a five-wave pattern, wave one, or three, or five will break down into additional five-wave patterns. This is called an extension.

Elliott Wave analysis has many critics because it is usually a subjective form of analysis. This chapter will show you how to make the most important part of Elliott Wave analysis—the pattern of waves three, four, and five—objective and totally mechanical.

TYPES OF FIVE-WAVE PATTERNS

The three possible five-wave patterns have been shown in Figure 13.1. The first two are the classic five-wave sequence and the double-top market. The mirror image of these patterns exists on the downside and, according to Tom Joseph, these two patterns account for 70 percent of all possible historical cases. Finally, when the market fails to hold its trend and the trend reverses, we have a *failed breakout sequence* pattern. The first two five-wave patterns consist of a large rally; then consolidation occurs, followed by a rally that tests the old highs or sets new ones. The failed breakout pattern occurs 30 percent of the time and is unpredictable. The classic five-way pattern can be traded as shown in Table 13.1.

Trading the five-wave pattern sounds easy, but the problem is that the current wave count depends on the time frame being analyzed. For

TABLE 13.1   TRADING THE ELLIOTT WAVE.

We can trade the basic five-wave pattern as follows:

1. Enter wave three in the direction of the trend.
2. Stay out of the market during wave four.
3. Enter the wave-five rally in the direction of the trend.
4. Take a countertrend trade at the top of wave five.

example, if we identify a wave three on both the weekly and daily charts, we have a low-risk, high-profit trading opportunity. If we are in a five-wave downward sequence on a weekly chart but a wave-three upward pattern on a daily chart, the trade would be a high-risk trade that may not be worth taking. When trading Elliott Waves, it is important to view the count on multiple time frames.

USING THE ELLIOTT WAVE OSCILLATOR TO IDENTIFY THE WAVE COUNT

Let's now learn how to objectively identify the classic five-wave pattern. In 1987, Tom Joseph, of Trading Techniques, Inc., discovered that using a five-period moving average minus a thirty-five-period moving average of the (High + Low)/2 produced an oscillator that is useful in counting Elliott Waves. He called this discovery the Elliott Wave oscillator. Using this oscillator and an expert system containing the rules for Elliott Wave, he produced software called Advanced GET, published by Trading Techniques, Inc. Advanced GET™ also has many Gann methods for trading, and seasonality and pattern matching are built into the package. GET does a good job of objectively analyzing Elliott Waves. It is available for MS-DOS, Windows, and for TradeStation. Tom agreed to share some of his research with us so that we can begin to develop our own TradeStation utility for Elliott Wave analysis.

The Elliott Wave oscillator produces a general pattern that correlates to where you are in the Elliott Wave count. Based on the research of Tom Joseph, we can explain this pattern by identifying a five-wave sequence to the upside. We start this sequence by first detecting the end of a five-wave sequence to the downside. The first rally that occurs after the market makes new lows but the Elliott Wave oscillator does not is called wave one. After the wave-one rally, the market will have a correction but will fail to set new lows. This is wave two, which can be one of two types. The first is *simple;* it may last for a few bars and have little effect on the oscillator. The second, less common type is a *complex* wave two. It will usually last longer, and the oscillator will pull back significantly. There is a relationship between wave two and wave four. If wave two is simple, wave four will be complex. If wave two is complex, wave four will be simple. After wave two is finished, both the market and the oscillator will begin to rise. This is the start of wave three. This move will accelerate as the market takes out the top of wave one. A characteristic of wave three is that both the market and the Elliott Wave oscillator reach new highs. After wave three, there is a profit-taking decline—wave four. After wave four, the market will begin to rally and will either create a double top or set new highs, but the Elliott Wave oscillator will fail to make new highs. This divergence is the classic sign of a wave five. The oscillator and prices could also make new highs after what looks like a wave four. At this point, we have to relabel our wave five a wave three. Another important point is that wave five can extend for a long time in a slow uptrend. For this reason, we cannot be sure the trend has changed until the Elliott Wave oscillator has retraced more than 138 percent of its wave-five peak.

TRADESTATION TOOLS FOR COUNTING ELLIOTT WAVES

The first step in developing our Elliott Wave analysis software is to develop the Elliott Wave oscillator. The code for this oscillator and a user function to tell us whether we are in a five-way sequence to the upside is shown in Table 13.2, coded in TradeStation EasyLanguage.

The user function in Table 13.2 starts with the trend set to zero. We initiated the trend based on which occurs first, the oscillator making a "Len" bar high or making it low. If the trend is up, it remains up until the Elliott Wave oscillator retraces the "Trigger" percent of the Len bar high and that high was greater than 0. The inverse is also true if the current trend is down. It will remain down until the market retraces the Trigger percent of the Len bar low as long as the low was less than 0.

This trend indicator normally will change trend at the top of wave one or when wave three takes out the top of one. For this reason, it is not a

TABLE 13.2 USER FUNCTIONS FOR ELLIOTT WAVE TOOL.

Copyright © 1996 Ruggiero Associates. This code for the Elliott Wave oscillator is only for personal use and is not to be used to create any commercial product.

```
Inputs: DataSet(Numeric)
Vars: Osc535(0),Price(0);
Price=(H of Data(DataSet)+L of Data(DataSet))/2;
If Average(Price,35)<>0 then begin
Osc535=Average(Price,5)-Average(Price,35);
end;
ElliottWaveOsc=Osc535;
```

Copyright 1996 Ruggiero Associates. This code for the Elliott trend indicator is only for personal use and is not to be used to create any commercial product.

```
Inputs: DataSet(Numeric),Len(Numeric),Trigger(Numeric);
Vars: Trend(0),Osc(0);
Osc=ElliottWaveOsc(DataSet);
If Osc=Highest(Osc,Len) and Trend=0 then Trend=1;
If Osc=Lowest(Osc,Len) and Trend=0 then Trend=-1;
If Lowest(Osc,Len)<0 and Trend=-1 and Osc>-1*Trigger*Lowest(Osc,Len) then
Trend=1;
If Highest(Osc,Len)>0 and Trend=1 and Osc<-1*Trigger*Highest(Osc,Len) then
Trend=-1;
ElliottTrend=Trend;
```

stand-alone system; it gives up too much of its trading profit on each trade before reversing. Even with this problem, it is still predictive and is profitable as a stand-alone system on many markets. Let's now use this Elliott Trend indicator to build a series of functions that can be used to count the classic 3,4,5 wave sequence. The code for the functions that count a five-wave sequence to the upside is shown in Table 13.3, stated in TradeStation's EasyLanguage.

The code in Table 13.3 has five inputs. The first is the data series we are applying the function to. For example, we could count the wave patterns on both an intraday and a daily time frame by simply calling this function twice, using different data series. Next, not wanting to call these functions many times because they are computationally expensive, we pass in both the Elliott Wave oscillator and the Elliott Trend indicator.

TABLE 13.3   SIMPLE ELLIOTT WAVE COUNTER FOR 3,4,5 UP.

```
Inputs: DataSet(Numeric),Osc(NumericSeries),ET(NumericSeries),Len(Numeric),
Trig(Numeric);
Vars: Price(0),Wave(0),HiOsc(-999),HiOsc2(-999),HiPrice(-999),HiPrice2(-999);
Price=(High of Data(DataSet)+Low of Data(DataSet))/2;
{ Is current wave sequence up or down}
{ When we change from down to up label it a wave 3}
{ and save current high osc and price}
If ET=1 and ET[1]=-1 and Osc>0 then begin;
HiOsc=Osc;
HiPrice=Price;
Wave=3;
end;
{ If wave 3 and oscillator makes new high save it}
if Wave=3 and HiOsc<Osc then HiOsc=Osc;
{ if wave 3 and price makes new high save it}
if Wave=3 and HiPrice<Price then HiPrice=Price;
{ If your in a wave 3 and the oscillator pulls back to zero
label it a wave 4}
if Wave=3 and Osc<=0 and ET=1 then Wave=4;
{ If you're in a wave 4 and the oscillator pulls back above zero and prices
break out then label it a wave 5 and set up second set of high oscillator and
price}
if Wave=4 and Price=Highest(Price,5) and Osc>=0 then begin
Wave=5;
HiOsc2=Osc;
HiPrice2=Price;
end;
if Wave=5 and HiOsc2<Osc then HiOsc2=Osc;
if Wave=5 and HiPrice2<Price then HiPrice2=Price;
{ If Oscillator sets a new high relabel this a wave 3 and reset wave 5 levels}
If HiOsc2>HiOsc and HiPrice2>HiPrice and Wave=5 and ET=1 then begin
Wave=3;
HiOsc=HiOsc2;
```

TABLE 13.3 *(Continued)*

```
HiPrice=HiPrice2;
HiOsc2=-999;
HiPrice2=-999;
end;
{ If the trend changes in a wave 5 label this a -3 or a wave three down}
{ and reset all variables}
If ET=-1 then begin
Wave=-3;
HiOsc=-999;
HiPrice=-999;
HiOsc2=-999;
HiPrice2=-999;
end;
Wave345Up=Wave;
```

Our final two arguments are (1) the Len used for the window to identify the wave counts and (2) the retracement level required to change the trend.

Let's now use these functions to create the Elliott Wave counter. This code is shown in Table 13.4.

The code in Table 13.3 sets the wave value to a three when the trend changes from −1 to 1. After that, it starts saving both the highest oscillator and price values. It continues to call this a wave three until the oscillator retraces to zero and the trend is still up. At this point, it will

TABLE 13.4   SIMPLE ELLIOTT WAVE COUNTER USER FUNCTION FOR THE UP WAVE SEQUENCE.

```
Inputs: DataSet(Numeric),Len(Numeric),Trig(Numeric);
Vars: WavCount(0);

WavCount=Wave345Up(DataSet,ElliottWaveOsc(DataSet),ElliottTrend(DataSet,
Len,Trig),Len,Trig);
Elliott345=WavCount;
```

label it a wave four. If we are currently in a wave four and the oscillator pulls above zero and the (High + Low)/2 makes a five-day high, we label this a wave five. We then set a second set of peak oscillator values. If the second peak is greater than the first, we change the count back to a wave three. Otherwise, it stays a wave five until the trend indicator flips to −1.

Let's see how to use our functions to develop a simple Elliott Wave trading system. The code for this system is shown in Table 13.5.

Our Elliott Wave system generates a buy signal when the wave count changes to a wave three. We reenter a long position when we move from a wave four to a wave five. Finally, we reenter a long position if the wave count changes from wave five back to wave three. Our exit is the same for all three entries, when the Elliott Wave oscillator retraces to zero.

The entries of this system are relatively good, but if this were a real trading system, we would have developed better exits. We tested this system of the D-Mark, using 67/99 type continuous contracts in the period from 2/13/75 to 3/18/96, and it performed well. Because our goal is to evaluate Elliott Wave analysis as a trading tool, we optimized the system across the complete data set in order to see whether the system was robust. We optimized across a large set of parameters (ranging from 20 to 180 for length, and from .5 to 1.0 for trig) and found that a broad range of parameters performed very well. The set of parameters using a length of 20 and a trigger of .66 produced the results shown in Table 13.6 for the period from 2/13/75 to 3/18/96 (with $50.00 deducted for slippage and commissions).

TABLE 13.5   CODE FOR ELLIOTT WAVE COUNTER TRADING SYSTEM.

```
Inputs: Len(80),Trig(.7);
Vars: WavCount(0),Osc(0);
Osc=ElliottWaveOsc(1);
WavCount=Elliott345(1,Len,Trig);
If WavCount=3 and WavCount[1]<=0 then buy at open;
If WavCount=5 and WavCount[1]=4 then buy at open;
If WavCount=3 and WavCount[1]=5 then buy at open;
If Osc<0 then exitlong at open;
```

TABLE 13.6   ELLIOTT WAVE COUNTER SYSTEM RESULTS D-MARK.

Net profit	$35,350.00
Trades	57
Percent profitable	51%
Average trade	$690.35
Drawdown	-$10,237.50
Profit factor	2.10

This was not just an isolated case: over 80 percent of the cases we tested in the above range produced profitable results.

After developing these parameters on the D-Mark, we tested them on the Yen. Once again, we used type 67/99 continuous contracts supplied by Genesis Financial Data Services. We used data for the period from 8/2/76 to 3/18/96. The amazing results (with $50.00 deducted for slippage and commissions) are shown in Table 13.7.

This same set of parameters did not work only on the D-Mark and Yen, it also worked on crude oil and coffee as well as many other commodities. These results show that Elliott Wave analysis is a powerful tool for use in developing trading systems. The work done in this chapter is only a starting point for developing mechanical trading systems based on Elliott Waves. Our wave counter needs logic added to detect the wave one and wave two sequence as well as adding ratio analysis of the length of each wave. Our system does not detect the top of wave three and wave five. If we can add that feature to the existing code and do even a fair job of detecting the end of both wave three and wave five, we may significantly improve our performance. We could also trade the short side of the market. Even with these issues, our basic mechanical Elliott Wave

TABLE 13.7   THE ELLIOTT WAVE COUNTER SYSTEM RESULTS ON THE YEN.

Net profit	$89,800.00
Trades	51
Percent profitable	51%
Average trade	$1,760.70
Drawdown	-$5,975.00
Profit factor	4.16

system shows that Elliott Wave analysis does have predictive value and can be used to develop filter trading systems that work when applied to various commodities.

EXAMPLES OF ELLIOTT WAVE SEQUENCES USING ADVANCED GET

We will discuss some examples using charts and Elliott Wave counts generated from Tom Joseph's Advanced GET software. Elliott Wave analysis can be applied to both the Futures markets and individual Stocks.

In the first example (Figure 13.2), the March 1997, British Pound is shown. From mid-September 1996 through November 1996, the British Pound traded in a very stong Wave Three rally. Then the market enters into a profit-taking stage followed by new highs into January 1997. However, the new high in prices fails to generate a new high in Tom Joseph's Elliott Oscillator, indicating the end of a Five Wave sequence. Once a Five Wave sequence is completed, the market changes its trend.

The daily chart of Boise Cascade is shown on Figure 13.3 trading in a Five Wave decline. The new lows in Wave Five does not generate a new

FIGURE 13.2   British Pound March 1997.

FIGURE 13.3   Boise Cascade—Daily Stock Chart.

FIGURE 13.4   British Pound with Profit Taking Index (PTI).

low in Tom Joseph's Elliott Oscillator, indicating the end of a Five Wave sequence. Once a Five Wave sequence is completed, the market changes its trend.

Using the Profit-Taking Index (PIT)

When a Wave Four is complete, the major question confronting the trader is whether the market will make a new high in Wave Five. Tom Joseph and his staff at Trading Techniques Inc., has devised a model that will predict the potential for a new high. This model is called the Profit Taking Index (PTI). The PTI is calculated by measuring the area under Wave Three and comparing it with the area under Wave Four. If the PTI is greater than 35, a new high is expected (Figure 13.4).

If the PTI is less than 35, the market fails to make a new high and will usually result in a failed Fifth Wave or Double Top (Figure 13.5).

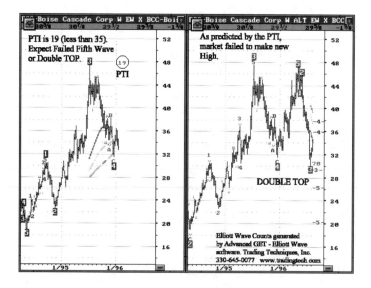

FIGURE 13.5   Weekly Boise Cascade Stock. Double Top.

Trading Techniques Inc. provides free information on mechanically counting Elliott Waves and other studies. They can be contacted at (330) 645-0077 or download from their web site www.tradingtech.com.

14

Mechanically Identifying and Testing Candlestick Patterns

Candlestick chart analysis is a subjective form of analysis. The analyst must first identify the patterns and then judge their significance. For example, a white hammer pattern is more bullish after a major downtrend. Several software vendors have developed software to automatically identify candlestick patterns. Some of these products also generate mechanical trading signals. Generally, these packages do well at identifying the patterns, but they have mixed results in using their mechanical trading signals.

In this chapter, we will use fuzzy logic to identify several candlestick patterns using TradeStation. We will also show you how to integrate other forms of technical analysis with candlesticks to develop mechanical trading signals.

HOW FUZZY LOGIC JUMPS OVER THE CANDLESTICK

Let's now see how fuzzy logic can be used to analyze candlestick charts. In our height example, we saw that the first step in developing a fuzzy logic application is to list the variables involved and then develop a list of

TABLE 14.1   A CANDLE'S ATTRIBUTES.

Color
White or black

Shape
Long, small, or about equal

Upper Shadow Size
Long, small, or about none

Lower Shadow Size
Long, small, or about none

---

attributes for each variable. For a single candlestick, the attributes are as shown in Table 14.1.

Not all variables require fuzzy logic. In our list, color does not, because color is simply the sign of the close minus the open. We will now develop a membership function for each of these variables. The "shape" candlestick variable is represented graphically in Figure 14.1.

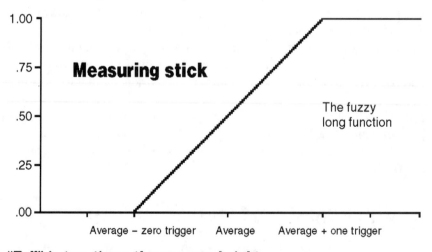

"Tall" is two times the average height.

FIGURE 14.1   A fuzzy logic function that identifies tall candlesticks.

FUZZY PRIMITIVES FOR CANDLESTICKS

A single candlestick has the following characteristics: color, shape, upper shadow size, and lower shadow size. Not all characteristics require fuzzy logic. As noted above, color does not require fuzzy logic. Let's look at an example of a fuzzy logic function that identifies a candle with a long shape. The code for this function in TradeStation's EasyLanguage is shown in Table 14.2.

The function in Table 14.2 will return a 1 when the current candle size is greater than or equal to OneCof times the average candle size over the last lookback days, and a zero when it is less than ZeroCof times the average size. When the candle size is between these range limits, it returns a scaled value between 0 and 1. This function can also handle a case where the previous candle was very long and the next candle should also be long, but, using the rule based on the average size, the candle would

TABLE 14.2   CODE FOR FUZZY LONG FUNCTION.

```
Inputs: OPrice(NUMERICSERIES),CPrice(NUMERICSERIES),LBack(NUMERIC),
OneCof(NUMERIC),ZeroCof(NUMERIC);
Vars: PrevLong(0),CRange(0),AveRange(0),ZTrig(0),OneTrig(0),Tall(0),Scale(0);
{ Calculate the range for the candle}
CRange=absvalue(OPrice-CPrice);
{ Calculate what level represents a 0}
ZTrig=Average(CRange,LBack)*ZeroCof;
{ Calculate what level represents a 1}
OneTrig=Average(CRange,LBack)*OneCof;
{ Calculate the difference between the zero and one level}
Scale=OneTrig-ZTrig;
{ If One Level and Zero Level are the same set to 99.99 so it can be a large bar}
if Scale=0 then Scale=99.99;
{ Calculate the fuzzy membership to tall}
Tall=maxlist(0,minlist(1,(CRange-OneTrig)/(Scale)));
{ If previous bar is big relax requirements}
if Tall[1]=1 and CRange[1]-ZTrig<>0 then Tall=maxlist(0,minlist(1,(CRange-
CRange[1])/(CRange[1]-ZTrig)));
FuzzyLong=Tall;
```

not have been identified correctly. We also handle divide-by-zero conditions that occur when the open, high, low, and close are all the same.

To identify most of the common candlestick patterns, we need functions that can classify all of the attributes associated with a candlestick. The shape of a candlestick can be long, small, or doji. The upper and lower wick can be large, small, or none. We also need to be able to identify whether there are gaps or whether one candle engulfs another. After we have developed functions to identify these attributes, we can start to identify more complex patterns.

DEVELOPING A CANDLESTICK RECOGNITION UTILITY STEP-BY-STEP

The first step in developing a candlestick recognition tool is to decide what patterns we want to identify. In this chapter, we will identify the following patterns: dark cloud, bullish engulf, and evening star. Next, we need to develop a profile of each of these patterns. The plates for the patterns have been illustrated by Steve Nison in his first book, *Japanese Candlestick Charting Techniques,* published by John Wiley & Sons, Inc., 1990.

Let's now describe each of these three patterns, beginning with the dark cloud cover. The dark cloud cover consists of two candlesticks: (1) a white candle with a significant body and (2) a black candle that opens above the high of the white candle but closes below the midpoint of the white candle. This is a bearish pattern in an uptrend.

The bullish engulfing pattern also consists of two candlesticks. The first is a black candle. The second is a white candle that engulfs the black candle. This is a bullish sign in a downtrend.

Our final pattern is an evening star. This pattern is a little more complex. It consists of three candles: (1) a significant white candle, (2) a small candle of either color, and (3) a black candle. The middle candle gaps above both the white and black candlesticks. The black candle opens higher than the close of the white but then closes below the midpoint of the white. This is a bearish pattern in an uptrend.

Let's now see how we can translate the candlestick definitions into TradeStation's EasyLanguage code.

The primitive functions that we will use in identifying the dark cloud, bullish engulf, and evening star are shown in Table 14.3.

TABLE 14.3   CANDLESTICK PRIMITIVE FUNCTIONS.

Candlestick Color
CandleColor(Open,Close)

Candlestick Shape
FuzzyLong(Open,Close,LookBack,OneTrigger,ZeroTrigger)
FuzzySmall(Open,Close,LookBack,OneTrigger,ZeroTrigger)

Miscellaneous Functions
EnGulfing(Open,Close,RefBar)
WindowDown(Open,High,Low,Close,LookBack)
WindowUp(Open,High,Low,Close,LookBack)

Let's now discuss some of the inputs to these functions, beginning with the parameter LookBack. This is the period used to calculate a moving average of the body size of each candlestick. The moving average is used as a reference point to compare how small or large the current candle is, relative to recent candles.

The OneTrigger is the percentage of the average candle size that will cause the function to output a 1, and the ZeroTrigger is the percentage of the average candle size for outputting a zero. The RefBar parameter is used by the engulfing function to reference which candlestick the current candlestick needs to engulf.

Another important issue when using these functions is that the OneTrigger is smaller than the ZeroTrigger for functions that identify small or doji candles. When using the long candle size function, the OneTrigger is larger than the ZeroTrigger.

The engulfing function returns a 1 if the current candle engulfs the RefBar candle. The window-up and window-down functions return a number greater than zero when there is a gap in the proper direction. The exact return value from these functions is based on the size of the gap relative to the average candle size over the past LookBack days.

Let's now see how to combine these functions to identify the three candlestick formations discussed earlier in the chapter. We will start with the dark cloud.

The dark cloud is a bearish formation. Many times, it signals a top in the market or at least the end of a trend and the start of a period of consolidation. The EasyLanguage code for the dark cloud is shown in Table 14.4.

TABLE 14.4   CODE FOR DARK CLOUD FORMATION.

```
Inputs: LookBack(Numeric),OneCof(Numeric),ZeroCof(Numeric);
Vars: Color(0),SBody(0);
Vars: FuzzyRange(0), Return(0);
Color=CandleColor(O,C);
{Fuzzy Small has the following arguments
FuzzySmall(Lookback,OneCof,ZeroCof)}
{We reversed OneCof and ZeroCof so that we can test for Not Small as input to
the dark cloud function}
SBody=FuzzySmall(O,C,LookBack,ZeroCof*.3,OneCof*1);
Return=0;
FuzzyRange=Close-(Open[1]+Close[1])/2;
if Color=-1 and Color[1]=1 and open>High[1] and FuzzyRange<0 then begin
Return=1-SBody[1];
end;
DarkCloud = Return;
```

Let's walk through the code in Table 14.4. First, we save the color of each candlestick. Next, we save the membership of each candlestick to the Fuzzy Small set. Notice that we inverted the OneCof and ZeroCof arguments. (The dark cloud requires the first white candle to have a significant body.) We did this by inverting the small membership function. If we had used the long membership function, we would have missed many dark clouds because the first candle was significant but not quite long. Next, we calculate whether the second candlestick is black and falls below the midpoint of the first candle that is white. The second candle must also open above the high of the first.

If the candle qualifies as a dark cloud, we return the fuzzy inverse membership of the first candle to the class Fuzzy Small as the value of the fuzzy dark cloud.

How do we identify a bullish engulfing pattern? The EasyLanguage code for this pattern is shown in Table 14.5.

When identifying a bullish engulf, the first thing we do is to evaluate the color and size of each candle. If the current candle is white and engulfs the first candle that is black, we have a possible bullish engulf. The significance of the bullish engulf pattern is measured by using our fuzzy

TABLE 14.5   CODE FOR BULLISH ENGULF PATTERN.

```
Inputs: LookBack(Numeric),OneCof(Numeric),ZeroCof(Numeric);
Vars: Color(0),SBody(0),LBody(0);
Color=CandleColor(O,C);
SBody=FuzzySmall(O,C,LookBack,OneCof*.3,ZeroCof*1);
LBody=FuzzyLong(O,C,LookBack,OneCof*2,ZeroCof*1);
if EnGulfing(O,C,1)=1 and Color=1 and Color[1]=-1 then BullEngulf=
minlist(SBody[1],LBody)
else
BullEngulf=0;
```

logic functions for candle size. We take a fuzzy "AND" between the membership of the previous candle in the Small class and the membership of the current candle in the Large class. This value measures the importance of the engulfing pattern. If the pattern does not qualify as a bullish engulfing pattern, we return a 0.

Table 14.6 shows the code of an evening star. The code first tests the color of each candle as well as its membership in the Small class. Next, we test to see where the close of the current candle falls in the range of the first candle in the formation.

TABLE 14.6   CODE FOR THE EVENING STAR PATTERN.

```
Inputs: LookBack(Numeric),OneCof(Numeric),ZeroCof(Numeric);
Vars: Color(0),SBody(0);
Vars:FuzzyRange(0),Return(0);
Color=CandleColor(O,C);
SBody=FuzzySmall(O,C,LookBack,OneCof*.3,ZeroCof*1);
Return=0;
FuzzyRange=Close-(Close[2]+Open[2])/2;
if Color=-1 and Color[2]=1 and WindowUp(O,H,L,C,1)[1]>0 and
open>open[1] and FuzzyRange<0 then begin
Return=minList(SBody[1],1-SBody[2]);
end;
EveningStar=Return;
```

For an evening star, we need a black current candle and a white candle two candlesticks ago. Next, we need the second candle in the formation to have gapped higher. Finally, the current candle must open higher than the middle candle but must close at or below the middle of the first candle. All of these requirements must be met in order for the formation to qualify as an evening star. We then return the fuzzy "AND" of one candle ago to the class Small and the "AND" of two candles ago to the inverse of the Small class. If the formation does not qualify as an evening star, the function returns a 0.

We can repeat this process to identify any candlestick patterns we wish. Once we have written a code, we need to test it. To test the codes given here, we used the plates from Nison's book *Japanese Candlestick Charting Techniques,* and tested our routines on the same charts. If you are not identifying the patterns you want, you can adjust the LookBack period as well as the scaling coefficients. In general, mechanical identification will miss some patterns that can be detected by the human eye. After you have developed routines to identify your candlestick patterns, you can use them to develop or improve various trading systems.

How can we use candlesticks to develop mechanical trading strategies? We will test use of the dark cloud cover pattern on Comex gold during the period from 8/1/86 to 12/26/95. We will go short on the next open when we identify a dark cloud cover pattern and have a 10-day RSI greater than 50. We will then exit at a five-day high.

Table 14.7 shows the code and results, without slippage and commissions.

TABLE 14.7   CODE AND RESULTS FOR SIMPLE DARK CLOUD SYSTEM.

```
Vars: DC(0);
DC=DarkCloud(15,1,1);
If DC>.5 and RSI(close,10)>50 then sell at open;
exitshort at highest(high,5) stop;
```

Net profit	$150.00
Trades	13
Wins	4
Losses	9
Win%	31
Average trade	$11.54

These results are horrible and cannot even cover slippage and commissions. Let's now see how combining the correlation analysis between the CRB and gold can improve the performance of the dark cloud cover pattern for trading Comex gold. In Chapter 10, we showed that gold normally trends only when it is highly correlated to the CRB. Let's use this information to develop two different exit rules for our dark cloud, combined with a 10-day RSI pattern. We will now exit using a 5-day high when the 50-day correlation between gold and the CRB is above .50. We will use a limit order at the entry price (−2 × average(range,10)) when the correlation is below .50. According to the theory, we use a trend type exit when the market should trend, and a limit order when the market has a low probability of trending. The code we are using for these rules, and the results without slippage and commissions, are shown in Table 14.8.

The performance of the dark cloud is incredibly improved by simply using intermarket analysis to select an exit method. There are not enough trades to prove whether this is a reliable trading method for gold. It is used only as an example of how to use candlestick patterns to develop mechanical trading systems.

TABLE 14.8   CODE AND RESULTS OF COMBINING INTERMARKET ANALYSIS AND CANDLESTICKS.

```
Vars: DC(0),Correl(0),CRB(0),GC(0);
CRB=Close of Data2;
GC=Close;
Correl=RACorrel(CRB,GC,50);
DC=DarkCloud(15,1,1);
If DC>.5 and RSI(close,10)>50 then sell at open;
If Correl>.5 then exitshort at highest(high,5) stop;
If Correl<.5 then exitshort at entryprice-2*average(range,10)
limit;
```

Net profit	$5,350.00
Trades	12
Wins	9
Losses	3
Win%	75
Average trade	$445.83

Combining candlesticks with other Western methods and with intermarket analysis is a hot area of research for developing mechanical trading systems. The ability to backtest candlestick patterns will help answer the question of how well any given candlestick pattern works in a given market. By evaluating candlestick patterns objectively, at least we know how well they worked in the past and how much heat we will take when trading them.

Part Four

TRADING SYSTEM DEVELOPMENT AND TESTING

15
Developing a Trading System

Developing a trading system can be a very difficult process if you do not understand the steps involved in building a reliable and profitable system. If you understand the steps and have trading methods that are sound, it is less difficult to build successful trading systems.

STEPS FOR DEVELOPING A TRADING SYSTEM

To give you an overview of how to build a trading system, the necessary steps are listed in Table 15.1.

Let's now discuss each of these steps in more detail.

SELECTING A MARKET FOR TRADING

You should select a market that offers you access to domain expertise. When developing a trading system for a given market, you need to understand what factors affect price movements in that market. If you want to develop a system that works on multiple markets, it is important to understand the potential markets well enough to find common technical characteristics that can be used in developing a multimarket trading

TABLE 15.1   STEPS IN DEVELOPING A SYSTEM.

1. Decide what market and time frame you want to trade.
2. Develop a premise that you will use to design your trading system.
3. Collect and organize the historical market data needed to develop your model into development, testing, and out-of-sample sets.
4. Based on the market you want to trade, and your premise, select trading methods that are predictive of that market and meet your own risk–reward criteria.
5. Design your entries and test them using simple exits.
6. Develop filters that improve your entry rules.
7. After you have developed your entries, design more advanced exit methods that will improve your system's performance.
8. When selecting the parameters that will be used in your trading system, base your selections not only on system performance but also on robustness.
9. After you have developed your rules and selected your parameters, test the system on your testing set to see how the system works on new data. If the system works well, continue to do more detailed testing. (This is covered in Chapter 16.)
10. Repeat steps 3 through 9 until you have a system that you want to test further.

system. After you have selected your market(s), it is very important to decide what time frame you want to trade on and to have an idea of how long you would like your average trade to last.

Selecting a time frame means deciding whether to use intraday, daily, or weekly data. Your decision on a time frame should be based on both how often you want to trade and how long each trade should last. When you use a shorter time frame, trading frequency increases and length of trades decreases.

Another little discussed issue is that each time frame and each market has its own traits. For example, on the intraday S&P500, the high and/or low of the day is most likely to occur in the first or last 90 minutes of the day.

When using daily data, you can have wide variation in trade length—from a few days to a year, depending on what types of methods are used to generate your signals. For example, many of the intermarket-based methods for trading T-Bonds, shown in Chapter 1, have an average trade length of 10 days, whereas a simple channel breakout system has an average trade length of 50 to 80 days.

Other issues also have an effect on your choice—how much money you have to trade, and your own risk–reward criteria. For example, if you only have $10,000.00, you would not develop an S&P500 system that holds an overnight position. A good choice would be T-Bonds.

DEVELOPING A PREMISE

The second and most important step in developing a trading system is to develop a premise or theory about the market you have selected. There are many rich sources for theories that are useful in developing systems for various markets. Some of these sources are listed in Table 15.2. Many of those listed were covered in earlier chapters of this book.

DEVELOPING DATA SETS

After you select the market and time frame you want to trade, you need to collect and organize your historical data into three sets: (1) the development set, which is used to develop your trading rules; (2) a test set, where your data are used to test these rules; and (3) a blind or out-of-sample set, which is used only after you have selected the final rules and parameters for your system. In developing many systems over the years, I have found that one of the important issues involved in collecting these

TABLE 15.2   PREMISES FOR TRADING SYSTEMS.

1. Intermarket analysis.
2. Sentiment indicators.
3. Market internals—for example, for the S&P500, we would use data such as breadth, arm index, the premium between the cash and futures, and so on.
4. Mechanical models of subjective methods.
5. Trend-based models.
6. Seasonality, day of week, month of year, and so on.
7. Models that analyze technical indicators or price-based patterns.

data is whether we should use individual contracts or continuous contracts for the futures data we need to use. It is much easier to use continuous contracts, at least for the development set, and the continuous contracts should be back adjusted. Depending on your premise, you might need to develop data sets not only for the market you are trading but also for related markets; that is, if we were developing a T-Bond system using intermarket analysis, we would want to also have a continuous contract for the CRB futures.

The next important issue is how much data you need. To develop reliable systems, you should have at least one bull and one bear market in your data set. Ideally, you should have examples of bull and bear markets in both your development set and your test set. I have found that having at least 10 years' daily data is a good rule of thumb.

SELECTING METHODS FOR DEVELOPING A TRADING SYSTEM

After you have developed your premise and selected the technologies that can be used to support it, you must prove that your premise is valid and that you actually can use it to predict the market you are trying to trade.

Another issue that you need to deal with is whether a system that is based on your premise will fit your trading personality. This issue is often overlooked but is very important. Let's suppose your premise is based on the fact that the currency markets trend. This approach will not work for you if you cannot accept losing at least half your trades or are unable to handle watching a system give up half or more of its profit on a given trade.

In another example, you might have a pattern-based premise that produced a high winning percentage but traded only 10 times a year. Many people, needing more action than this, would take other trades not based on a system and would start losing money.

Let's now look at several different premises and how they are implemented. This information, plus the pros and cons of each premise, is shown in Table 15.3.

After you have selected your method, you need to test it. Let's suppose your premise was that T-Bond prices can be predicted based on

TABLE 15.3   TYPES OF TRADING METHODS
AND IMPLEMENTATION.

Premise	Implementation	Pro/Cons
Trend following	Moving averages Channel breakout Consecutive closes	All trend-following methods work badly in nontrending markets. The channel breakout and consecutive closes are the most robust implementations. You will win only 30 percent to 50 percent of your trades.
Countertrend methods	Oscillator divergence and cycle-based methods	Don't trade often. These offer higher winning percentages than trend-following methods, but they can suffer large losing trades.
Cause and effect (intermarket and fundamental analysis)	Technical analysis, comparing two or more data series	These systems can work only on the markets they were developed to trade. They can suffer high drawdowns but yield a good winning percentage.
Pattern and statistically based methods	Simple rules of three or more conditions	Don't trade often. These need to be tested to make sure they are not curve-fitted. They have a good winning percentage and drawdown if they are robust.

inflation. As in Chapter 1, several different commodities can be used as measures on inflation; for example, the CRB index, copper, and gold can all be used to predict T-Bonds. Next, you need to test your premise that inflation can be used to predict T-Bonds. When inflation is rising and T-Bonds are also rising, you sell T-Bonds. If inflation is falling and so are T-Bonds, you buy T-Bonds. You can then test this simple divergence premise using either the price momentum or prices relative to a moving average. Once you have proven that your premise is predictive, you can use a simple reversal system and start to develop your entries and exits.

DESIGNING ENTRIES

The simplest type of system is the classic reversal, which has been shown several times in this book. For example, the channel breakout system shown in Chapter 4 is a reversal-type system. This type of system can be either long or short—a feature that creates problems because sometimes a reversal-type system can produce very large losing trades.

Having discussed the simplest type of system entry, let's now examine the entries themselves. There are two major types of entries: (1) simple and (2) complex. Simple entries signal a trade when a condition is true. Complex entries need an event to be true, and another "trigger" event must occur to actually produce the entry. A simple entry will enter a trade on the next open or on today's close, if a given event is true. For example, the following rule is a simple entry:

If today = Monday and T-Bonds > T-Bonds[5], then buy S&P500 at open.

The rule's conditional part, before the "then," can be as complex as needed, but the actual order must always occur when the rule is true. Complex entries use a rule combined with a trigger, for example:

If today = Monday and T-Bonds > T-Bonds[5], then buy S&P500 at open + .3 × range stop.

This is a complex entry rule because we do not buy only when the rule is true. We require the trigger event (being 30 percent of yesterday's range above the open) to occur, or we will not enter the trade.

For both types of entries, the part of the rule before the "then" states the events that give a statistical edge. In the above examples, Mondays in which T-Bonds are in an uptrend have a statistically significant upward bias. Triggers are really filters that increase the statistical edge. Suppose, for day-trading the S&P500, we use a trigger that buys a breakout of 30 percent of yesterday's range above the open. This works because once a market moves 30 percent above or below the open in a given direction, the chance of a large-range day counter to that move drops significantly. This is important because the biggest problem a trading system can have is very large losing trades. They increase the drawdown and can make the system untradable.

The top traders in the world use these types of complex entries; for example, many of Larry Williams's patterns are based on buying or selling on a stop based on the open, plus or minus a percentage of yesterday's range when a condition is true.

Now that you have a basic understanding of developing entries, you need to learn how to test them. When testing entries, you should use simple exits. Among the simple exits I use are: holding a position for N bars, using target profits, and exiting on first profitable opening. Another test of entries is to use a simple exit and then lag when you actually get into the trade. I normally test lags between 1 to 5 bars. The less a small lag affects the results, the more robust the entry. Another thing you can learn is that, sometimes, when using intermarket or fundamental analysis, lagging your entries by a few bars can actually help performance. Testing your entries using simple exits will help you not only to develop better entries but also to test them for robustness.

When you have found entry methods that work well, see whether there are any patterns that produce either substandard performance or superior performance. These patterns can be used as filters for your entry rules.

DEVELOPING FILTERS FOR ENTRY RULES

Developing filters for entry rules is a very important step in the system development process. Filters are normally discovered during the process of testing entries; for example, you might find out that your entry rules do not work well during September and October. You can use this information to filter out trades in those months.

Another popular type of filter is a trend detection indicator, like ADX, for filtering a trend-following system. The goal in using these types of filters is to filter out trades that have lower expectations than the overall trades produced by a given pattern. For example, our correlation filter in Chapter 8 was applied to our buy on Monday, when T-Bonds were above their 26-day moving-average rule. It succeeded in filtering out about 60 trades that produced only $6.00 a trade. With the average trade over $200.00, filtering out these trades greatly improved the results of this pattern. This is an example of what a well-designed filter is meant to do. After you have developed your entries, filtered them, and finished testing them, you can develop your exits.

DESIGNING EXITS

Exits are much more complex than entries. In general, there are two different types: (1) an exit used to protect a profit or limit a loss, and (2) an exit used after an event or a target occurs.

Let's first discuss the protective-type exits. They exit the market when the market moves against a trader's position to a given level. The classic exit of this type is the *N* days low for buys and the *N* days high for sell.

Sometimes, depending on the entry, we cannot use this type of exit—at least early in the trade. For example, if we enter a trade on the long side, based on intermarket divergence, we will often be entering at a five-day low. We will then either want to wait a few days before we use this exit or will want to use a longer-period low and tighten it as the trade progresses.

Money management stops are another type of protective exit. These stops exit a trade at a fixed level of loss—for example, when the open position loss exceeds $750.00. A modification of this type of exit is a trailing stop. You exit once you have lost more than $750.00 of the maximum open position profit for the trade.

Another classic method that works well in trend-following applications is a trailing stop that tightens the longer you are in a trade. One example of this method is the parabolic indicator developed by Welles Wilder. A simpler example is to set initial stops at yesterday's low minus three times yesterday's range for long trades, and yesterday's high plus three times yesterday's range for short trades. As the trade progresses, this multiplier for the range and reference for yesterday's high and low is reduced. After 20 or more days in the trade, the stop is positioned a few ticks away from yesterday's high or low. This allows us to elegantly protect our profits. How the multiplier is adjusted can be based on many different methods—for example, using the current dominant cycle versus the current number of days in the trade. This type of exit is very powerful and useful in developing exits for classic trend-following systems.

There are many event-type exits. For example, you might exit on the first profitable opening—a classic exit used by Larry Williams. Or, you might exit on a target profit. Another example that works well is to exit a trade based on the action of a given technical indicator; for example, we can exit a position once we see divergence between price and an oscillator.

PARAMETER SELECTION AND OPTIMIZATION

After you have designed the entries and exits for your system, you need to select the proper parameters to use in each rule. For example, if you exit at an N-day low on a long position, what should be the proper value for N? This process is normally done using optimization. Optimization is often misunderstood. If used correctly, it can actually help you judge whether a given set of rules and parameters should continue to work in the future. Let's now overview the steps of properly using optimization.

Use your development set and optimize across a large range of parameters. When you have the results of the optimizations, begin to analyze them. When analyzing parameters based on an optimization, you are looking for traits that will produce a robust system. On the basis of all of my research, I have found that reliable sets of parameters have given traits. You should almost never select the most profitable set of parameters. The rare exception to this rule would be if the most profitable pair is surrounded by almost equally profitable pairs. Next, you want to have the highest possible number of neighboring parameters with similar performance. You also want reasonable drawdowns, and you do not want too much of the total profit produced by only one or two trades. It is also important to have the profits evenly distributed and to have a system that has an upward sloping equity curve.

UNDERSTANDING THE SYSTEM TESTING AND DEVELOPMENT CYCLE

Once you have found a set of parameters and a system that, based on these criteria, works well, you are ready to test the system on the testing set. A system that performs well on the testing set is worth testing further. The complete process of system testing will be covered in the next chapter.

DESIGNING AN ACTUAL SYSTEM

Let's now use what we have learned to build an actual trading system. Our first step is to select the market(s) and time frame(s) we want to trade. In this case, we want to trade three major currencies—the D-Mark, the Yen, and the Swiss Franc—using daily data. Second, we need to develop a premise. Our premise is simple: the currency markets' trend.

Because trend-following systems are based on a single series of price data, we will need to collect continuous contract data for the D-Mark, the Yen, and the Swiss Franc. We will use data for the period from 1/1/80 to 7/26/96. The reason we select a starting point of 1/1/80 is that the currency markets had just started trading in 1975, and the early years do not represent how these markets currently trade. We will break our data into three sets:

1. The period from 1/1/80 to 12/31/91 = the development set.
2. The period from 1/1/92 to 12/31/95 = the test set.
3. The period from 1/1/96 to 7/26/96 = the sample set.

Let's now select the technology to use in developing our system based on our premise. Because our premise is based on trend following, we will use the best trend-following method we have: adaptive channel breakouts, as described in Chapter 7. Briefly, this method simply buys and sells at the highest high and lowest low of the past dominant cycle days.

Now that we have selected our method, let's develop our entries. We start with the basic entries used by the adaptive channel breakout system. These are as follows:

Buy at Highest (High, DCycle) stop;

Sell at Lowest (Low, DCycle) stop;

where DCycle is the current dominant cycle.

This basic system is simply a stop and reverse. The results of this system for all three markets during the development period are shown in Table 15.4 (with $50.00 deducted for slippage and commissions).

TABLE 15.4   RESULTS ON THE CURRENCIES FOR THE STANDARD ADAPTIVE CHANNEL BREAKOUT SYSTEM.

SMarket	Net Profit	Trades	Win%	Average Trade	Drawdown
D-Mark	$ 69,137.50	76	41%	$ 909.70	−$11,312.50
Yen	95,512.50	74	39	1,304.22	−6,100.00
Swiss Franc	102,462.50	78	38	1,313.62	−12,412.50

What happens when we test our simple entries by holding a position for *N* days? We tested *N* from 10 to 30 days in steps of 2. Our results showed that our simple entries were very robust across the complete set of holding periods. When trading the D-Mark, every holding period from 10 to 30 days produced at least 75 percent of the profits of the standard reversal system. Some of the holding periods even outperformed the original system—for example, using a 26-day holding period produced $71,112.50 with 53 percent winning trades and a −$10,187.50 drawdown. Using a fixed holding period also improved the winning percentage. Every test we ran on the D-Mark won 50 percent or more of its trades. We also increased the number of trades to a range from 117 to 194 (versus 76, using the standard reversal system). This concept of holding for 26 days also worked well on the Yen, but not as well as the standard system. On the Yen, a 26-day holding period produced only a few hundred dollars less in profit but increased the drawdown to −$9,425.00 as compared to the original system. The winning percentage also increased to 51 percent. On the Swiss Franc, a 28-day holding period worked best, making a little over $89,000.00. The 26-day holding period finished third at $83,000.00. Both of these holding periods won more than 50 percent of their trades, but they increased the drawdown to −$14,350.00 as compared to the original system.

Next, we tested various target profits. Our target profits ranged from $750.00 to $2,000.00 in steps of $250.00. Once we entered a position, we could exit either on a target profit or when we got a signal in the opposite direction. Once again, our entries worked well for the complete range of target profits. For example, on the Swiss Franc, our target profits produced between $83,000.00 and almost $93,000.00. The net profit increased as we increased the size of our target profit. We also had a very high percentage of winning trades; for example, a $750.00 target won 82 percent of its trade, and a $2,000.00 target won 63 percent of its trades. The drawdown increased slightly, ranging from −$13,500.00 to −$14,812.50. The number of trades ranged from 193 for a $2,000.00 target to 392 for a $750.00 target. The results were similar for the other two currencies. For example, the Yen profits ranged from $77,700.00 for a $750.00 target to $99,162.50 for a $2,000.00 target, and had between 63 percent and 79 percent winning trades, respectively.

After testing the fixed holding period and the target profit, we tested these entries by lagging the trade by 1 to 5 days. Once a signal was generated, we entered on the first open after the lag period. When testing these small lags, we were surprised at their minimal effect on net profit. The results, using various lags on the Yen, are shown in Table 15.5 (with $50.00 deducted for slippage and commissions).

You can see in Table 15.5 that the lag has little effect on the Yen. The stability in profit, using small lags, also shows how robust our entry rules are. We can enter up to five days late and still produce about the same profit as the original signals. The results were similar for the other currencies; the lag did not cut the profits significantly. In the case of the Swiss Franc, a one-day lag produced the best (about $87,000.00) profits and a five-day lag produced the worst (about $73,000.00).

These three tests supply valuable information during the system development process. First, they can be used to develop better entries and exits. Second, the fact that our entries produced very stable results across all three currencies, over the complete sets of test, shows the robustness of the adaptive channel breakout method.

Now that we know that our basic entries are robust, let's try to find filters that will improve the performance of our system. The first filter we will use is the trend filter shown in Chapter 7. The indicator shown in Table 7.1 defined a trend based on how long prices stay above a

TABLE 15.5   RESULTS OF ADAPTIVE CHANNEL BREAKOUT WITH LAGGED ENTRIES.

Lag	Net Profit	Trades	Win%	Average Trade	Drawdown
4	$95,312.50	73	41%	$1,305.65	−$8,925.00
5	93,125.00	72	38	1,293.40	−9,650.00
1	89,637.50	72	39	1,244.97	−8,600.00
2	85,550.00	72	40	1,188.19	−9,212.50
3	85,175.00	72	42	1,182.99	−9,262.50

TABLE 15.6   RESULTS OF ADAPTIVE CHANNEL BREAKOUT WITH SIMPLE CYCLE BASED TREND FILTER.

Market	Net Profit	Trades	Win%	Average Trade	Drawdown
D-Mark	$49,987.50	56	48%	$ 892.63	−$6,412.50
Yen	89,537.50	53	45	1,689.39	−5,100.00
Swiss Franc	87,462.50	51	47	1,714.95	−7,562.50

full-period moving average. We used the same window size of 30, with 6 poles, to calculate the length of the dominant cycle for the breakout. Because a channel breakout system works better in trending markets, we will use this indicator to filter our entries. For the development period, using this filter for our entries and exiting on a dominant cycle day high or low produced the results shown in Table 15.6 (with $50.00 deducted for slippage and commissions).

This filter improved the winning percentage and drawdown across all three currencies, but did reduce the profits slightly.

The next filter used a simple 10-day ADX above 30 in order to take a trade. The results using the ADX filter are shown in Table 15.7 (with $50.00 deducted for slippage and commissions).

Comparing these two filters, only the trend filter based on the dominant cycle improved the performance across all three currencies. If we were trying to develop a system for trading only one market, we could have used the ADX on the Yen, for example, since it produced amazing results. Because we want a system that works well across all three currencies, we will use the filter originally shown in Table 7.1 to filter our entries.

TABLE 15.7   RESULTS OF ADAPTIVE CHANNEL BREAKOUT WITH ADX TREND FILTERS.

Market	Net Profit	Trades	Win%	Average Trade	Drawdown
D-Mark	$49,162.50	56	39%	$ 877.90	−$ 7,337.50
Yen	75,712.50	33	67	2,294.32	−5,537.50
Swiss Franc	96,337.50	53	47	1,817.69	−15,537.50

Having developed our entries and filters, we need to develop our exits.

Many breakouts fail early in a trade, and these failures often lead to large losing trades. We can help solve this problem by using a tighter stop early in the trade. In the currency system example, we used this tighter stop for 10 days. We selected 10 days because exiting a trade blindly after 10 days did not cause a large drop in profits. Using this concept, we designed the following exit:

MarketPosition = 1 and BarsSinceEntry < 10 then ExitShort at Highest(High,CycleLen/2) stop

MarketPosition = −1 and BarsSince Entry < 10 then ExitLong at Lowest(Low,CycleLen/2) stop

This simple exit was then combined with our original exits to improve the performance of the system. The concept of using a special exit within the first few days of a trade is very powerful; for example, if we are trading divergence using stochastics, we want that trade to be profitable within a few days or else we exit it.

Let's now put all the pieces together. The code for our currency trading system is shown in Table 15.8.

TABLE 15.8 MODIFIED ADAPTIVE CHANNEL BREAKOUT CURRENCY SYSTEM.

Vars: CycleLen(0);

value2=RSCycleTrend(close,30,6);

{shortest cycle detectable is 6 and longest is 50. We are using 30 bars of data and six poles}

CycleLen=Round(RSMemCycle1.2(close,6,50,30,6,0),0);

if value2=1 then Buy Highest(High,CycleLen) stop;

If value2=1 then Sell at Lowest(Low,CycleLen) stop;

If MarketPosition=-1 and BarsSinceEntry<10 then ExitShort Highest(High,.5*CycleLen) stop;

If MarketPosition=1 and BarsSinceEntry<10 then exitlong at Lowest(Low,.5*CycleLen) stop;

ExitShort Highest(High,CycleLen) stop;

ExitLong at Lowest(Low,CycleLen) stop;

TABLE 15.9   RESULTS OF MODIFIED ADAPTIVE CHANNEL
BREAKOUT SYSTEM DEVELOPMENT SET.

Market	Net Profit	Trades	Win%	Average Trade	Drawdown
D-Mark	$50,400.00	62	45%	$ 812.90	−$6,575.00
Yen	89,662.50	54	44	1,664.12	−4,762.50
Swiss Franc	91,125.00	53	51	1,734.43	−7,950.00

How did this system perform on the development set for all three currencies? These results are shown in Table 15.9 (with $50.00 deducted for slippage and commissions).

The stop reduced the drawdown slightly, compared to the version using only the trend filter. The stop also slightly increased the profits.

Now that we have selected our system, let's test it on the test set, the data set for the period from 1/1/92 to 12/31/95. The results during these four years, as well as the average yearly returns for the development set, are shown in Table 15.10 (with $50.00 deducted for slippage and commissions).

When evaluating the performance of a trading system, it is important that the system's performance is similar in both the development set and the test set. A system can be said to have similar performance when the

TABLE 15.10   RESULTS OF DEVELOPMENT AND TEST SET FOR
MODIFIED ADAPTIVE CHANNEL BREAKOUT SYSTEM.

Market	Net Profit	Trades	Win%	Drawdown	Yearly Development Set	Yearly Test Set
D-Mark	$ 7,337.50	18	39%	−$8,450.00	$4,200.00	$ 1,834.37
Yen	63,487.50	18	50	−4,187.50	7,471.87	15,871.88
Swiss Franc	27,400.00	22	50	−7,950.00	7,593.75	6,850.00
	Average Returns for Development Set per Year				$19,265.62	
	Average Returns for Test Set per Year				$24,556.25	

results between the two data sets are within the standard error. The standard error is calculated as follows:

$$\text{Standard error} = \frac{1}{\sqrt{N}}$$

where N is the number of trades.

Table 15.10 shows that this system has averaged over $15,000.00 per year on the Yen during this period. This profit is the result of one large winning trade that produced over $31,000.00 in seven months. If we remove that trade, we would have made only $31,712.50 on the Yen over 3.41 years, or $9,299.85 per year. If we use these numbers, then our average yearly returns are $17,984.20, or within 7.12 percent of the numbers generated during the development set period. This one Yen trade is a major outlier that should be excluded to get a more realistic view of the system's performance.

The standard error for our system is $1/\sqrt{58}$ because we have a total of 58 trades. This means that the standard error is 13.1 percent.

Because the difference of 7.12 percent between the average annual returns of the development set and the test set is within the standard error of 13.1 percent, we can conclude that this system is most likely robust and is worth testing further.

16

Testing, Evaluating, and Trading a Mechanical Trading System

The previous chapter showed you how to design a trading system. This chapter shows you how to properly test and evaluate a mechanical trading system. Testing and evaluating a trading system involves three major issues:

1. How well can the system be expected to perform, and what are the risks?
2. How likely is it that the system will continue to work in the future?
3. Can we predict when and if the system's performance will either temporarily degrade or fail completely?

Addressing these issues requires a deep understanding of the trading system being evaluated—not only how the system generates its trading signals but a statistical analysis of the system via the development set, the testing set, and an out-of-sample set. Prediction of future system performance during live trading requires a statistical analysis that compares the system performance for both live trading and historical test periods.

THE STEPS FOR TESTING AND EVALUATING A TRADING SYSTEM

Table 16.1 gives a general outline for both evaluating and trading a mechanical trading system. This section discusses each of these steps in more detail.

Historical System Performance and Data Collection

In this stage of our analysis, we need to collect statistics about system performance. Data are collected on the system over the development, testing, and out-of-sample periods. Data are collected for the complete periods as well as for a moving window of these periods. Data collection is important for both historical and live system evaluation and analysis. Collecting statistical performance data on a trading system is the most important step in analyzing a system. The data should be collected over various time frames, as well as for long, short, and combined trading performance, for the development, testing, and out-of-sample sets. If the system is being traded, data since the system went live should also be collected. Useful ways to collect these data are: on a yearly basis, or using a moving window with a one-year time frame.

Table 16.2 shows some of the statistics that can be collected using the TradeStation's backtester.

A lot of other valuable statistics can be collected—for example, a simple equity curve and a moving average of equity curve. Scatter and bar charts can also tell you a lot about a trading system. Some of the more valuable types of charts that I use are listed in Table 16.3.

Other statistical tests can be run on your system. Using the statistics collected over the development, testing, and out-of-sample periods, you

TABLE 16.1   STEPS IN TESTING A TRADING SYSTEM.

1. Historical system performance and data collection.
2. Historical system evaluation and analysis.
3. System trading.
4. Live system performance data collection.
5. Live system evaluation and analysis.
6. Repeat steps 1 to 5.

TABLE 16.2   SYSTEM STATISTICS COLLECTED BY TRADESTATION™.

Number of periods in test

Total net profit, gross profit, and gross loss

Total number of trades, percent profitable, number of winning trades, number of losing trades

Largest winning trade, largest losing trade

Average winning trade, average losing trade

Ratio of average wins/average losses

Average trade (wins and losses)

Maximum consecutive winners, maximum consecutive losers

Average number of bars in winners, average number of bars in losers

Maximum intraday drawdown

Profit factor

Trade-by-trade history

might try to show that the results are similar over all three periods. Or, you might compare the live trading results to the preliminary periods. The more similar these periods' statistical traits are, the more likely the system is robust. You might also run statistics that try to estimate the true average trade of the system within a given confidence level.

Historical System Evaluation and Analysis

By analyzing the data we have collected, we can address some issues relating to system performance, reliability, and tradability, as shown in Table 16.4.

TABLE 16.3   TYPES OF CHARTS TO USE FOR SYSTEM ANALYSIS.

1. Distribution chart of trade profits (all trades over various data-collection period(s)).
2. Distribution chart of trade drawdowns (all trades over various data-collection period(s)).
3. Scatter chart of trade profit versus volatility.
4. Scatter chart of average N period profit versus next M period profit.
5. Scatter chart of current values of a given technical indicator versus future trading profits.

TABLE 16.4   IMPORTANT SYSTEM ISSUES.

1. How profitable is the system on a risk-adjusted basis?
2. When a trader is using the system's own risk/reward criteria, will he or she be able to have the discipline to follow all of the system's signals?
3. What are the system's statistical traits? Our goal is to build a collection of systems with statistical characteristics that can be used like a DNA system.
4. On the basis of our analysis of the historical test results of this system, how likely is it to continue to work into the future?

Let's discuss evaluating a system on a risk-adjusted basis. Trading results are defined by three things: (1) risk, (2) margin, and (3) profits. The most popular measure of risk is maximum drawdown. A simple measure of risk-adjusted performance is net profit/maximum drawdown. Another measure relating to risk is called the *Sharpe ratio*, which is defined as:

$$\text{Sharpe} = \frac{(RA - RF)}{S}$$

where RA is average returns, RF is risk-free returns, and S is standard deviation of returns.

The higher the Sharpe ratio, the more stable the returns. If two systems have the same returns, the one with the higher Sharpe ratio has less risk. These are just a few ideas about measuring risk-adjusted performance. There are many other methods that are beyond the scope of this chapter.

When using a mechanical trading system, it is important to trade all of the system's signals. Profitable mechanical trading systems make money over time either by winning a high percentage of their trades or by having the average winner much greater than the average loser. If you do not take trades from the system that turn out to be very profitable, you have changed the statistical basis of your expected returns and, in fact, could even lose money on a profitable system. For this reason, the trader should spend time analyzing the system so that he or she understands its risks and rewards. Only then will the trader be able to trade the system correctly, using the correct required capital.

When we collect statistical data on a trading system, our analysis can give us an internal look at the system's traits—a kind of system DNA test. Let's look at a few system traits that we can capture. The first is a distribution chart of trade profits. Most trend-following systems will only win less than 50 percent of their trades. They make money by having a non-standard distribution in which there are many more large winning trades than in a standard distribution. An example of this type of distribution chart, for a standard channel breakout system on the Yen, is shown in Figure 16.1. This is a distribution chart for a simple trend-following system. Another type of chart might show trading profits versus volatility. Trend-following systems usually make more money with higher volatility. (An example of this type of chart has been shown as Figure 10.1.)

These are only a few ideas of how to capture a view of a system's personality. Almost any comparison of system performance that makes sense can be used. Once this information is collected, it can be used like a system DNA test.

Statistical analysis is very useful to tell whether a system will continue to work in the future. First, if the system was optimized, you should make sure that the parameters chosen were stable. If they were not, the system could fail badly in the future. Second, you should collect system traits over the development, testing, and out-of-sample periods. For all three periods, these traits should remain constant. They can change slightly, but radical changes would be a warning sign that the system is not

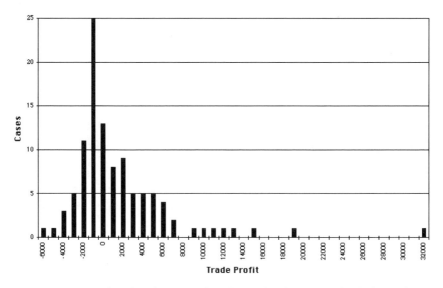

FIGURE 16.1 The distribution of trade profits for a standard channel breakout system on the Yen.

robust. Third, you should analyze both an equity curve and a one-year moving window of equity. The equity curve should be stable and upward sloping. The one-year moving window of equity should be above 0 at least 70 percent of the time. It should spend more time above zero than below it. A short and choppy moving window of equity is a danger sign for a trading system. Also, the moving window of equity should slope upward. Another measure I use is a ratio of system profits to standard deviation for the testing set versus the development set and out-of-sample set test periods. These ratios should always be above .5 and, for a reliable system, above .7.

System Trading

System trading can be either real trading or paper trading. What is important is that the data used are collected after the development of the system is finished. Two trading records should be kept when a system is trading with real money: (1) the results based on simulated trading performance, and (2) the true profits and losses achieved by the trader using the system. This information will be valuable. If all the trading signals of the system were followed, the result of these two records should be the same except for errors in estimating slippage. When the records match, we can use these results to improve our slippage estimates. When they are different, it means that the trader did not follow all of the system's trading signals. We must discover the gaps because this practice makes all of the profitability analysis for the system invalid. The cause could be either the trader's lack of discipline or an underestimation of the perceived risk of trading the system.

Live System Performance Data Collection

This data collection process is identical to the one used for historical data except that it uses only data issued since the release date of the system. These data, along with the historical data collection, will be used to predict future systems performance.

Live System Evaluation and Analysis

Live system evaluation and analysis consist of not only evaluating current system profitability but also trying to predict future system performance.

This is done by comparing the statistical characteristics of the system over both the development and the live trading periods. The more similar their performance, the more likely the system will perform well in the future. Let's look at an example. Suppose we have a trend-following system that made an average of $12,000.00 per year trading the currencies during the development period, and it still made $11,500.00 over the current twelve months of live trading. The system could still be dangerous to trade if the statistical characteristics of the system have changed. If we compare charts of system trading profit distributions during the development period and the live trading period, and they are dissimilar, the assumptions we made about the system and the trending nature of the currencies during the system's development may have changed. The system could still make money by winning a higher percentage of its trades, even if the original assumption of a nonstandard distribution of larger winning trades must be discarded. This would mean that the system's backtested results are no longer valid and the system is not safe to trade. We can also look for simple relationships in the live data, such as only trading the system when the equity curve is upward sloping. These are only a few examples of this type of analysis.

If the analysis shows the system is still safe to trade, you can continue to trade the system and repeat steps 3, 4, and 5 in Table 16.1.

TESTING A REAL TRADING SYSTEM

Now that you have an overview of how to test, evaluate, and trade a mechanical trading system, we will walk through an example of using these ideas for the system development described in the previous chapter.

Historical System Performance and Data Collection

Let's start by collecting statistics for our currency trading system. The first set of statistics we will collect has been outputted by TradeStation's backtest for the development, testing, and out-of-sample sets. The list of statistics was shown earlier, in Table 16.2.

We will now examine the statistics for our system over three different sets of data: (1) the development set, (2) the testing set, and (3) a combined set. We are using a combined set because the blind set has too few trades to be significant. Data comparing these numbers for three currencies—the Yen, the D-Mark, and the Swiss Franc—are shown in Table 16.5.

Next, we need to develop the series of charts discussed earlier, to create a system "footprint" or DNA. Three of these charts will be compiled for all three data sets in Table 16.5:

1. A distribution chart of trading profits.

2. An equity curve.

3. A one-year moving window of equity.

The first step in collecting our needed data is to modify our system slightly by adding the following line of code:

Print(file("d:\articles\sysva12\equity.txt"),Date,",",",NetProfit);

This will trigger TradeStation, when the system is run, to create a text file that can be used to analyze the system's equity curve.

After adding this line of code, we then run the system using the development, testing, and combined sets. This approach is valid because the testing set was not used as part of the optimization process. Analysis of the optimization results is very important; it helps us to predict future system performance. Next, each data set is run through the system, and the summary and trade-by-trade results are saved for a spreadsheet compatible file. (This process is covered in the TradeStation manual.) This process must be completed for the development, testing, and combined data sets.

Having collected a data profile, we can show graphically the footprint of the system, using the charts in Table 16.5.

A distribution chart of trade profits is developed by using the trade-by-trade history that TradeStation saves for each data set in a spreadsheet format. A distribution bar chart can be developed, using the trade profit column of the spreadsheet. Other charts can be developed using the file created by the extra line of code we added to the system, which entered the date and the net profit to a file. To develop a simple equity curve, we just plot the date and net profit. To develop a one-year moving window of equity, we add one more column to the spreadsheet. The new column

TABLE 16.5   TESTING RESULTS FOR A CURRENCY TRADING SYSTEM.

	Development Set	Testing Set	Combined Set
Yen			
Net profit	$89,862.50	$63,487.50	$63,187.50
Trades	54	18	20
Win%	44	50	50
Win/Loss	4.84	7.00	6.08
Max. consec. winners	4	4	4
Max. consec. losers	8	3	3
Ave. bars, winners	81	79	73
Ave. bars, losers	15	10	11
Profit factor	3.87	7.00	6.08
Drawdown	−$4,537.50	−$4,187.50	−$4,187.50
Annual ROA*	157.25%	379%	329.62%
D-Mark			
Net profit	$50,400.00	$7,337.50	$9,250.00
Trades	62	18	19
Win%	45	39	42
Win/Loss	2.86	2.22	2.09
Max. consec. winners	4	2	2
Max. consec. losers	8	3	3
Ave. bars, winners	64	72	69
Ave. bars, losers	15	21	21
Profit factor	2.35	1.41	1.52
Drawdown	−$6,575.00	−$8,450.00	−$8,450.00
Annual ROA	63.91%	21.75%	23.59%
Swiss Franc			
Net Profit	$91,925.00	$27,400.00	$31,700.00
Trades	53	22	25
Win%	51	50	48
Win/Loss	3.45	2.43	2.63
Max. consec. winners	7	6	6
Max. consec. losers	4	4	4
Ave. bars, winners	67	53	58
Ave. bars, losers	16	16	15
Profit factor	3.58	2.43	2.43
Drawdown	−$7,950.00	−$7,950.00	−$7,950.00
Annual ROA	96.33%	86.25%	86.27%

*ROA (return on account) is just returns based on net profit and drawdown with no margins.

contains a formula that subtracts the current net profit from the net profit 255 trading days ago. When we plot the date versus this column, we have created a one-year moving window of equity.

Let's look at examples of some of these charts for our currency trading.

Figure 16.2 shows our system's profit distribution chart for the development period for the Yen.

As in the classic channel breakout system, Figure 16.2 has more large winning trades than a standard distribution. Another interesting feature of this chart is the very large number of small winning trades between $0.00 and $1,000.00. These small trades are caused by the time-based exit method we added to our system. Without this exit, many of these small trades would have become losing trades.

Figure 16.3 shows a profit distribution chart for the combined testing and out-of-sample periods for the Yen. Notice that both Figure 16.2 and Figure 16.3 have large positive tails and the same high number of small winning trades. It is very important that this two charts are similar. Even if the system has similar profitability during both periods, it would be risky to trade if these charts were not similar, because the distribution of

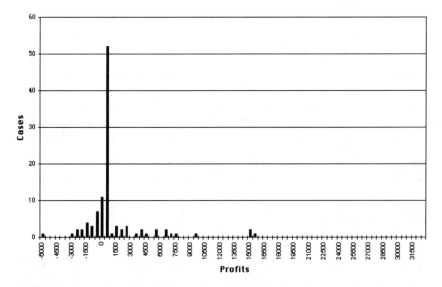

FIGURE 16.2   The distribution of trade profits for the adaptive channel breakout system, using the development set in Chapter 15.

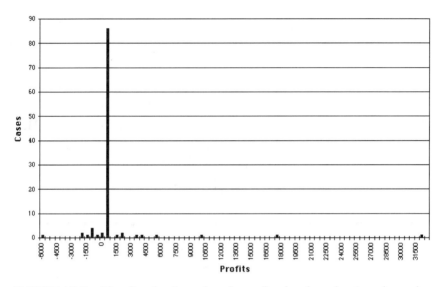

FIGURE 16.3   The distribution of trade profits for the adaptive channel breakout system, using the combined testing and out-of-sample sets in Chapter 15.

trades would have changed. Most of my research has shown that the distribution of trades changes prior to a system's failure. This change will often occur in the distribution of trades of a profitable system before a system actually starts losing money.

Figure 16.4 shows a one-year moving window of equity for the development set for the Yen. The one-year moving window of equity is almost always above zero and, in general, has an upward slope.

Let's now briefly analyze this system. First, we learned that it has a very stable performance when it is viewed as trading a basket of currencies. For example, the system has not performed well on the D-Mark over the past few years but has done better than expected on the Yen. When we view the results as a basket, they have remained similar over the development, testing, and combined sets. (We showed this for the development and testing sets in Chapter 15.) We also see that the distribution of trades has remained similar for the Yen during both the development and the combined sets, as shown in Figures 16.2 and 16.3. The results for the other two currencies are also similar enough to give us confidence in this

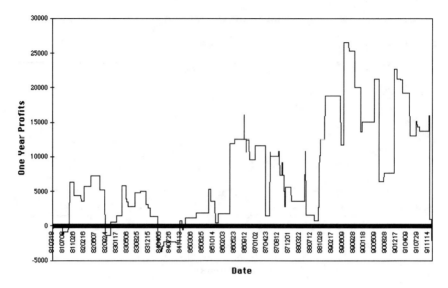

FIGURE 16.4 The one-year moving average of equity for the channel breakout system on the Yen, using the development set.

system. Many factors, such as the average length of winning and losing trades, have also been relatively constant on the basis of a basket of currencies. The one-year moving window of equity for the Yen (Figure 16.4) is above zero most of the time and has a general upward bias on the development set.

On the basis of our analysis, we can conclude that this system has a good probability of continuing to work well for this basket of three currencies for some time to come. Now that we think we have a reliable system, we need to discuss actually trading it.

System Trading

To trade our system on all three currencies, we would need a minimum of $60,000.00. This amount would give good returns and limit the maximum drawdown to about 33 percent, with returns on the account of about 31 percent per year. Because winning trades last about four months and losing trades last about three weeks, it will take some discipline to trade this model. The problem is that if we don't follow the system exactly, we could lose money even if the system continues to work. Most mechanical trading systems make money based on the results of a few large winning trades. This makes it very important to follow each and every trade that the system generates. If we know we are not disciplined enough to trade the model, we can still trade it by giving it to a broker who is equipped to trade the system. The broker can be given a limited power of attorney and would be legally obligated to follow all of the system's signals. We will use the results of the system's live performance to adjust our slippage estimates and collect live trading performance data.

Live System Performance Data Collection

The live data collection process is the same as the historical data collection process, except that it is based on results recorded since the system has gone on line.

During the process of trading the system, we collect data on the system just as we did during the historical testing period. We use these data to develop the same characteristic benchmarks we had during the development periods. We compare these to make sure that the live trading period is still similar to our previous results. This process is the same as comparing the development set to the testing set or the out-of-sample set. If they are similar within the standard error of the samples, then the system is still tradable. Any change in the profile of the system's performance must be explained—even an increased percentage of winning trades.

Live System Evaluation

Let's look at some danger signs for a system. One bad sign would be a 150 percent increase in maximum drawdown since the development period. Another would be a 150 percent increase in the number of maximum consecutive losing trades.

If the system performance degrades, you should stop trading the system. If the system is performing well, you should continue collecting the live data (using the data collection process) and analyzing the data at regular intervals. In this way, if a problem occurs, you can stop trading the system while minimizing losses. If the system is performing well, your analysis will give you confidence to trade the system and maximize your profits.

Part Five

USING ADVANCED TECHNOLOGIES TO DEVELOP TRADING STRATEGIES

17
Data Preprocessing and Postprocessing

Preprocessing and postprocessing data involve transforming data to make relationships more obvious or to extract information from raw data. Preprocessing refers to transforming raw data into a form that makes it easier for a modeling method, such as a neural network or machine induction, to find hidden relationships in the data, which can be used for forecasting. Postprocessing is the act of processing results from a model in order to extract all of the knowledge the model has learned. To illustrate, many neural-network-based models require postprocessing to make the forecasts useful. For example, we might find that the model is more accurate when the output of the neural network is above a given threshold.

DEVELOPING GOOD PREPROCESSING—AN OVERVIEW

There are many steps in developing good preprocessing. These steps are shown in Table 17.1.

Now that we have overviewed the steps involved in preprocessing, let us discuss them in more detail.

TABLE 17.1   STEPS IN DEVELOPING A MODEL.

1. Select the modeling method you are going to use.

2. Decide on the half-life of the model you want to build. For example, you might want to develop a model that you must retrain every 20 days (or every 3 or 6 months, or once a year). This issue is not as easy to resolve as picking the longest period, because the longer the life you want your model to have, the more data you need to develop it. In general, the more data you use, the better your raw data selection and preprocessing must be.

3. Select what your model is going to predict. This is important for any type of model, whether based on a neural network, machine learning, or a genetic algorithm, because your preprocessing should be designed to be predictive of your desired target.

4. Select and collect raw data that will be predictive of your desired output. These raw inputs can be different data series, such as the S&P500 or T-Bonds, or non-price-based data like the COT report or the traders' sentiment numbers (a report of what percentage of a given group of traders are bullish or bearish).

5. Select data transforms that can be tested to see how predictive they are of your target.

6. Using statistical analysis, evaluate which transforms work best in predicting your desired target. These transforms can be based on engineering methods, technical indicators, or standard statistical analysis.

7. When you find transforms that are predictive, you must decide how to sample them. Sampling is the process of selecting from a series data points that allow a modeling method to develop a reliable model based on the least possible data. This is important because using too many inputs will lower the reliability of the model.

8. After you have selected your inputs and sampling, you need to break your data into development, testing, and out-of-sample sets.

9. Develop your model and then start the cycle of eliminating inputs and rebuilding the model. If the model improves or performs the same after eliminating one of the inputs, remove that input from your preprocessing. Continue this process until you have developed the best model with the fewest inputs.

SELECTING A MODELING METHOD

The first step in building a model is to decide what analysis method to use. Neural networks are very powerful but will not allow you to see the rules used. In fact, a neural network is the best modeling method if you need to predict a continuous output. Neural networks are not easy to use with discrete variables such as day of week. To use a discrete variable, you need to convert it into a binary variable. Machine induction methods like C4.5 or rough sets will show you the rules but do not work well on continuous data. When using a machine induction method, you need to break continuous data into bins, so that it becomes a series of discrete or symbolic values for both the inputs and the output(s).

When developing preprocessing, I have found that it is easier to convert continuous-data-type preprocessing (the kind you would use in a neural network) into a discrete type that can be used in a method like C4.5 or rough sets than to convert discrete preprocessing into preprocessing that would work well in a neural network. This issue is important because, often, applying different methods to the same data will produce different models. One of my methods is to use the same data for both a neural network and a rough set model. I have found that when they both agree, the best trades are made.

THE LIFE SPAN OF A MODEL

How long you want your model to work before retraining also has a big effect on your preprocessing. In general, the shorter the life of the model, the easier it is to develop the preprocessing. This is because a model with a shorter-term life span does not require development of preprocessing to detect general market conditions such as bear and bull markets. For example, it is easier to develop a neural network that uses 1 year of history—to train it, test it for 6 weeks, and trade it for 6 weeks—than it is to develop a neural network trained on 10 years of data, which can be tested on 1.5 years and traded for 1.5 years before retraining. Believe it or not, this extra level of complexity in preprocessing can increase the required development time by an order of magnitude. On the other hand, you don't want to build a model with a very short life span because, often, this type of model will stop working unexpectedly. This happens because it has learned short-term patterns that may exist for only several months. Because the testing period is short for these types of models, you will not have enough statistical data to see a failure coming, before it results in large losses.

Another factor that affects the life span is what you are trying to predict. In general, neural networks that predict smoother targets and technical indicators, or are based on intermarket analysis, will have a longer life than models based on price-only data that predict price changes directly.

The modeling tool you use is also important. In general, machine-induction-based models, in which you can select rules based on simplicity, will have a longer life than neural networks, even when developed on the same data. The reason for using a neural network, however, is that these rules might cover only 20 percent of the total cases, whereas a robust neural network can produce a reliable forecast 60 to 80 percent of the time.

DEVELOPING TARGET OUTPUT(S) FOR A NEURAL NETWORK

The decision on what target to use for a neural network should be based on several factors: (1) the desired trade frequency; (2) the risk/reward criteria; and (3) the expertise available for building market-timing neural network models. We can predict three major classes of outputs. The easiest to predict is forward-shifted technical indicators. Many modeling methods perform better when predicting a smooth target. Next, we can make a direct price forecast, i.e., the percent of change five days into the future, or whether today's bar is a top or a bottom. These types of indicators are harder to predict, because of the effect of noise in financial data. The final type of target we will discuss is non-price-based forecasts. These include targets that predict the error in one forecasting method, switch between systems, or make consensus forecasts. These are very powerful targets that have been used in many successful trading applications.

Technical Indicator Prediction

There are two classes of indicators that we can predict: (1) classic technical indicators such as Moving Average Convergence/Divergence

(MACD) or even a simple moving-average crossover, and (2) designer indicators that have been developed for the purpose of being predictable by a modeling method such as a neural network. We will look at three examples of designer indicators:

1. Forward percent K.
2. Forward oscillators.
3. Forward momentum (of various types).

The forward percent K indicator is calculated as follows:

$$\text{Forward K} = (\text{Highest}(\text{High}_{+N}, N) - \text{Close})/(\text{Highest}(\text{High}_{+N}, N) - \text{Lowest}(\text{Low}_{+N}, N))$$

where $+N$ is a price N days into the future, and N is the number of days into the future.

When this indicator is high, it is a good time to buy. When it is low, it is a good time to sell. We can also take a short-term moving average of this indicator, that is, a three-period average so that we can remove some of the noise.*

Another designer indicator is a forward oscillator. An example of this, a forward price relative to the current moving average, is calculated as follows:

$$\text{Close}_{+N} - \text{Average}(\text{Close}, X)$$

where $+N$ is days into the future, and X is the length of the moving average.

If this indicator is positive, then it is bullish. If it is negative, then it is bearish. This type of forward oscillator was discussed in Paul Refene's book, *Neural Networks in the Capital Markets* (John Wiley & Sons, Inc., 1995).

---

*This indicator was presented as a target for a neural network at the Artificial Intelligence Application on Wall Street Conference, April 1993, by Gia Shuh Jang and Feipei Lai.

Another forward oscillator I have used in several applications follows the general uptrends and downtrends of a given market but is resistant to short periods of adverse movement. It is defined as follows:

$$\text{Average}((\text{Close}_{+5} - \text{Lowest}(\text{Close}_{+5}, 5))/(\text{Highest}(\text{Close}_{+5}, 5)$$
$$- \text{Lowest}(\text{Close}_{+5}, 5)), 5)$$

This output was used in a T-Bond neural network that I discussed in *Futures* Magazine May, June 1995. I showed how this target has a 0.77 correlation with a five-day percent change five days into the future over the training and testing sets, and is much smoother than predicting raw price change. Predicting this target with reasonable accuracy will lead to developing a very profitable model.

Another example of a designer output uses a percent change based on a smooth low-lag version of price. This type of output could be developed using classic exponential moving averages (EMAs), but more often we could develop it using a Kalman filter to smooth the price data before taking the momentum. A Kalman filter is a special moving average that uses feedback to make a prediction of the next values in order to remove some of the lag.

One of the outputs of this type that I have used in many different projects is based on Mark Jurik's adaptive moving average. When I use this adaptive filter, I use a very short period smoothing constant (e.g., 3), which induces about one bar of lag. I then have been able to predict this curve successfully 3 to 5 bars into the future.

Predicting a forward Pearson's correlation between intermarkets is also a good target for a neural network or other modeling method. We can find a predictive correlation between the intermarket and the market we are trading. This curve is relatively smooth and, if we know it, we can then use current changes in an intermarket to trade with high accuracy the market we are interested in. Considering the results using intermarket analysis without correlation analysis, and how using standard prediction correlation can improve results, just imagine what predictive correlation can do. We can also predict other indicators such as volatility, which can be used to trade options.

Now that we have discussed predicting various technical indicators, let us examine some targets that are based on raw price. Predicting raw-price-based outputs is relatively easy on weekly or monthly data but much harder on daily data.

Price-Based Targets

The classic price-based target is to predict percent of change over the next N days. When predicting this type of target, it is easier to predict a five-day change than a one-day change, because noise has a smaller effect on the five-day change. When using this type of target, you can predict the raw change or just the sign of the change. If you want to predict short-term moves or day trades, you can predict the difference between tomorrow's open and close. This type of target is a good tool for developing day trading systems that do not even require intraday data.

Another often used target is predicting tops and bottoms. Normally, for these predictions, you will have one model for predicting tops and another for predicting bottoms. You will also filter cases so that you will develop your models based only on cases that can be possible tops or bottoms. For example, if the price is higher than 3 days ago, today cannot be a bottom. One way to define a top or bottom is to use a swing high or low of a given number of days. You can either make your output a 1 at the turning points or make it a scaled value based on how far off the turning the market moved during the definition period. For example, if we identify a 5-day swing high, we can output a 0.5 if we fall less than .25 percent, a 0.75 if we fall more than .50 percent, and a 1 if we fall more than 1.0 percent. Another type of target that can be used to predict tops or bottoms with a neural network, outputs the number of days to the next top or bottom. This type of target has been discussed by Casey Klimassauskas.

Model-Based Targets

Model-based outputs are based on the output of another system or modeling method. There are several categories of these types of outputs, as listed in Table 17.2.

Let us now discuss some examples of these targets, beginning with developing targets based on system performance. One of the simplest system-performance-based targets is either predicting a simple change in the equity curve or predicting a moving-average crossover of equity.

TABLE 17.2   TYPES OF NEURAL NETWORK OUTPUTS.

1. Predicting system performance.
2. Selecting between models.
3. Developing a consensus based on many different models.
4. Predicting error correction values for a given model.
5. Predicting non-price-based indicators such as the current dominant cycle.

These types of targets can be used as filters for an existing trading system or model.

Another application is to develop a model using a neural network or genetic algorithm that has multiple outputs and encodes which system or systems should be traded.

The concept of developing a consensus system is another example of this technology. Your output would be the same as a simple model, but your inputs would be the result of multiple models plus other data. The goal of a consensus-type system is to take many models that are 60 percent or so accurate, and create a consensus model that is better than any of the individual models.

SELECTING RAW INPUTS

The next major step is to decide what raw input data to use in the model. This decision is based on two factors: (1) what influences the price of the market you want to trade, and (2) data availability.

First, you need to look at the factors that affect the prices of what you want to trade. You can start with the actual open–close, high–low of the market you are trading. Next, you should think about any related markets. For example, if you are developing preprocessing for T-Bonds, you would use data for markets like Eurodollars, CRB, XAU, and so on. If we were predicting the S&P500, we would use T-Bonds but we could also use factors like an advance–decline line or a put/call ratio. Commitment of traders (COT) data can also be valuable.

In general, any data series that logically has an effect on the market you are predicting is worth collecting and analyzing for use in developing inputs to your model.

Data availability is also an important issue. For example, many data series have only 3 to 5 years of daily data available. Even if they have been very predictive over this period of time, they do not give us enough data to work with. In general, we would like a minimum of 8 to 10 years of data in order to use a series in developing a model. Another issue relating to data availability is that when you use fundamental data, the data are often revised and the question becomes: How do you deal with the revised data? For example, do you replace the original data or do you deal with the revision in some other way?

DEVELOPING DATA TRANSFORMS

There is an almost infinite number of different types of transforms you can use to preprocess data. Let's discuss some of the general types of transforms, shown in Table 17.3.

Let's now discuss each of these in detail.

Standard Technical Indicators

Standard technical indicators and proprietary indicators used by market analysts are great sources for data transforms for preprocessing. The most popular indicators to use in a neural network are MACD, stochastics, and

TABLE 17.3   TYPES OF DATA TRANSFORMS.

1. Standard technical indicators, as well as components used to calculate these indicators.
2. Data normalization.
3. Percent or raw differences and log transforms.
4. Percent or raw differences and log transforms relative to moving average.
5. Multibit encoding.
6. Prefiltering raw data before further processing.
7. Trading system signals.
8. Correlation between price action and indicators or other markets.
9. Outputs of various other modeling methods.

ADX. Usually, these three are used together because stochastics work in trading range markets and MACD works in trending ones. ADX is used to identify when the market is trending versus not trending.

Another use of technical indicators as data transforms is to further transform the output of one or more indicators to extract what an indicator is trying to reveal about the market. (Several examples of this were given in Chapter 4.)

When using technical indicators in a neural network, I have found that the intermediate calculations used to make the indicators are often powerful inputs for a model. As an example, let's look at RSI, which is calculated as follows:

$$RSI = 100 - (100/(1 + RS))$$

where RS = average of net up closes for a selected number of days/average of net down closes for a selected number of days. We can use each of these averages as input to a neural network.

Data Normalization

Data normalization is a very important data transform in developing preprocessing for almost every modeling method. Let's now examine two classic methods of normalization:

1. Normalize the data from 0 to 1 and use the formula as follows:

X = Value – Lowest (Value, N)/(Highest (Value, n) – Lowest (Value, n))

If you want to scale between –1 and 1, subtract 0.5 and then multiply by 2.

2. Normalize relative to the mean and standard deviation. An example of this calculation is as follows:

$$X = \frac{X - \overline{X}}{\sigma}$$

where $\overline{X}$ = mean of the data set, and σ = standard deviation.

Percent or Raw Differences

One of the most common transforms used in developing any predictive model is the difference or momentum type of transform. There are several widely used transforms of this type, as follows:

$$X = \text{Value} - \text{Value}_n$$
$$X = \text{Log}(\text{Value}/\text{Value}_n)$$
$$X = (\text{Value} - \text{Value}_n)/\text{Value}$$

Value_n is the value of the series n bars ago.

Percent or Raw Differences Relative to the Mean

Percent or raw differences from the mean are also popular data transforms. There are many different variations on these transforms, and many different types of moving averages can even be used. Some of the basic variations for this type of transform are shown in Table 17.4. The moving average (MA) can be of any type or length.

Another variation on this theme is the difference between price and a block moving average. An example of this is as follows:

$$X = \text{Value1} - \text{MA}[\text{centered } n]$$

where MA[centered n] is a moving average centered n days ago.

We can also have a log transform or percent transform on this theme:

$$X = \text{Log}(\text{Value1}/\text{MA}[\text{centered } n])$$
$$X = (\text{Value1} - \text{MA}[\text{centered } n])/\text{MA centered } n$$

TABLE 17.4 MOVING AVERAGE TRANSFORMS.

X = Value – MA
X = Log(Value/MA)
X = MAShort – MALong
X = Log(MAShort/MALong)
X = (Value – MA)/Value

Multibit Encoding

The next type of data transform we will discuss is multibit encoding, a type of encoding that is valuable in many different types of transforms. One good use of it is for encoding day of week or month of year. When developing a model, you should not code days of the week by using a single number. For instance, you should not use 2 for Tuesday because a 3 for Wednesday might be considered (incorrectly) a higher value for output. The effects of the day of week coding are not based on the actual day's values. Instead, these values need to be encoded into discrete values, as shown here:

M	T	W	T	F
0	1	0	0	0

This encoding would be for a Tuesday.

Another type of encoding uses a thermometer-type scale. Here is how we would encode ADX into a thermometer-type encoding:

>10	>20	>30	>40
1	1	1	0

This encoding would represent an ADX value between 30 and 40.

This type of encoding works well when the critical levels of raw input are known. This encoding also makes a good output transform because if the encoding output from a model is not correct, we know that the forecast may not be reliable. For example, if bit one was a 0, we could not be sure that ADX is really over 30 (it does not follow our encoding). The reliability of a forecast can often be judged by designing a multiple bit output—for example, two outputs, one of which is the opposite of the other. We would take the predictions only when they agree. This method is frequently used in neural network applications.

Prefiltering Raw Data before Further Processing

One of my best methods, when I am predicting short-term time frames all the way from daily to intraday data, is to first process the data using a low-lag filter, before applying other data transforms. Low-lag filters are a special type of adaptive moving average. For example, a Kalman filter is a moving average with a predictive component added to remove most of the lag.

In my research in this area, I use a moving average called the Jurik AMA, developed by Jurik Research. I apply it to the raw data with a very fast smoothing constant of three. This removes a lot of the noise and induces only about one bar of lag. After applying the Jurik AMA, I then transform the data normally. When developing a target for these models, I use the smooth data.

Trading System Signals

Another data transform you can use is trading signals from simple trading systems. For example, you can use the signals generated by some of the systems you have seen in this book as inputs to a neural network. To illustrate, if your system is long, output a 1; if short, output a −1. You could also output a 2 for the initial long signal, a −2 for the initial short signal, and just a 1 or −1 for staying long or short. If you don't use the signal, the components that generate the signals are often very good transforms for your models.

Correlation Analysis

Intermarket relationships are a very powerful source of preprocessing for your models. As we have discussed earlier in this book, intermarket relationships do not always work, but by using Pearson's correlation we can judge how strong the relationship currently is and how much weight to put on it. One of the classic ways to do this is to take the correlation between another transform and your target shifted back in time, and use that correlation as an input to your neural network.

Outputs of Various Other Modeling Methods

Another powerful method is to use the input produced by various other modeling methods. For example, you can use the dominant cycle, prediction, or phase produced from MEM, and then apply data transform to those data. One valuable transform is to take a simple rate of change in the dominant cycle. This transform is valuable because, without it, when the dominant cycle is getting longer, you will be too early in predicting turning points, and when it is getting shorter, you will be too late.

EVALUATING DATA TRANSFORMS

Having discussed many different data transforms, how do we decide which ones to use? The general rule is: Select transforms performed on data that are predictive of your desired output. The transforms you select can be used either as inputs into your model or to split the data set into multiple models. For example, we would split the data records into two sets, one for when the market is trending and the other for nontrending conditions. Another alternative is to split the data into a possible top set and possible bottom set by splitting it based on whether the market is lower or higher than N days ago.

Subdividing the data sets based on variables that are very predictive is a powerful tool in developing reliable high-performance models. Let's now see how to judge the value of a given input set in predicting our desired output.

Scatter Charts

One of the simplest methods for evaluating a data transform is to use scatter charts, plotting the output on the Y axis and the data transform on the X axis. When analyzing these charts, we look for either linear shapes or nonlinear patterns. If we have a cloud around the axis, there is no relationship between the transform and the desired output. Let's look at an example of a linear relationship between an input variable and an output variable. Figure 17.1 shows the CRB index on the X axis and gold futures on the Y axis. In general, these have a linear relationship when gold is below $600.00 an ounce.

Figure 17.2 shows the nonlinear relationship between T-Bond prices and gold. In general, T-Bonds and gold futures are negatively correlated until the T-Bond price rises above 90. When the price of T-Bonds rises above 90, the relationship between T-Bonds and gold becomes positively correlated until the T-Bond price rises to 110. At 110, the correlation once again becomes negative.

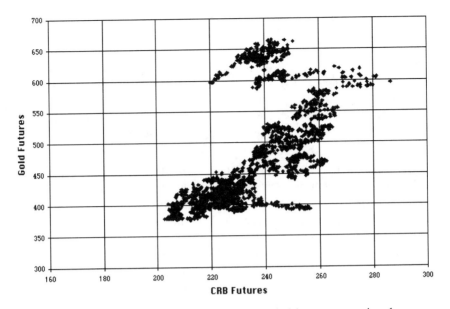

FIGURE 17.1 A scatter chart of CRB versus gold—an example of a linear relationship.

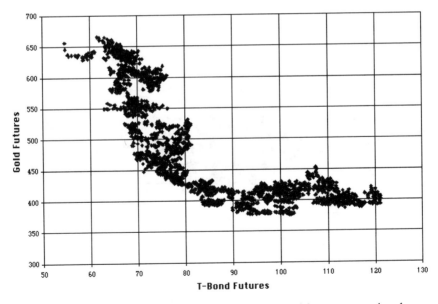

FIGURE 17.2 A scatter chart of T-Bond versus gold—an example of a nonlinear relationship.

255

Figure 17.3 shows a typical pattern when there is no relationship between two variables. In this example, we are using the one-day change 10 days ago on the X axis, and the current one-day change on the Y axis for gold futures. This chart shows that the one-day change in gold 10 days ago is not predictive of the price change tomorrow.

When analyzing these charts, you can use the current value of your transforms or past values. Many times, a variable's relationship with a multiperiod lag is not as clear as when using the current value.

Scatter charts are a great tool, but simple numerical methods for evaluating how predictive a transform will be are also available. Let's now discuss some of these methods.

The first method is to take a simple Pearson correlation between the data transforms and the desired output. This method will detect only linear correlations, and, often, even correlations that are known to exist and are used to build trading systems will be missed during simple correlation analysis. However, if you have a strong correlation, you should use that input in your model.

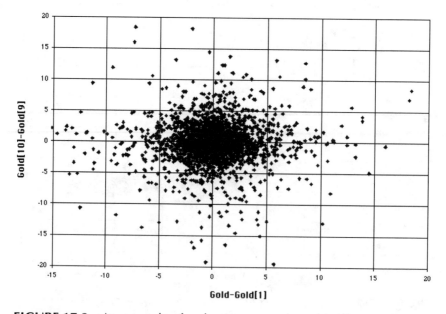

FIGURE 17.3   An example of a classic scatter chart that shows no relationship between the variables.

Both scatter charts and correlation analysis can be used to help you select inputs, but, besides these methods, you can use a modeling method such as C4.5 or rough sets to select input transforms. Using one of the machine induction methods, you would use all of your transforms to build a model. You would then select the inputs that, according to these methods, made the biggest contribution to predicting your output.

DATA SAMPLING

When developing preprocessing, you do not merely want to use all of the past values of each transform in your models because using all of the data will result in a less robust model. On the other hand, because the model method often needs to "see" patterns in the transform to use them effectively, you cannot use only the current value. You can solve this problem by sampling the data. When I sample data, I normally use the following scheme: 0,1,2,3,5,7,10,15,20,30,50. This approach was discussed by Mark Jurik (*Futures* Magazine, October 1992). This sequence allows detection of short-, medium-, and long-term patterns without sampling every bar.

DEVELOPING DEVELOPMENT, TESTING, AND OUT-OF-SAMPLE SETS

After you have selected transforms and sampling that are predictive of your desired output, you must develop your data sets. You can develop either one development/testing/out-of-sample unit based on the complete data set, or multiple sets, in which each set contains cases that meet given criteria. For example, suppose the market is trending or the last Fed move was a tightening. Subdividing the data sets can often produce good results if the criteria used for subdividing are truly predictive. When developing your data sets, your development set should contain at least 5 times the desired life of your model. If you have 5 years of data in your development set, you can expect the model to predict for about a year (at most) after the end of the development set. This means you can test for 6 months and trade for 6 months. If you want to develop models using 10 or more years of data, subdividing the data based on very predictive relationships can help.

When developing your models, you should have at least 30 cases per input. The higher this ratio, the more robust your model will be. The goal in developing your data sets is to have as few inputs as possible while producing the best possible results.

An iterative process of developing a model uses a neural network or other methods. This process deletes one variable at a time and then re-trains the model. You should try to reduce the number of connections if you are training a neural network. If the performance of the model improves or stays the same, you can remove that variable or hidden node. This process is repeated until the best model is found.

Often overlooked is the process of examining when the model is correct and when it is wrong. If you can find a pattern in these cases, it may reveal a need for a new input. Adding such inputs will often greatly improve your results.

DATA POSTPROCESSING

Postprocessing uses the output from one or more models and applies data transforms to extract knowledge contained in the model(s). Let's now discuss some of the most common methods. Postprocessing is often used for neural-network-based models. One example of this type of postprocessing uses the signals from the neural network only when they are above or below a given threshold. For example, if our neural network predicted the 5-day percent change, we would go long only if the network outputted a value greater than 1 percent and would go short only if it outputted a value below −1 percent. This is because neural network outputs that are too close to zero are within the error of the model and are not reliable.

Another form of postprocessing for a neural network model takes an average of the output of several models trained on the same data. This method will often produce better results than any of the networks alone.

Postprocessing can also be used to help you decide when a neural network needs retraining. You must run a correlation between the output of the neural network and the actual target. If this correlation drops below a given threshold based on the standard deviation of past correlations, you can turn the network off.

Preprocessing and postprocessing are the most important steps in developing models using advanced technologies. We will use what we learned here to build a neural network for the S&P500 in Chapter 18.

18

Developing a Neural Network Based on Standard Rule-Based Systems

One of the most powerful but easiest approaches for building a neural-network-based model begins with an existing tradable rule-based system. In this approach, we break a rule-based model into its components, which can be used in developing a neural network. This process allows us to develop a tradable neural network model because our goal is to improve the existing system, not to develop a new one from scratch.

A NEURAL NETWORK BASED ON AN EXISTING TRADING SYSTEM

Let's investigate the process of developing a neural network based on an existing trading system. The steps involved are overviewed in Table 18.1.

Table 18.2 lists some of the applications of neural networks that are developed using existing trading systems. As you can see, the range of applications is broad.

TABLE 18.1   STEPS IN BUILDING A NEURAL NETWORK MODEL.

1. Develop a good rule-based system first, using as few parameters as possible. Ideally, use fewer than four parameters in the system. Keep the system simple, without any fancy filters or exit rules. It will be the neural network's job to use the extra information you are supplying to improve your results. These extra inputs can include any information that you would have used to filter the original system.

2. Analyze the results of your rule-based system. Examine where your entries and exits occur, and take into account the premise of the system. Analyze the trade-by-trade results to try to discover how a discretionary trader might have used the system as an indicator and outperformed the system.

3. Use your analysis to develop your target output.

4. After selecting your output, develop your inputs based on the original indicators used in your rule-based system, plus any filters you would have used. Add inputs based on how a human expert trader would have used this system as part of his or her discretionary trading.

5. Develop your data sets, using the first 80 percent to train your model. The remaining 20 percent will be used for the testing set and the out-of-sample set. Normally, 15 percent of the data is used for the testing set and the remaining 5 percent is used for the out-of-sample set. These numbers are not set in stone; they are only guides.

6. Train your model, then test it on the testing set. Repeat this process three to five times, using different initial weights. Neural networks that perform well on both the training set and the testing set, and perform similarly across multiple trainings, are more likely to continue their performance into the future.

7. After you have developed a good neural network that performs well and is stable, analyze it to see whether it can be improved. One method I use is to analyze the training period to see whether there are any periods in which it has performed badly for an extended time. Next, compare these results to the original system. If both the network and the system performed badly during the same period, add new indicators that can filter out the times when the premise the system is based on performs badly. If the network performs badly while the original system performs well, change the transforms used on the original data.

8. When you have developed an acceptable model, start a process of eliminating inputs and retraining and testing the model to produce the best possible model with the smallest number of inputs and hidden nodes.

9. After you have finished developing your neural network, analyze the model so that you can develop the best possible trading strategy based on this model. Often, patterns in the output of neural networks can tell you when a given forecast may be right or wrong. One of the simplest and most common relationships is that the accuracy of a forecast is often higher when the absolute value of the output of the neural network is above a given level.

TABLE 18.2   TYPES OF NEURAL NETWORKS THAT CAN BE DEVELOPED USING AN EXISTING TRADING SYSTEM.

1. Breakout-type systems.
2. Moving-average crossover systems.
3. Oscillator-type countertrend systems.
4. Intermarket divergence-type systems.

We can use a neural network to supercharge systems based on the concepts in Table 18.2, as well as many other types of systems. Let's first overview how we can develop neural networks based on the applications in Table 18.2. Later in the chapter, we will explore a real example using an intermarket divergence system for the S&P500.

Neural Networks and Breakout Systems

Neural networks can be used to improve a classic channel breakout system or the adaptive channel breakout systems shown in Chapter 7. Because a standard channel breakout system does not trade very often, we must increase the number of trades if we are going to use neural networks to improve our model. We will accomplish this increase by exiting our trades when a target profit is reached, or exiting after a fixed number of days if the target is not reached. We tested this basic concept using adaptive channel breakout on the Swiss Franc over the period from 1/1/80 to 10/1/96. The target profit was $1,000.00, and we had a 10-day holding period. How this model performed relative to the original adaptive channel breakout (with $50.00 allowed for slippage and commissions) is shown in Table 18.3.

The net profit dropped 39 percent, and the number of trades increased by almost 5 to 1. The winning percentage went up to 69 percent, and drawdown was only slightly higher at −$14,950.00. The problem with this system is the high drawdown, which resulted from several large losing trades. If we can develop a neural network that will at least filter out these large losing trades and will possibly select the most profitable breakouts, we can have a great short- to medium-term currency trading system with a high winning percentage and low drawdown.

TABLE 18.3   ADAPTIVE CHANNEL BREAKOUT
ON SWISS FRANC REVISITED.

	Original Channel Breakout	Target + Hold
Net profit	$129,750.00	$80,325.00
Trades	107	512
Win%	44	69
Largest losing trade	−$6,287.50	−$6,337.50
Drawdown	−$12,412.50	−$14,950.00

We can develop a neural network for this application. Our target is 1 when the market is $1,000.00 higher within the 10 days following a breakout, or else it is 0. Our analysis should include only cases that are breakouts.

One of the most important issues in developing this type of model is the problem of having only about 500 cases for training a network. We can solve this problem by normalizing our inputs so that we can use data from three major currencies—the D-Mark, the Yen, and the Swiss Franc—in developing our model. This would give us about 1,500 cases: 1,250 for training, 200 for testing, and 50 for out-of-sample data. The first step in developing inputs for such a neural network would be to use standard indicators, such as ADX, as part of the preprocessing. In this type of application, we would use both the raw ADX value and simple differences of ADX. Next, we should use many of the outputs from the maximum entropy method (MEM)—for example, the dominant cycle, phase, and MEM predictions. For the dominant cycle, we should use both the value and the simple differences over the past several bars. We should also preprocess the price series data by using standardized price differences—for example, $\log(\text{close}/\text{close}_n) \times 100$. These types of inputs, when sampled, will allow the network to learn patterns that produce good channel breakouts. For example, when an upside breakout is preceded by the market's rallying for 3 or more days in a row, the breakout will normally fail. These are the types of patterns that the network can learn and implement to improve the performance of a channel breakout system.

This method offers promise; in fact, one of my clients claims to have produced $25,000.00 a year trading a 1 lot of the Swiss Franc using this type of method.

Neural Network Moving-Average Crossover Systems

One of the most often used trading systems is a simple moving-average crossover. Neural networks can be used to supercharge this classic system by predicting a moving-average crossover a few days into the future. For example, suppose we want to predict the difference between a 20-day and a 40-day moving average, 2 days into the future. This approach works well in many different markets and will even work on individual stocks. It is a good application because it is easy to predict a moving-average crossover, even with only a basic understanding of neural networks and the markets.

The key is that the base moving-average pair must be profitable and reliable before you try to predict it. Predicting a crossover enhances the original system but will not make a bad set of parameters a good one. On average, a well-designed neural network can improve the net profit and drawdown of a moving-average crossover system by 30 percent to as much as 300 percent. Even though this method works well, it is not always possible to find a reliable moving-average crossover system. In cases where we cannot find a robust moving-average crossover combination, we can use other predictive indicators.

Using Neural Networks to Enhance Oscillator-Type Systems

Oscillator-type indicators, such as stochastics and RSI, are often used to develop trading systems that try to enter near tops or bottoms. They are usually based on divergence between the price and the oscillator. We learned in Chapter 4 that, in order to trade bounded oscillators like stochastics and RSI effectively, their period must be set to 50 percent of the current dominant cycle. This type of system works well in a trading range market, but it works badly in a trending one. We can use this relationship to help a neural network improve standard oscillator systems. In developing this network, we would first include the current and sampled versions of the oscillator, as well as its rate of change. Next, we would include normalized price differences. Because these systems work best when the market is not trending, we should include ADX and simple differences of ADX, to allow the network to know when the oscillator system is likely to work well. Cycle information—the current dominant cycle, the rate of change of the dominant cycle, and the phase angle calculated using

MEM—could also help a neural network. We should develop two separate networks, one for tops and another for bottoms. Our target for this neural network could be tops and bottoms identified using divergence based on a human expert trader. This type of application may not always give enough cases to train a neural network on daily bars, so we want to either (1) standardize the data so we can train it using data from multiple markets, or (2) use it on intraday applications where we will have enough cases.

Using Intermarket Divergence to Develop a Neural Network

Intermarket divergence systems are countertrend trading systems that try to predict turning points based on the divergence between two fundamentally linked markets. In general, these systems are early, are on time, or totally miss a major move. They usually produce a high percentage of winning trades but will sometimes produce large losing trades. These losing trades occur because either the markets become so correlated that divergences are not generated, or they decouple for long periods of time and the market being traded becomes controlled by other technical or fundamental forces. We can combine the concept of intermarket divergence with neural networks to develop powerful predictive neural-network-based models. One target I often predict, using this application, is an N-day percentage change smoothed with a Y-day moving average. Most often, I use a 5-day percentage change with a 3-day moving average. Another target I use is a forward stochastic, as discussed in Chapter 17. After choosing our target, we can add other information—for example, correlation and predictive correlation—to help the model. Finally, we should add technical indicators such as ADX and stochastics. They allow the neural network to trade the market technically when it has detected, based on both correlation and predictive correlation, that intermarket analysis is currently not working.

DEVELOPING A WORKING EXAMPLE STEP-BY-STEP

During my research in developing intermarket divergence-based neural networks, I have found that they will trade much more often than the original intermarket-based system, sometimes yielding three to five times as many trades. This is very desirable because filtering an intermarket divergence system often leads to too few trades to make the system fit the needs of most shorter-term traders. Besides increasing the number of trades, you can often increase profits and reduce drawdown. Let's now look at an example of developing an intermarket divergence neural network for the S&P500, using T-Bonds as the intermarket. In this example, we will discuss the theory behind developing the preprocessing for this type of application. Let's now develop our S&P500 neural network.

Developing an S&P500 Intermarket Neural Network

We begin our development of our neural network by revisiting trading the S&P500 based on intermarket divergence, using T-Bonds as our intermarket. Our development set used in optimization is the period from 4/21/82 to 12/31/94. Our combined testing and out-of-sample set uses data for the period from 1/1/95 to 8/30/96. On the basis of our analysis using intermarket divergence, we found that the following rules produced good results:

1. If S&P500 < Average (S&P500, 12) and T-Bonds > Average (T-Bonds, 26), then buy at open.
2. If S&P500 > Average (S&P500, 12) and T-Bonds < Average (T-Bonds, 26), then sell at open.

During the development period (with $50.00 deducted for slippage and commissions), these basic rules produced the results shown in Table 18.4.

TABLE 18.4 DEVELOPMENT SET RESULTS FOR SIMPLE INTERMARKET DIVERGENCE OF THE S&P500 AND T-BONDS FOR TRADING THE S&P500.

Net profit	$321,275.00
Trades	118
Win%	69
Average trade	$2,722.67
Largest losing trade	−$17,800
Drawdown	−$26,125.00
Profit factor	3.92

We then tested this method on our combined testing and out-of-sample set (again allowing for $50.00 slippage and commissions) and produced the results shown in Table 18.5.

This system produced great results during the development period, but only $12,200.00 during the combined testing period. One of the main reasons for the substandard performance was a −$20,750.00 losing trade that occurred during the period from 1/23/96 to 6/7/96. There was also a −$6,100.00 losing trade during the period from 7/15/96 to 7/29/96. The first trade was a short signal given during this year's correction in the T-Bond market. During this period, T-Bonds and the S&P500 decoupled. The second trade was a buy signal during a period when bonds rallied as a safe haven to the correction going on the stock market. In general intermarket systems, the S&P500 underperforms the market during bull markets and outperforms it during bear markets. This system is based on a sound concept and, over a long period of time, should continue to be profitable and will profit greatly when the bear market finally occurs.

Intermarket Divergence—A Closer Look

In general, T-Bonds are predictive of the S&P500. Our goal in using a neural network is to extract from the data more information than can be extracted using the simple system. In order to accomplish this, we need to take a closer look at intermarket divergence. In Table 18.6, we show some of the strengths and weaknesses of the intermarket divergence approach.

TABLE 18.5   COMBINED SET RESULTS FOR SIMPLE INTERMARKET DIVERGENCE OF S&P500 AND T-BONDS FOR TRADING THE S&P500.

Net profit	$12,200.00
Trades	16
Win%	63
Average trade	$762.50
Largest losing trade	−$20,750.00
Drawdown	−$33,725.00
Profit factor	1.22

TABLE 18.6   PROS AND CONS OF INTERMARKET DIVERGENCE.

Strengths of Intermarket Divergence

The percentage of winning trades is high (often 60% to 80%).

Good profits per year are realized.

The basic premise is sound, if correct intermarkets are used.

This approach can pick tops and bottoms.

Weaknesses of an Intermarket Divergence System

Occasionally, large losing trades occur.

Sometimes, drawdowns will make the system untradable, even though they are still only 10%–15% of net profit.

A long period of flat equity occurs when intermarket relationships decouple.

Many systems have long average holding periods.

We can help to correct some of these weak points by using correlation and predictive correlation analysis, as discussed in Chapter 8. Intermarket correlation analysis can be used to filter out the occasional large losing trades and cut the drawdown of these systems. The problem is that using these filters significantly cuts the number of trades and increases the holding period, but the resulting systems are more tradable. Intermarket divergence is a powerful concept that can produce very profitable trading systems, but the simple rules we are using cannot capture many of the inefficiencies that can be exploited when using these intermarket relationships. To understand these systems better, we need to study how they work and where they enter and exit the market.

Anatomy of an Intermarket Divergence System

Intermarket divergence systems are countertrend trading systems that try to predict turning points. In general, these systems are either early or on time. They produce a high percentage of winning trades but sometimes, when correlated intermarkets do not diverge, they will miss a major market move. For example, a period in which the S&P500 and T-Bonds move together with a very high correlation may fail to generate a divergence signal for the S&P500 in the direction of bonds. Without that divergence, we would be trapped in the wrong direction and the result would be a very large losing trade. Another problem is that sometimes markets will decouple and a standard intermarket divergence-based system will lose money unless a correlation filter is applied.

Let's now look at some of the trades from our S&P500, T-Bond intermarket divergence system.

Figure 18.1 shows the system for the period from mid-December 1993 to mid-September 1994. The short signals that we entered on 2/23/94 produced a large correction, which at one time accounted for 35 points of open position profit. The problem was that the S&P500 and T-Bonds failed to have a bullish divergence in order to exit the trade. This caused the system to give back most of the profit in late August of 1994. Luckily, the market corrected again just before Thanksgiving, and this time it generated a bullish divergence that allowed us to exit this trade with a $13,750.00 profit on November 25, 1994. Even though this trade was a big winner, the inefficiency of our simple intermarket divergence rules was clear.

Figure 18.2 shows the period from December 1995 to August 1996. During this period, several trading signals were generated from our divergence model. For example, a buy signal in late January 1996 produced a

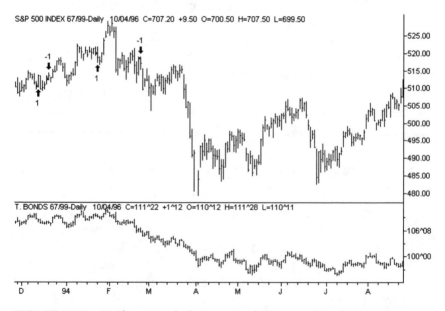

FIGURE 18.1   Trading signals from a simple intermarket divergence system, mid-December 1993 to mid-September 1994.

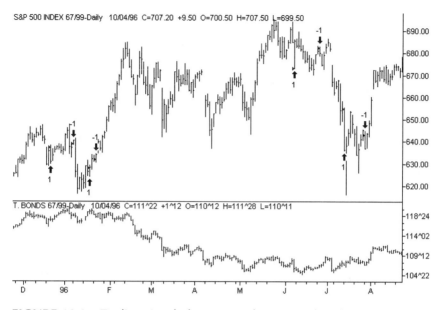

S&P 500 INDEX 67/99-Daily 10/04/96 C=707.20 +9.50 O=700.50 H=707.50 L=699.50

T. BONDS 67/99-Daily 10/04/96 C=111^22 +1^12 O=110^12 H=111^28 L=110^11

FIGURE 18.2 Trading signals from a simple intermarket divergence system, December 1995 to August 1996.

$1,750.00 winning trade. Unfortunately, when T-Bonds collapsed in February 1996, our system went short and remained short until June 7, 1996. This intermarket divergence trade lost over $20,000.00. It was caught on the wrong side of an explosive move in the S&P500—almost 60 points in about 6 weeks. A human expert trader would have gone long, based on momentum, well before the move ended. For example, one logical place to go long would have been at 642.00. This was one tick above the previous record high of $641.95, set on January 4, 1996. This would have limited the loss to only $8,150.00, and the reversal signal would have produced profit of over $15,000.00 if we had exited our trade based on the next short signal from our system. This change in the trading sequence would have produced about a $7,000.00 profit instead of a loss of over $20,000.00. This type of expert interpretation, combining intermarket analysis with classic technical analysis, can be a powerful concept that is not easy to express using simple rules, but it can greatly improve a standard intermarket divergence system.

Another method that can be used to improve an intermarket-based system is correlation analysis, which was discussed in Chapter 8. Correlation analysis has many uses. For example, it can be used to turn the system on and off, or to detect when a market will have a sustainable trend. The problem is to integrate all of these concepts into one system without curve fitting. A neural network can be used to integrate multiple trading methods into one model. In addition, a neural network can perform both pattern matching and modeling in the same model and can make use of all of the information that we can extract from intermarket analysis. Our goal now is to develop an S&P500 model based on the relationship between the S&P500 and T-Bonds, as well as technical analysis to forecast a price-based target.

An Intermarket Divergence Neural Network for the S&P500

To develop a neural network model based on our intermarket divergence example for the S&P500, we will use a forward-feed neural network. This type of network includes all of the variations on backpropagation. On the basis of my research, I have found that the following neural network products, all based on variations of backpropagation, work best: Braincel from Promised Land Technologies, Inc.; N-Train™, from Scientific Consultant Services; and Predict, from NeuralWare.

Before we select our target and design our preprocessing, we need to understand how a human expert trader would use our simple system and intermarket analysis as a tool for his or her discretionary trading. If we can understand how a great trader processes this information, we can develop preprocessing that will allow a neural network to extract from these data the same information that a human expert would look for.

The first priority of a human expert would be patterns between the oscillators for the intermarket and the market we are trading. For example, if the intermarket oscillator for T-Bonds makes higher highs and the oscillator for the S&P500 makes lower highs, it might mean that the market will move with a choppy upward bias. On the other hand, if the S&P500 oscillator is making lower lows while T-Bonds are making higher highs, then we could be on the verge of a major rally in the S&P500. This is only one example of the kinds of patterns an expert trader can learn to identify. A human expert learns how to identify these patterns by seeing how each pattern affects future price changes in the market he or she is trading. The trader may not even be aware of exactly what rules he or she is using.

In Chapter 8, we discussed using correlation analysis to improve the performance of trading systems based on intermarket analysis. We used two very powerful methods: (1) looking at the level of the actual correlation, and (2) the concept of predictive correlation. The level of the actual correlation can give insight about how a given intermarket-based system will work currently and about whether the market being traded is about to have a major trend. For example, when fundamentally linked markets like the S&P500 and T-Bonds currently have a strong correlation that is well above historical averages, the dependent market (in this case, the S&P500) will often trend. The sign of the correlation can tell us a lot about the fundamental forces in place. If we look at the relationship between gold and T-Bonds, we find that the largest moves in gold occur when gold is positively correlated to T-Bonds. This is because when interest rates fall quickly, inflation fears are fueled and can cause a major rally in gold. This type of information is very valuable when trading using intermarket analysis.

The second important tool that can improve the performance of intermarket analysis-based systems is the concept of predictive correlation. Briefly, the concept works as follows. Let's say we are trading the S&P500 using T-Bonds. We could correlate a five-day change in the T-Bonds five days ago to the current five-day change in the S&P500. Effectively, we would learn how predictive the past changes in T-Bonds are with regard to future price changes in the S&P500 over the period used in the correlation. If the predictive correlations remained constant, which they do not, we would effectively be able to predict future price changes and direction using intermarket oscillators, price changes, and the predictive correlations. But they do not remain constant, so we need some way for the model to estimate these correlations in the future. We can attempt this estimate by using rates of change of the predictive correlation in our model.

Developing Preprocessing for Intermarket Neural Networks

Now that we have a general understanding of how we can use intermarket divergences to predict future market price action, let's discuss our preprocessor based on intermarket divergence.

The first step is to decide what target to use for the neural network. In our example, we will use a five-period percentage change with a smooth three-bar moving average. The smoothing makes this an easier target for the network to predict, but the prediction is still made up of all future data. This target follows future trends but is resistant to daily noise. We can predict a price-based target because intermarket analysis can be used to infer future price changes based on the equilibrium between strongly linked markets. This relationship is strong enough that we can consider intermarket analysis a form of real-time fundamental analysis.

After we have selected our target, we need to design a preprocessor based on a combination of technical and intermarket analysis. We selected the periods used in our indicators on the basis of the profitability and robustness of simple rule-based intermarket divergence systems that used these same indicators.

Our preprocessor used nine different classes of indicators that were sampled using the method discussed in Chapter 17. This preprocessing is shown in Table 18.7.

The inputs and target shown in Table 18.7 are a good starting point for developing even a generic intermarket and technical analysis neural network preprocessor. This preprocessing model works best on the S&P500 but also produces acceptable results on T-Bonds using the CRB index as well as on T-Bonds using the UTY index.

Let's now discuss how we selected the inputs used in our preprocessor. The first inputs we used were technically based indicators. In this case, we used both ADX and stochastic. We used a 10-bar period for ADX, and both a two-day and a five-day difference. The ADX value tells us whether the market is trending, and the difference tells us whether the trend is getting stronger or weaker.

Next, we used a 14-day SlowK and SlowD (SlowK – SlowD) and a five-day rate of change of SlowK. Stochastics can tell us whether the market is overbought or oversold. Another little known use of stochastics is in predicting a price target for a given move. George Lane, in a seminar at Futures West in September 1996, showed that when a cycle-tuned FastK crosses above 75, we have reached the midpoint of a given rally, and when it crosses at 25, we have reached a midpoint of a given decline. The SlowK and SlowD crossings are useful in developing filters for detecting a possible market turning point. Finally, the most important stochastic signal is divergence between the price and the oscillator. Because we are using a five-period difference in SlowK and the same period log ratio for the price series, we have given the neural network what it needs to detect divergence between stochastics and price. Divergences, as we have shown earlier, occur at tops and bottoms.

TABLE 18.7   INPUTS TO AN INTERMARKET DIVERGENCE NEURAL NETWORK.

1. *Standard Technical Indicators*
ADX with a period of 10
ADX Difference 2 day
ADX Difference 5 day
SlowK 14 day
SlowD 14 day
SlowK – SlowD
Slowk – SlowK[5]
Sample five-day difference both two and five days back

2. *Intermarket Inputs*
Let Inter equal the close of the intermarket.
Let TrMarket equal the close of the market we are trading.
$N = N$ bars ago.
$+N = N$ bars into the future.

3. *Intermarket Oscillators*

$$InterOsc = Log\ \frac{Inter}{Inter_N}\ or$$

$$InterOsc = Log\ \frac{Inter}{Average(Inter, N)}$$

Sample these indicators using bars that are 0,2,5,10,15,20,25 bars ago.

4. *Intermarket Percent Change*

$$InterPerChg = \frac{Inter - Inter_N}{Inter} * 100$$

Sampled using 2,5,7,10,15,25 bars ago.

5. *Traded Market Oscillators*
    Let $N = 5$

$$TrMarketOsc = Log\ \frac{TrMarket}{TrMarket_N}\ or$$

$$TrMarketOsc = Log\ \frac{TrMarket}{Average(TrMarket, N)}$$

Sample these indicators using bars that are 0,2,5,10,15,20,25 bars ago.

(continued)

TABLE 18.7   (Continued)

---

6. *Intermarket Percent Change*
Let $N = 5$

$$TrPerChg = \frac{TrMarket - TrMarket_N}{TrMarket} *100$$

Sampled using 0,2,5,7,10,15,25 bars ago.

7. *Intermarket Correlation*
IntCor = Correlation(Inter,TrMarket,N)
Sampled using 0,2,5,10 bars ago.
IntCorLong = Correlation(Inter,TrMarket,Y)
Use a long-term correlation (for example, 40 or 50 bars) and only use today's value.

8. *Predictive Correlation*
PredCorrel = Correlation(InterOsc[5],Average(TrPerChg,3);
Sampled using 0,2,5,10 bars ago.

9. *Predictive Correlation Differences*
PredCorrel2 = PredCorrel – PredCorrel$_2$
PredCorrel5 = PredCorrel – PredCorrel$_5$
PredCorrel5 = PredCorrel – PredCorrel$_{10}$
These inputs were used to predict the following output:

$$Target = Average \frac{TrMarket - TrMarket_N}{TrMarket} *100$$

After our technical indicators, we have the components of our inter-market divergence system. Because we want to normalize our inputs, we will use logs of ratios to express simple differences. Our preprocessor will use the log ratio of either the current price to past prices, or the current price to a moving average of price. This is done both for the market we are trading and for the intermarket. In our S&P500 example, we will use prices relative to a moving average for both the S&P500 and T-Bonds.

Next, we calculate a five-period percentage change for both the inter-market and the market we are trading.

After we have added our correlation inputs, we use both a long-term and a short-term correlation between the market we are trading and the intermarket. The long-term correlation is used as a switch so that we can tell whether the market should continue to trend based on correlation. The short-term correlation is the same type of filter we discussed in Chapter 8. The predictive correlation between our intermarket oscillator five days ago and our target is actually one of the most important inputs in our model. This correlation gives us a measure of how currently predictive an intermarket oscillator is of our target, which, in turn, helps the neural network develop price-based forecasts. Predictive correlations are not constant, so we need a way of judging future values of these predictive correlations. We have attempted to supply this information to the network by using simple rates of change of the predictive correlation values.

We used these inputs to develop a preprocessor coded in TradeStation's EasyLanguage. We then applied this preprocessor to a multidata chart in TradeStation, using continuous backadjusted contracts for both the S&P500 and T-Bonds for the period from 4/21/82 to 8/30/96. We will use data for the period from 4/21/82 to 12/31/94 for training our neural network. Our testing set will be from 1/1/95 to 3/1/96, and our out-of-sample set will be from 3/2/96 to 8/30/96.

We used the results of our original intermarket-divergence S&P500/T-Bond system, as well as several systems that filtered our original model using correlation and predictive correlation for discovering the best periods to use for our preprocessed inputs. Table 18.8 shows the periods selected on the basis of our research.

We generated a comma separated values (CSV) file, which we imported into Excel. We split our data into the training (development), testing, and out-of-sample sets, and trained our neural network using Braincel 3.0. Our

**TABLE 18.8   PARAMETERS USED TO GENERATE
A NEURAL NETWORK FOR THE S&P500.**

We used prices relative to a moving average for both the intermarket and trading market oscillators, and the following periods for our indicators:

S&P500 moving average length	12
T-Bond moving average length	26
Short-term correlation length	15
Long-term correlation length	40
Length used in predictive correlation	15

preprocessor created 49 inputs and 1 output. We tested various configurations using between 6 and 12 hidden nodes. We used an initial weight range of ± .10 and an initial learning rate of .10. Braincel has an auto-learning rate adjuster that we had to disable.

We trained each network for between 150 and 350 cycles. Each configuration was trained at least five times. We had to train each configuration multiple times because training a neural network is an optimization problem. If we start with different sets of initial weights, we will get different solutions to our problems. In general, a neural network that produces similar results when trained with different sets of initial weights is more robust and has a better chance of holding up in the future.

When developing a neural network, it is best to use the lowest number of hidden nodes that will still produce good results. The reason is: When evaluating the robustness of a neural network, you want to develop a network with as high a ratio of training cases to weights as possible. The higher this ratio is, the better chance that the network will continue to work in the future. We first trained our neural network for the S&P500, using all of our inputs. We found that using 10 hidden nodes worked best. We then tested it after removing various inputs and found that, even though we could remove some of these inputs without degrading performance based on the correlation to our target output, we did degrade its trading performance. Removing those inputs changed the distribution of error between the target and our output. In this case, the network had the same correlation and percentage of accuracy on the direction of our target, but the distribution of errors changed. We now had more larger errors that led to larger losing trades. Based on these results, we decided to use the original set of inputs.

Table 18.9 shows how two of the neural networks that were trained to use 10 hidden nodes performed. Note the percent correct on direction and the correlation to the target for the training and the combined testing/out-of-sample sets, as well as the out-of-sample set by itself.

The network was constant over all three sets in predicting direction (measured by the percentage of the time the sign of the target was predicted correctly). All of the networks that we trained using 10 hidden nodes and our original inputs trained well and produced consistent results. Our networks all had a lower correlation during the testing period than during the training set. This is normal and was within an acceptable range.

TABLE 18.9   RAW RESULTS OF S&P500 NEURAL NETWORK
ON TRAINING, TESTING, AND OUT-OF-SAMPLE SETS.

	Network 1	Network 2
Training:		
% Correct	63.7%	64.2%
Correlation	.570	.574
Testing/Out-of-sample combined set:		
% Correct	63.5%	67.6%
Correlation	.373	.353
Out-of-sample set:		
% Correct	68.8%	66.4%
Correlation	.400	.369

Neural networks are not magic; they must be used as part of a larger system. If we use the raw output of a neural network and primitive rules, we can create a very profitable system, but it will often have properties that will make it untradable, such as large losing trades or high drawdown. Let's now see how Network 1 in Table 18.9 would have worked in a very simple trading system. Our simple rule is: We will go long when this network crosses above zero, and short when it crosses below zero.

Let's see how this simple system performed during our training and combined testing/out-of-sample sets. This network was trained on August 30, 1996. We will include results up to October 4, 1996. These extra data are truly out-of-sample.

The results to October 4, 1996, for Network 1 (with $50.00 allowed for slippage and commissions) are shown in Table 18.10.

Our total profit over the complete data set was $423,625.00 with a drawdown of −$43,225.00. This is about the same ratio of drawdown to profit as our original model, but we had almost 800 trades during this period, or about six times more trades than our original model. More important, this model has done much better than the original model since January 1995: it has made over seven times more money! The network has held up well, from its training, on August 30, 1996, until the testing was completed on October 4, 1996. Over a two-month period, this network made $15,450.00 per contract, including open equity. The problem is that this system is untradable because of the high drawdown and large losing

TABLE 18.10   TRADING RESULTS OF OUR SELECTED NEURAL NETWORK.

	Training Set	Combined Testing and Out-of-Sample Set
Net profit	$329,575.00	$94,050.00 + open $8,600.00
Trades	591	101 + open
Win%	50	54
Profit factor	1.68	1.80
Drawdown	−$43,225.00	−$33,825.00

trades. In general, most neural networks are not tradable when using such primitive rules.

Let's now try to develop a more tradable system using this neural network. Our first change is to use a two-day average of our neural network output to generate our signals. Next, we correlate a five-day percentage change smoothed using a three-day average with our neural network output five days ago. In effect, we are doing a predictive correlation between our neural network output and our target. We also found that when the simple five-day difference of this correlation drops below −.20 we should not take any entry signals. Next, we found that the neural network threshold should be above .10 for our buy signals and below −.10 for our sell signals. We exit long positions when the neural two-day average output crosses below zero, and short positions when it crosses above zero.

This system significantly outperformed our original simple network system; in fact, it produced a good S&P500 trading model. Our results,

TABLE 18.11   NEURAL NETWORK TRADING RESULTS USING THRESHOLDS AND CORRELATION FILTER.

	Training Set	Combined Testing and Out-of-Sample Set
Net profit	$383,175.00	$122,050.00 + $8,100.00
Trades	374	62 + open
Win%	55	66
Profit factor	2.27	2.74
Drawdown	−$22,850	−$22,950.00

until October 4, 1996, for both the training period and the combined testing/out-of-sample period, are shown in Table 18.11.

These results show how much better this system performed. Our new neural-network-based system made $513,325.00 during the period from 4/21/82 to 10/4/96, while the buy and hold profit was only $217,000.00. Our profits on the short side were $114,025.00 during the training set and $30,800.00 during the combined testing and out-of-sample set. This shows that the model outperforms the S&P500 during both bear and bull markets.

This was not the outcome for our rule-based simple divergence model. During the period from 8/30/96 to 10/4/96, we took the following trades:

Entry Date	Exit Date	Profit
1. 8/16/96 (buy)	9/6/96	$8,200.00
2. 9/10/96 (buy)	9/16/96	$7,650.00

A third and final trade was a buy on 9/23/96 at 697.05. We exited this trade with a $4,150.00 profit on 10/10/96. Our results show that this technology can be used to develop a profitable and tradable S&P500 neural network.

Our early analysis also shows that this intermarket divergence preprocessing model can be used to develop neural networks in other markets where intermarket divergence can produce profitable trading systems. Neural networks have fallen out of favor on Wall Street, but the reports of their death have been grossly exaggerated.

19

Machine Learning Methods for Developing Trading Strategies

Machine induction methods extract rules from data. We discussed the theory behind some of these methods in Chapter 11. This chapter gives an overview of how to use machine induction in various trading applications.

Table 19.1 lists some of the ways in which machine induction can be used to develop trading strategies.

The examples given in Table 19.1 use machine induction either to develop or to improve a trading strategy. In the first four examples in the table, the rules developed by the machine induction method are used directly as part of a trading strategy. In the fifth example in the table, the information generated by machine induction helps in selecting which

TABLE 19.1   USES OF MACHINE INDUCTION.

1. Developing trading rules.

2. Extracting rules from a neural network.

3. Combining trading strategies.

4. Developing postprocessing for a neural network.

5. Eliminating inputs for use in other modeling methods such as neural networks.

variables are needed to train a neural network with maximum performance and a minimum of architecture.

USING MACHINE INDUCTION FOR DEVELOPING TRADING RULES

The classic use of machine induction is to develop sets of rules that classify a target output based on input variables. We can use machine induction methods to develop trading strategies by developing rules that predict the output class of a target. For example, we can predict whether the market will be higher or lower five days from now. When developing rules using a machine induction method such as C4.5 or rough sets, which are based on supervised learning, the process is very similar to the one used for a neural network. Our first step is to select the target we want to predict. Next, we need to develop preprocessing that is predictive of that target. The main difference between developing a machine induction application and one using neural networks is that both the inputs and the outputs must be made into discrete variables.

When developing our output classes, we use human expertise to either select a discrete set of outputs or convert a continuous output into a series of discrete values. One very simple but useful method is to use the sign of a standard continuous output class like a five-day percentage change—for example, negative output $= -1$ and positive output $= +1$. When using more complex output classes, we should limit the number of classes to less than 1 class per 500 training cases.

Let's now discuss how we can use a human expert to develop discrete values for our input variables. A human expert might set the number of classes and their levels, or just the number of classes. We can then use statistical analysis or machine learning methods to find the correct levels. As an example, if we were using SlowK as an input, we could break it into three classes: (1) overbought, (2) neutral, and (3) oversold. We could set the level based on domain expertise. Normally, in this case, we would use 30 and 70. We could also use various statistical and machine learning methods to find these levels. For example, when analyzing the T-Bond market, I found that the critical levels for Slow K are 30 and 62. These are close to our standard values, and if we were to collect these statistics across multiple markets, they would probably be even closer to the standard levels, but we can fine-tune performance in a given market using these analytical methods.

One problem with using automatic methods for generating classes is that sometimes the classes will cover a very small range of values and be based on a statistical artifact without any cause-and-effect relationship. For example, if we have 10 cases when stochastics were between 51 and 53, and all 10 times the market rose, our statistical methods might develop an input class with a range between 51 and 53. A human expert would know that this is just curve fitting and would not use such a class. Machine generated classes are usually good, but they should be filtered with the expertise of a human trader.

After developing our input and output classes, we need to divide our data into the development, testing, and out-of-sample sets. We then apply the machine learning method to the data. If we are using C4.5 or another decision-tree-type method, we can develop these trees and then prune their leaves in order to develop the best rules with the fewest terms. These rules then need to be tested further. If we are using rough sets, which are currently available only as DataLogic/R from Reduct Systems, we need to assign a roughness level and a precision to our model. The roughness level controls the complexity of the rules, and the precision determines the accuracy of the rules in identifying the output classes. If we use a high level of roughness, such as .90, we will develop very simple rules with few terms, and these should generalize well. This removes the step of pruning that is normal when developing rules based on a commercial decision-tree-type product.

After we have developed our rules, we will select the best candidates for trading. This process is discussed later in this chapter.

When we have finished this selection process, we need to develop a trading strategy. For example, if we are predicting whether a market will be higher or lower five days from now, we must decide how we are going to exit the trade. We can use any number of classic exit methods, or we can just hold our position for the lookahead period of the target. We must be careful not to write our exits so that we exit and reenter in the same direction and at the same price on the same day. This would happen, for example, if we exited on the next open after being in a trade for five days, and our rule for entering the market also generated our exit. We also must realize that when we predict a classic target like percentage change and use it as part of a trading strategy, the number of trades will be much less than the number of supporting cases for the rules, because a rule will often be true for several days in a row.

EXTRACTING RULES FROM A NEURAL NETWORK

One of the biggest problems with neural networks is that a trader cannot see how they arrived at their answers. This is a problem because it is hard to place a trade based on a black box when the premise that produces the signal is unknown. Given this problem, why don't we just directly generate the rules from the data instead of using the neural network? The answer is: Training the neural network gives us an input–output mapping without any conflicts. This mapping can be converted into rules very easily because it does not contain any noise or conflicting cases. For the same reason, it will often generate rules that are different from those directly generated from the original data.

The concept of inducting rules from a neural network has been used by many successful high-tech money management firms. LBS Capital Management used sensitivity analysis to develop rules from a neural network. LBS adjusted the level of the inputs, recorded the changes in output, and then used this information to develop rules. However, this method is very time-intensive, and the number of combinations that can be used for the inputs, even in a small neural network with 20 inputs using real numbers, is so large that they could not be all tested in our lifetime.

We could use machine induction and a library of generated cases to develop an approximate set of rules for our neural network. We could then use sensitivity analysis to test only cases at the edge of the rules. For example, if one condition of a given rule is Slow K > 60, we could test 59.5, 59.0, 58.5, and so on, until the output value changes class. This will make the problem solvable and will allow us to generate an approximate rule set for the neural network.

The rules we generate from our neural network will give us some idea of the reliability of our neural network for a given set of input values. For example, when we analyze the rules from the network, we might find that an area of the solution space is based on relationships that do not have any theoretical basis. This is very valuable information and could allow us to use a neural network with more confidence. We can also learn whether there are any areas of the solution space where the network's performance is substandard. For example, our network might be 69 percent accurate overall, but when ADX is below 20, we might find that it is only 55 percent accurate based on the rules for this condition. Also, when the neural network is not performing well, the rules will help us judge whether the neural network is beginning to fail or whether the market is currently in a mode where it is not performing well even during the training set. This information can be very valuable when either developing trading strategy or evaluating its real-time performance.

Let's now itemize the steps involved in arriving at rules for a neural network using machine induction:

1. Generate new cases using valid real-world input combinations. At least 50 cases per weight should be generated, and their distribution should be based on the density of the occurrence of a given value in real-world data.
2. Have the network output a value for each case.
3. Induce rules using either rough sets or a decision-tree algorithm like C4.5. The resulting rules will not be exactly the rules used by the neural network, but will be a good first approximation.
4. Use sensitivity analysis to fine-tune the rules by testing values at the boundaries of the rules.
5. Repeat the sensitivity analysis until you have generated a satisfactory rule set.

COMBINING TRADING STRATEGIES

Another valuable use for machine-induced rules is combining of multiple trading methods or switching between trading methods. Let's discuss an example. Suppose we have two different methods; one is a channel breakout and the other is a trading system based on stochastics. Each of these systems is profitable on its own. We then notice that these systems' equity curves are negatively correlated. This is a good example of why you should use machine induction to combine trading systems.

Our first step in developing such an application is to select our output. In this case, we will have three discrete output classes: one for when we should be trading the channel breakout, one for when we should not be

TABLE 19.2   INPUTS FOR AN IMPROVED CHANNEL BREAKOUT NEURAL NETWORK BASED SYSTEM.

Current position for both trading methods.

Trade performance information for both systems.

ADX and simple differences of ADX.

Stochastic and difference of stochastic.

Current dominant cycle and rates of change of the dominant cycle.

Current phase and rates of change of phase.

Normalized price momentum data: either simple differences or price relative to a moving average.

trading either system, and one for when we should be trading the stochastic system. In this application, we should use the types of inputs shown in Table 19.2.

We should sample all of these types of inputs when developing a model. Our goal is to develop a model that is better than either existing model in trading the market these systems were designed for.

This type of application works well and has been discussed by Paul Refene in several different articles. The inputs listed in Table 19.2 are predictive of which model to use for our example. In my research, as well as research published by Refene, the trading results over the last three to five trades for each method we are switching between are actually among the most important inputs to our model. Both the cycle-based inputs and ADX are used to tell whether the market is in a trending, cycle, or consolidation mode. Stochastics and price data interact to give us information that can be used to help predict which method is currently the best to trade. The concept of developing a switching model has been little discussed outside of academia, but should become a hot area of research over the next few years.

POSTPROCESSING A NEURAL NETWORK

One of the most powerful applications of machine induction is for postprocessing the results based on another modeling method, such as neural networks. For example, we could use the past outputs from a neural network and some other preprocessed inputs to try to predict whether the neural network's next forecast will be right or wrong. I have used rough sets in several different systems to try to filter out periods when a given neural network will perform at a substandard level. Often, simple patterns exist that can tell the reliability of a given forecast. For example, the higher the absolute value of the network's output, the more likely that it will be correct. When developing this type of application, it is often a good idea to develop a different set of rules for different output classes from the neural network. For example, you might want one set of rules for when the current forecast is positive and another for when it is negative. In these types of models, you would use either raw or preprocessed past values produced by the neural network, as well as other inputs that may not have been included in the original model—for example, you could add month of year. This is often a good input to add when generating rules because it is hard to preprocess for a neural network and would require some type of thermometer encoding. In my research, I have found that the accuracy of some neural networks differs greatly, based on month of year, for example this is very important in the T-Bond market. You can also include data that the original network used, because rough sets or C4.5 will generate a model different from the original model, which was generated using the neural network. The process of filtering a neural network in this way is very powerful. Filtering out only a few large losing trades can make a huge difference in the overall performance of the network.

VARIABLE ELIMINATION USING MACHINE INDUCTION

In the previous chapter, we learned that, when developing a neural network, it is important to eliminate variables that do not contribute to the performance of the model, because the reliability of a neural network is proportional to the ratio of the training cases to the number of connections. In Chapter 18, we discussed using brute force to try to eliminate inputs that do not improve the performance of the neural network. Using a brute force search can be impossible for even a small neural network (30 inputs) and could require days of using a genetic algorithm to speed up the search. We can use machine induction to select inputs for our model, induce rules, and then use only the inputs that are used in these rules. This process is similar to developing standard rules using machine induction, except that we allow more curve fitting. For example, we might use more than one output class per 500 cases. We also might divide our input classes further, using as many as 10 classes for an indicator like stochastics. In this application, we actually want to curve-fit because if the variables are not used in overfitted rules, they most likely are not necessary to the solution. If we are using C4.5, we would use all of the variables in the rules except the ones at the leaves of the decision tree. If we are using rough sets, we would use a roughness of .60 and a rules precision of 55 percent to select our variables using DataLogic/R. These levels are near the middle of the range. Roughness varies from 0 to 1, and rule precision from 0 percent to 100 percent. This method can often produce networks with reduced inputs but the same accuracy of direction, as well as the same correlation between the neural network output and the target as in the original configuration. One problem is that sometimes the distribution of errors will change and the network will not be as profitable. In these cases, we start with the inputs used by this method and then, using either brute force or a genetic algorithm, we try readding the variable that has been removed and continuing until we develop a satisfactory model.

EVALUATING THE RELIABILITY OF MACHINE-GENERATED RULES

How can you judge the probability that a given rule(s) will continue to work into the future?

The first step in estimating the future reliability of any set of rules is to rank the rules based on the number of conditions each rule contains. The fewer conditions a rule contains, the higher its ranking. The next step is to divide the ratio of supporting cases by the number of conditions. The higher this ratio, the higher the probability that the rule will continue to work in the future.

In general, when selecting rules generated using machine induction methods in trading, we will select only rules that are at least 60 percent accurate when discriminating output, and are supported by a minimum of 5 percent of the cases in that output class in the database. Next, we examine where each case occurred in the data set and score rules higher based on how the uniform distribution of cases occurred.

After rule selection based on these criteria, we need to have them analyzed by a human expert. This expert will select rules that he or she feels are based on a sound premise and should continue to work well in the future, and will eliminate rules that are based on statistical artifacts (e.g., it rains every time I wash my car, so I can make it rain by washing my car). This is a necessary step because each rule we trade should be based on a valid premise and should have a cause-and-effect relationship that makes sense.

Next we need to have these rules coded for use in a trading simulating and real-time trading tool like Omega Research's TradeStation with EasyLanguage. We then test these rules on the development, testing, and out-of-sample sets. We evaluate these rules on the development set, to judge the tradability of a given rule. We need this analysis because, using most machine learning methods with a standard target like percent change, we can judge only the percent correct for a given output or class, normally above or below zero, and no other criteria like drawdown or average trade. It is possible to have rules that are 70 percent or more accurate and yet are not tradable because of a small average trade or a high drawdown. We will also analyze the uniformity of the performance of a given rule over the development set. The more uniform the performance, the more likely a given rule will continue to work in the future.

After selecting rules that we feel are robust and tradable, we test them in the testing set.

Once we have collected the statistical information about our rules' performance via both the development and the testing sets, we use this information to select rules that have performed similarly during both sets of data. If the rules do not show similar performance but the performance is good across both sets, we try to find other variables that can explain these differences. One example of this would be a higher average trade in the testing set because of an increase in volatility over the past three years. If this is the case, we then standardize our trading results, for both the development and the testing periods, based on the average N-day range for the market we are trading. After this normalization, the results for good rules are often within the standard error.

When our selection is finished based on the development and testing sets, we make our final selection, using a blind data set if enough cases are available. If we do not have enough data to make a testing and blind set statistically valid, we can use a set that combines the testing set and one of our sample sets, and then measure the performance using a moving window for our analysis. In this case, we would want an upward sloping equity curve at the end of our combined data period.

This chapter has presented several ways to use machine induction to develop trading strategies. This technology is not the egghead approach once reserved for the university laboratory. Some of the methods discussed here can greatly improve your trading performance and help you research how markets actually work. Machine induction will grow in use over the next few years, and will give traders who use this technology an important edge to increase their performance in rapidly changing markets.

20
Using Genetic Algorithms for Trading Applications

In Chapter 11, we discussed the basics of genetic algorithms. In this chapter, we show how they can be used in a broad range of trading applications. We will first discuss several different applications for genetic algorithms in trading. Next, we will overview the steps involved in developing a solution using a genetic algorithm. Finally, we will show how to develop a real trading system by evolving rules based on both technical and intermarket analysis.

USES OF GENETIC ALGORITHMS IN TRADING

Genetic algorithms have many uses in developing trading applications. Some of these are listed in Table 20.1.

Let's now overview how genetic algorithms are used in each of these applications.

Genetic Algorithms and Neural Networks

Genetic algorithms are useful in evolving neural networks. This application is actually two different types of applications. The first is to evolve inputs and/or the configuration of a network. Genetic algorithms can find

**TABLE 20.1   APPLICATIONS OF A
GENETIC ALGORITHM.**

1. Evolving a neural network.
2. Evolving trading rules.
3. Combining or selecting multiple trading strategies.
4. Money management applications.

near optimal solutions for what are called NP Complete-type problems. NP Complete means that the problem is so complex that the time required to solve it cannot be determined using a polynomial. These are problems in which the number of combinations makes it impossible to try all of them in our lifetime. Genetic algorithms can intelligently search subsets of these solutions to find a near optimal solution for these problems in hours or days, even via a desktop computer. Using genetic algorithms makes it practical to search for the best possible inputs and configurations for our neural network architecture.

The second type of application actually evolves the connection weights for a neural network. Why would we use a genetic algorithm to evolve weights for a neural network? The reason is simple. Most neural network algorithms use error functions that are not optimal for developing trading applications. For example, in many backpropagation-like algorithms, the error function is usually a root mean squared error. This error function will produce a model with a distribution of errors that produces small errors on the more common small moves but allows larger errors on the rarer large moves. This will result in large losing trades that will often make a neural network untradable. If we use a genetic algorithm to evolve the weights, we can then use an error function more appropriate for market timing applications. This is impossible using standard neural networks because the mathematics involved in the trading algorithm often restrict the error functions. One example occurs in the standard backpropagation type of network: the error function must have a derivative that is a continuous function. Using a genetic algorithm, we have no such restriction.

Evolving Trading Rules Using Genetic Algorithms

Another classic application of genetic algorithms is in evolving trading rules. Just as when using genetic algorithms to develop a neural network, we can develop a fitness function that is optimal for our application. I have used genetic algorithms to develop trading rules in two different ways. The first is to design a genetic algorithm to find both the structure and parameters for a given rule. The second is to use the genetic algorithm to combine and optimize predefined rule templates. We will discuss this application later in this chapter.

Combining Trading Methods Using Genetic Algorithms

Genetic algorithms can also be used to either combine forecasts from multiple models or select the best model to trade at any given time. These functions allow us to discover hidden patterns between models that can be used to maximize trading performance.

Let's discuss these applications in a little more detail. To combine the output of several different neural networks, we use genetic algorithms to develop weighting factors that can be applied to the output of the neural networks. This weighting can be different, based on technical factors such as where we are in the business cycle. We can combine different models by developing a new forecast based on a combination of models, including neural networks, rules-based models, or statistics-based models. For example, we could use one set of rules that trades T-Bonds using the CRB, and another set that uses UTY. We then could add month of year, CPI data, and other fundamental data to the model and have the genetic algorithm develop a new model that will give us a combined forecast. We can also use a genetic algorithm to tell us which of two or more models we should be using to trade tomorrow.

Using Genetic Algorithms for Money Management Applications

Genetic algorithms can be used as part of a money management strategy. They can search millions of combinations and find near optimal solutions. If we apply a money management method like optimal f to a large portfolio of commodities, the number of combinations that we need to try to calculate our optimal f value for the portfolio can make this analysis an NP Complete problem. In this case, we can use genetic algorithms to intelligently search these combinations and make it possible to quickly solve optimal f over a basket of commodities. In this case, we would set up our optimal f equations and simply use the genetic algorithm to plug in numbers and then evaluate the fitness of each solution.

DEVELOPING TRADING RULES USING A GENETIC ALGORITHM—AN EXAMPLE

Now that we have overviewed some of the uses of genetic algorithms in trading applications, let's develop an actual application. We will use a genetic algorithm to combine and optimize template rules that will generate entry signals for trading the T-Bond market. In this example, we will have a genetic algorithm combine and optimize parameters for three rule templates that will be banded together. We will only develop rules to trade the long side of the market. Our rule template will allow us to use intermarket analysis combined with stochastics. The basic form of our rule templates is shown in Table 20.2.

We will use the momentum and moving-average templates not only for the market we are trading, but also for different intermarkets used in our analysis.

Let's now apply this basic concept to the T-Bond market. We will trade T-Bond futures using two different intermarkets in our analysis: (1) Eurodollars and (2) the XAU index. Our development period will be from 1/1/86 to 12/31/94. Our combined testing and out-of-sample period will be from 1/1/95 to 10/4/96. We will use a product called TSEvolve, developed by Ruggiero Associates and Scientific Consultant Services, Inc., to evolve these rules in TradeStation.

Our first step is to define our problem. We need to design both our basic rule templates and how they interface to our chromosome so that, by changing the values on the chromosome, we can develop any valid solution to our problem. Often, to solve a given problem, we will divide it into subproblems. These subproblems can be thought of as multiple genes on a chromosome. We will then allow mating only between genes of the same type. In solving our problem, we will use three independent genes, one for each of the rules we are "anding" together. We will allow each rule to use up to four parameters. This gives us a chromosome with twelve elements.

TABLE 20.2   TYPES OF RULE TEMPLATE.

Momentum above or below a given threshold.
Comparing two exponential moving averages to determine which one is higher.
FastD above or below a given trigger.

Let's now discuss how these four elements on each gene are used. The first position on each gene is the rule number for which we are currently optimizing the parameters and combining them with the rules from the other two genes.

Positions 2 through 4 are different parameters that can be used by the rules we are combining. In our genetic algorithm code, we will give these numbers a range from 1 to 1,000, and in the interface to our rules, we will map them back into valid numbers for our domain. Our chromosome is a set of three of these genes.

Let's now look at the code from TSEvolve, in TradeStation, to evolve our rules. We will start with the code for our rule templates, shown in Table 20.3.

The rules templates stored in CalcRules are combined and optimized by the genetic algorithm to develop combinations of three trading rules to buy T-Bonds at the next day's open. We used the following rule to exit our long position:

If BarsSinceEntry>4 then exitlong at low−.5*Average(TrueRange,3) stop;

This exit rule will exit our long position on a stop after the fourth day of the trade if the market breaks yesterday's low by more than 50 percent of the three-day average TrueRange.

Let's now see how the CalcRules function is used in evolving our rules. The code, written in TradeStation's EasyLanguage and using TSEvolve, is shown in Table 20.4.

Let's now discuss this code. Our main module is a system we optimize (using the TradeStation optimizer) to evolve actual rules. We initialize twelve elements that form three genes of four elements each. This makes up our chromosomes. We next initialize our genes. The first element of any gene stores the rule number. We initialize these in a range from 1 to 14.99. When using these values, we take the floor of these numbers in order to produce an integer number that is used to assign a rule number to a given gene. The floor will return the integer portion of a number. We initialize the next three elements on a gene between 1 and 1,000. The CalcRules function will map them back into a parameter range that can be used by a given rule.

TABLE 20.3   CODE FOR CALCRULES FUNCTION.

```
User Function CalcRules
{
We define 4 inputs. These completely specify a rule and its parameters.
Normally, these inputs are the elements of a rule-specifying gene.
}
   Inputs: v1(NumericSimple), v2(NumericSimple);
   Inputs: v3(NumericSimple), v4(NumericSimple);
{
Declare some local variables.
}
   Vars: Norm(0), Norm2(0), Norm3(0), Ka(0), Kb(0), Thr(0);
{
Initialize some variables. We want CalcRule to have a value of 0 unless some
rule fires. We want all thresholds expressed in a market-scale-independent way.
Hence, the use of a normalization factor, Norm.
}
   CalcRule=0;
   Norm=Average(TrueRange, 100);
   Norm2=Average(TrueRange Of Data2, 100);
   Norm3=Average(TrueRange Of Data3, 100);
{
Finally, we implement our rules!
The first rule is a simple momentum threshold rule with a maximum lookback of
100 bars and a normalized threshold that takes into consideration both market
volatility and momentum period.
}
   If Floor(v1)=1 Then Begin { Simple momentum threshold rule }
      Ka Floor ((v2*v2)/10000); { Integer, 0..100 }
      Kb=Floor ((v3*v3)/10000); { Integer, 0..100 }
      Thr=Norm*SquareRoot (AbsValue (Ka-Kb))*(v4-500)/200;
      If C[Ka]-C[Kb]>Thr Then CalcRule=1;
   End;
{
Rule #2 compares two exponential moving averages.
It is real simple!
}
   If Floor(v1)=2 Then Begin { Moving average comparison }
      Ka=Floor (1+(v2*v2)/10000); { Integer, 1..100 }
      Kb=Floor (1+(v3*v3)/10000); { Integer, 1..100 }
      If ExpAvg(C, Ka) > ExpAvg(C, Kb) Then CalcRule=1;
   End;
```

(continued)

TABLE 20.3   *(Continued)*

```
{
Rule #3 compares the Stochastic to a threshold for countertrend signals.
}
   If Floor(v1)=3 Then Begin { Stochastic comparison }
      If FastD(14)<(v2/10) Then CalcRule=1;
   End;
{
Rule #4 compares the Stochastic to a threshold for with-trend signals.
}
   If Floor(v1)=4 Then Begin { Stochastic comparison }
      If FastD(14)>(v2/10) Then CalcRule=1;
   End;
{
Rule #5 is same as #1, momentum threshold, but for Data2
}
   If Floor(v1)=5 Then Begin { Simple momentum threshold rule }
      Ka=Floor ((v2*v2)/10000); { Integer, 0..100 }
      Kb=Floor ((v3*v3) / 10000); { Integer, 0..100 }
      Thr=Norm2*SquareRoot (AbsValue (Ka-Kb)*(v4-500)/200;
      If C[Ka] Of Data2-C[Kb] Of Data2>Thr Then CalcRule=1;
   End;
{
Rule #6 is same as #1, but for Data3
}
   If Floor(v1)=6 Then Begin { Simple momentum threshold rule }
      Ka=Floor ((v2*v2)/10000); { Integer, 0..100 }
      Kb=Floor ((v3*v3)/10000); { Integer, 0..100 }
      Thr=Norm3 * SquareRoot (AbsValue (Ka-Kb))*(v4-500)/200;
      If C[Ka] Of Data3 - C[Kb] Of Data3 > Thr Then CalcRule=1;
   End;
{
Rule #7 is same as #2 but for Data2
}
   If Floor(v1)=7 Then Begin { Moving average comparison }
      Ka=Floor (1+(v2*v2)/10000); { Integer, 1..100 }
      Kb=Floor (1+(v3*v3)/10000); { Integer, 1..100 }
      If ExpAvg(C of Data2, Ka)>ExpAvg(C of Data2, Kb) Then CalcRule=1;
   End;
```

TABLE 20.3 *(Continued)*

```
{
Rule #8 is same as #2 but for Data3
}
   If Floor(v1)=8 Then Begin { Moving average comparison }
      Ka=Floor (1+(v2*v2)/10000); { Integer, 1..100 }
      Kb=Floor (1+(v3*v3)/10000); { Integer, 1..100 }
      If ExpAvg(C of Data3, Ka)>ExpAvg(C of Data3, Kb) Then CalcRule=1;
   End;
{
Rule #9 is same as #2 but moving average Ka is less than Kb
}
   If Floor(v1)=9 Then Begin { Moving average comparison }
      Ka=Floor (1+(v2*v2)/10000); { Integer, 1..100 }
      Kb=Floor (1+(v3*v3)/10000); { Integer, 1..100 }
      If ExpAvg(C of Data, Ka) < ExpAvg(C of Data, Kb) Then CalcRule=1;
   End;
{
Rule #10 is same as #9 but for Data2
}
   If Floor(v1)=10 Then Begin { Moving average comparison }
      Ka=Floor (1+(v2*v2)/10000); { Integer, 1..100 }
      Kb=Floor (1+(v3*v3)/10000); { Integer, 1..100 }
      If ExpAvg(C of Data2, Ka) < ExpAvg(C of Data2, Kb) Then CalcRule=1;
   End;
{
Rule #11 is same as #9 but for Data3
}
   If Floor(v1)=11 Then Begin { Moving average comparison }
      Ka=Floor (1+(v2*v2)/10000); { Integer, 1..100 }
      Kb=Floor (1+(v3*v3)/10000); { Integer, 1..100 }
      If ExpAvg(C, Ka) < ExpAvg(C, Kb) Then CalcRule=1;
   End;
{
Rule #12 is inverse rule of rule 1
}
   If Floor(v1)=12 Then Begin { Simple momentum threshold rule }
      Ka=Floor ((v2*v2)/10000); { Integer, 0..100 }
      Kb=Floor ((v3*v3)/10000); { Integer, 0..100 }
      Thr=Norm*SquareRoot (AbsValue (Ka-Kb))*(v4-500)/200;
      If C[Ka]-C[Kb]<-Thr Then CalcRule=1;
   End;
```

(continued)

TABLE 20.3   *(Continued)*

```
{
Rule #13 is inverse rule of rule 1 but for Data2
}
   If Floor(v1)=13 Then Begin { Simple momentum threshold rule }
     Ka=Floor ((v2*v2)/10000); { Integer, 0..100 }
     Kb=Floor ((v3*v3)/10000); { Integer, 0..100 }
     Thr=Norm2*SquareRoot (AbsValue (Ka-Kb))*(v4-500)/200;
     If C[Ka] Of Data2-C[Kb] Of Data2<-Thr Then CalcRule=1;
   End;
{
Rule #14 is inverse rule of rule 1 but for Data3
}
   If Floor(v1)=14 Then Begin { Simple momentum threshold rule }
     Ka=Floor ((v2*v2)/10000); { Integer, 0..100 }
     Kb=Floor ((v3*v3)/10000); { Integer, 0..100 }
     Thr=Norm3*SquareRoot (AbsValue (Ka-Kb))*(v4-500)/200;
     If C[Ka] Of Data3-C[Kb] Of Data3<-Thr Then CalcRule=1;
   End;
```

**TABLE 20.4   SIMPLE GENETIC TEMPLATE FOR
EVOLVING COMBINATION OF THREE RULES.**

```
{
TSEvolve™ for TradeStation™.
Copyright © 1995, 1996. All Rights Reserved.
Ruggiero Associates and Scientific Consultant Services, Inc.
Tel: (US) 203-469-0880
```

This is the code for a trading system which uses TSEvolve to discover good trading rules. It illustrates just how this may be done. The "inputs" allow us to use the TradeStation optimizer to loop through generations, with TSEvolve providing the actual parameter-vector (rule set) guesses. If the generation number is less than the number of records saved to the solutions file, then we read the solutions file for our parameter vector. If the generation number is greater than what is in the solutions file, then we use TSEvolve to provide us with a parameter vector guess.
This way, we can select the desired solution in the standard TradeStation manner without needing to play with our code!

```
}
```

TABLE 20.4 *(Continued)*

Input: Gen(1); { Generation Number = 1...N }
{
We define some local variables that we need in the code that follows.
}
  Vars: RecCnt(0), EFlag(0), Fitness(0);
  Vars: v1(0), v2(0), v3(0), v4(0), K(0);
  Vars: Res1(0), Res2(0), Res3(0);
  Vars: FilePtr(0);

{
We need to initialize TSEvolve once before using it. This code accomplishes the initialization on the first bar of the first generation. Note that TEST.SOL is our current solutions file that will contain all parameter sets (rule sets) generated, and that 12 is the number of parameters which is also equal to the record size of TEST.SOL Each rule consists of 4 numbers, and we are allowing 3 rules in each complete gene string.
}
  If CurrentBar = 1 Then Begin
    RecCnt = ChromSize("C:\TEST.SOL," 12); { Record count }
    If Gen > RecCnt Then EFlag = 1; { Set evolve mode }
    If Gen < = RecCnt Then EFlag = 0; { Set retrieve mode }
    If Gen = 1 And EFlag = 1 Then Begin { If evolve mode.. }
      GA_Init (12, 500); { 12 = no. parameters 50 = population size }
      For K = 0 To 2 Begin { 3 genes, each with 4 numbers }
        GA_Scale (0 + 4 * K, 1, 14.99); { Range 1..14.99 }
        GA_Scale (1 + 4 * K, 1, 1000); { Range 1..1000 }
        GA_Scale (2 + 4 * K, 1, 1000); { Range 1..1000 }
        GA_Scale (3 + 4 * K, 1, 1000); { Range 1..1000 }
      End;
      GA_Chunk (4); { Set gene or block size to 4 }
      GA_Random (93); { Randomize population with seed=93 }
      GA_Mut (0.30); { Set mutation rate to 0.30 }
      GA_Cross (0.30); { Set crossover rate to 0.30 }
    End;
  End;
{
Now we either retrieve a guess as to the optimal parameters (rules) from TSEvolve, or we retrieve a previously evolved solution from our solutions file. We place the newly-generated guess or the retrieved solution into memory.
}

(continued)

TABLE 20.4 *(Continued)*

```
If CurrentBar = 1 Then Begin { On the first bar.. }
  If EFlag = 1 Then Begin { If we are evolving.. }
    GA_Guess (1); { We get a guess and place it in VR #1 }
    GA_Save (1, 12, Gen, "C:\TEST.SOL"); { And we save it! }
  End;
  If EFlag = 0 Then Begin { If we are running a saved solution.. }
    GA_Load (1, 12, Gen, "C:\TEST.SOL"); { Load it into VR #1}
  End;
End;
{
```
Run the actual trading rules. We retrieve gene data. CalcRule then returns a 1 (True) or a 0 (False) based on the application of the rule defined by its gene-data inputs. The inputs, of course, are taken from a gene in the gene string. We are allowing 3 genes, hence rules, and requiring all rules be True in order to take a trade.
```
}
  GetGeneElem (1, 0, &v1); { Get first element of first gene }
  GetGeneElem (1, 1, &v2); { Get second element of first gene }
  GetGeneElem (1, 2, &v3); { Get third element of first gene }
  GetGeneElem (1, 3, &v4); { Get fourth element of first gene }
  Res1 = CalcRule (v1, v2, v3, v4); { run the rule }
  GetGeneElem (1, 4, &v1); { Get first element of second gene }
  GetGeneElem (1, 5, &v2); { Get second element of second gene }
  GetGeneElem (1, 6, &v3); { Get third element of second gene }
  GetGeneElem (1, 7, &v4); { Get fourth element of second gene }
  Res2 = CalcRule (v1, v2, v3, v4); { run the rule }
  GetGeneElem (1, 8, &v1); { Get first element of third gene }
  GetGeneElem (1, 9, &v2); { Get second element of third gene }
  GetGeneElem (1, 10, &v3); { Get third element of third gene }
  GetGeneElem (1, 11, &v4); { Get fourth element of third gene }
  Res3 = CalcRule (v1, v2, v3, v4); { run the rule }

  If Res1 = 1 And Res2 = 1 And Res3 = 1 Then Begin
    If MarketPosition < = 0 Then Buy At Open;
  End;
  If MarketPosition > 0 Then Begin
    If BarsSinceEntry(0) > 4 Then ExitLong At Low-.5*Average(TrueRange,3) stop;
  End;
{
```

TABLE 20.4 *(Continued)*

Finally, we need to tell TSEvolve how "good" its guess was. That is, we need to report the "fitness" of the guess it provided. Using the information, TSEvolve will be able to provide better and better guesses as the population maintained internal to TSEvolve evolves. Of course, we must do this only on the last bar of each generation, when all backtest/simulation data have been processed for that generation's guess as to the best chromosome (i.e., set of rules). The Date = LastCalcDate clause in the if.. statement below provides us with a crude way to detect the last bar of a run. Of course, we only need to do this if we are evolving, so we also have the EFlag = 1 clause in the if.. statement that follows.

```
}
    If EFlag = 1 And Date = LastCalcDate Then Begin
        Fitness = NetProfit-2*MaxIDDrawDown; { We will maximize NetProfit }
        GA_Fit (Fitness); { Tell TSEvolve goodness of current guess }
        { Write out some useful info to a text file }
        SC_Fopen (&FilePtr, "C:\TEST.TXT", "AT");
        SC_Fprintf (&FilePtr, "%6.1f ", Gen); { Generation }
        For K = 0 To 11 Begin
            GetChromElem(1, K, &Value1); { Gene data }
            If K = 4 Or K = 8 Then
                SC_Fprintf (&FilePtr, ",", 1);
            SC_Fprintf (&FilePtr, "%7.1f", Value1); { Genes, 1 per line }
            If K = 3 Or K = 7 Or K = 11 Then
                SC_Fprintf (&FilePtr, "N", 1); { New line }
        End;
        SC_Fprintf (&FilePtr, "%10.2f", NetProfit);
        SC_Fprintf (&FilePtr, "%10.2f", GrossProfit);
        SC_Fprintf (&FilePtr, "%10.2f", PercentProfit);
        SC_Fprintf (&FilePtr, "%10.2f", TotalTrades);
        SC_Fprintf (&FilePtr, "%10.2f N", MaxIDDrawdown);
        SC_Fclose (&FilePtr);
    End;
{
```

We are done. Verify this code, set up TradeStation's built-in optimizer to step the single input Gen from 1 to whatever number of generations you want to run. Use an increment of one. To run the system, set Gen to whatever generation you liked best as determined from studying the data. To do another evolution run, change the solutions file name or delete the existing solutions file from your disk (otherwise you will be retrieving old solutions rather than evolving new ones).

```
}
```

On the first bar of every run, we get a chromosome that was the result of the last mating operation. We then use the values on each gene to test our defined set of three rules which will be anded together. We will buy when all three of these rules are true. We hold our position for at least four bars and exit it after that period on a stop at 50 percent of a three-day average true range below yesterday's low.

When we are in an evolution mode, we evaluate the fitness of a given rule set based on the trading performance as reported in TradeStation. We use a simple fitness function in this evaluation: NetProfit $- 2 \times$ MaxID-DrawDown. This function will produce profitable combinations with a good drawdown-to-profit ratio. If instead of this measure we use a measure such as profit factor, the genetic algorithm might have evolved a solution with five or fewer trades, all of which are winners and have a profit factor of 100. These systems have too few trades and most likely will not be profitable in the future because they are curve-fitted systems.

We then write to both a solution file "test.sol," used by TSEvolve to reload solutions into TradeStation once we are done evolving, and an information file "test.txt," which we can use to analyze our results and select the generation we would want to trade.

The way this code is written, it will evolve a generation if the value passed to the system is greater than the maximum value stored in the solution file. If the value passed is less than the maximum generation in this file, it will run that generation to produce its trading signal.

Let's now discuss the code for CalcRules. This code first initializes the return value of this function to false and then calculates normalization factors based on 100-day average true ranges for Data1, Data2, and Data3. Next, we find the rule that is being requested. Let's look at each of these rule templates.

Rule 1 wants to see whether a momentum is above a given threshold. Both the lookbacks and the threshold are found using the genetic algorithm. Rule 2 compares two exponential moving averages and is true when the first one is greater than the second. The genetic algorithm also sets the periods used in these moving averages.

Rule 3 is true when a FastD is below a threshold, and Rule 4 is true when a FastD is above a threshold. Rule 5 is the same as Rule 1 but uses Data2; so is Rule 6, but now for Data3. Rules 7 and 8 are the same as Rule 2 but use Data2 and Data3, respectively. Rule 9 is when the first moving average is less than the second and is applied to Data1. Rules 10 and 11 are the same as Rule 9 but are applied to Data2 and Data3. Rule 12 is just like Rule 1, but the value must be below a given $-1 \times$ threshold rule. Rules 13 and 14 are the same as Rule 12, but are used for Data2 and Data3.

We evolved these rules with a population size of 500, a crossover rate of .30, and a mutation rate of .30. They were evolved for 3,000 generations. A generation is a single mating of the population. We found that, in general, we had a number of good solutions. We then tested them, from 1/1/95 to 10/4/96. Four of them performed very well in both the development set and the testing set. One of the nice features about TSEvolve is that we are able to rerun any generation without coding the rules. The chromosomes for each generation are stored in a solution file and can be used by TradeStation to reload a given set of rules without any coding.

Let's now see how these four generations/solutions performed during both the development and combined testing/out-of-sample sets (allowing $50.00 for slippage and commissions). Our development set period was from 1/1/86 to 12/31/94, and our combined set period was from 1/1/95 to 10/4/96. Note that we used 210 for maxbars back, so that the first 10 months of data did not generate any trades on the development set. The results are shown in Table 20.5.

We then translated our trading rules into both EasyLanguage and English so that we could see whether they would make sense to a domain expert. These restated rules are shown in Table 20.6.

Note that we can use genetic algorithms to induce rules that we can translate into both EasyLanguage and English, and then have them studied by a domain expert. We analyzed these rules and found several examples of some of the theories discussed in earlier chapters. For example, the rule from generation 1909 has, as one of its conditions, that the XAU has not gone up too much. This rule confirms the existence of the concept of intermarket inversion, which we discussed earlier. Briefly, the concept is that intermarket relationships will sometimes invert. Positive ones become negative and negative ones become positive for some markets, when these markets move too quickly. The classic example of this effect is that, when interest rates drop too quickly or gold rises too fast, the inverse relationship between gold and T-Bonds will invert and they will become positively correlated. Another example of this occurs with

TABLE 20.5   RESULTS OF SELECTED GENERATION OF RULES FOR T-BONDS USING OUR TEMPLATE.

	Development Set	Combined Testing/Out-of-Sample Set
Generation 1197		
Net profit	$34,300.00	$10,681.25
Trades	74	17
Average trade	$463.51	$628.31
Win%	66	65
Drawdown	−$5,668.75	−$5,175.00
Profit factor	1.96	2.48
Generation 1723		
Net profit	$32,175.00	$11,900.00
Trades	74	17
Average trade	$434.80	$700.00
Win%	66	65
Drawdown	−$6,400.00	−$5,175.00
Profit factor	1.90	2.65
Generation 1909		
Net profit	$38,350.00	$6,906.25
Trades	68	15
Average trade	$563.97	$460.42
Win%	66	60
Drawdown	−$5,068.00	−$4,537.50
Profit factor	2.47	2.06
Generation 2329		
Net profit	$34,156.00	$5,718.75
Trades	50	10
Average trade	$683.13	$571.88
Win%	68	80
Drawdown	−$5,618.75	−$4,331.25
Profit factor	2.51	1.91

Eurodollars in generation 1197. Eurodollars often rally very quickly during times of crisis, and this rally does not always follow through in the T-Bond market.

We found that the rules we selected make sense and use parameters similar to those of many of the rule templates that we are combining. For

TABLE 20.6   TRANSLATION OF SELECTED RULES INTO BOTH ENGLISH AND EASYLANGUAGE.

Let Data1=T-Bonds
Let Data2=Eurodollars
Let Data3=XAU index

Generation 1197

EasyLanguage:
If FastD(14)<61.9 and C[40] of Data2 -C[19] of Data2>-
6.69*Average(TrueRange of Data2,100) and XAverage(C,8)>XAverage(C,14) then
buy at open;
If BarsSinceEntry>4 then exitlong at Low-.5*Average(TrueRange,3) stop;

English:
If FastD is not too high and Eurodollars did not go up too much between 19
days ago and 40 days ago and the T-Bond eight-day average is above the 14-day
average, then buy.

Generation 1723

EasyLanguage:
If FastD(14)<61.9 and FastD(14)>31.9 and XAverage(C,7)>XAverage(C,15) then
buy at open;
If BarsSinceEntry>4 then exitlong at Low-.5*Average(TrueRange,3) stop;

English:
If Fast D is in the middle of the range and the trend is up, then buy at open;

Generation 1909

EasyLanguage:
If C[8] of Data3- C[1] of Data3>-1.53*Average(TrueRange of Data3,100) and
C[84] of Data3-C[9] of Data3>2.16*Average(TrueRange of Data3,100) and
C[61] of Data2-C[32] of Data2>-5.23*Average(TrueRange of Data2,100) then
buy at open;
If BarsSinceEntry>4 then exitlong at Low-.5*Average(TrueRange,3) stop;

English:
If the recent XAU is not going up too much and the past XAU is going down
and Eurodollars are either up or only slightly lower, then buy.

Generation 2329

EasyLanguage:
If FastD(14)>46.8 and C[48] of Data2-C[3] of Data2>-13.52*Average
(TrueRange of Data2,100) and XAverage(C,7) > XAverage(C,15) then buy.

English:
If FastD is not too low and Eurodollars are not down too much, then buy if
T-Bonds are in a uptrend.

example, in three of the four generations, we have one condition that is true when a short-term EMA is above a long-term EMA. The genetic algorithm used either 7 or 8 for the short-term EMA and 14 or 15 for the long-term EMA—an indication of the stability of these pairs of parameters.

This chapter has shown how genetic algorithms can be used for a broad range of trading applications and can also incorporate human trader expertise into the solutions. Given these capacities, I feel that genetic algorithms will be one of the hottest areas of research in advanced technologies for trading well into the next century.

References and Readings

Articles by Murray A. Ruggiero, Jr.
In *Futures* Magazine (Chronological Order)

"Getting the lag out," April 1994, pages 46–48.

"Interpreting feedback to build a better system," July 1994, pages 46–48.

"Training neural nets for intermarket analysis," August 1994, pages 42–44.

"How to build an artificial trader," September 1994, pages 56–58.

"Putting the components before the system," October 1994, pages 42–44.

"How to build a system framework," November 1994, pages 50–56.

"Turning the key," December 1994, pages 38–40.

"Artificial trader jumps candlesticks," February 1995, pages 42–44.

"Testing the black box system that feeds you," March 1995, pages 44–46.

"Testing a real system," April 1995, pages 46–48.

"Nothing like net for intermarket analysis," May 1995, pages 46–47.

"Build a real neural net," June 1995, pages 44–46.

"Evolution of a trader," July 1995, pages 44–46.

"Taking evolution into warp speed," August 1995, pages 42–44.

"Fine-tuning money management with *f*," September 1995, pages 48–50.

"Tips to develop smarter exits," October 1995, pages 54–58.

"Building a system one day at a time," November 1995, pages 52–54.

"Building a real day-trading system," December 1995, pages 50–52.

"How to adapt systems to survive changing markets," January 1996, pages 48–50.

"Using correlation analysis to predict trends," February 1996, pages 46–49.

"Building the wave," April 1996, pages 46–48.

"How to predict tomorrow's indicators today," May 1996, pages 44–48.

"Fundamentals pave way to predicting interest rates," September 1996, pages 46–48.

In *AI in Finance*

"Building a great artificial trader," Premier Issue 1994, pages 39–44.

"Rules are made to be traded," Fall 1994, pages 35–40.

"Neural networks: Tahiti or bust," Spring 1995, pages 15–20.

Articles by Other Authors

Jurik, Mark. "The care and feeding of a neural network," *Futures* Magazine, October 1992, pages 40–44.

Meyers, Dennis. "The electric utility bond market indicator," *Technical Analysis of Stocks & Commodities,* January 1996, pages 18–31.

Pawlak, Zdzislaw, Grzymala-Busse, Slowinski, R., and Ziarko, W., "Rough sets," unpublished manuscript, 1995, pages 1–17.

Books

Azoff, E. Michael. *Neural Network Time Series Forecasting of Financial Markets.* New York: John Wiley & Sons, Inc., 1994.

Deboeck, Guido. *Trading on the Edge.* New York: John Wiley & Sons, Inc., 1994.

Ehlers, John. *MESA and Trading Market Cycles.* New York: John Wiley & Sons, Inc., 1992.

Joseph, Tom. *Mechanical Elliott Wave Seminar.* Cleveland, OH: Trading Techniques, Inc., 1993.

Kaufman, Perry J. *The New Commodity Trading Systems and Methods.* New York: John Wiley & Sons, Inc., 1987.

Lipschutz, Seymour. *Theory and Problems of Finite Mathematics.* New York: McGraw-Hill Book Co., 1966.

MESA '96 for TradeStation's User's Manual. Copyright 1996, MESA Software, P.O. Box 1801, Goleta, CA 93116.

Murphy, John J. *Intermarket Technical Analysis.* New York: John Wiley & Sons, Inc., 1991.

Murphy, John J. *Technical Analysis of the Futures Market: A Comprehensive Guide to Trading Methods and Applications.* Englewood Cliffs, NJ: Prentice-Hall (NY Institute of Finance), 1986.

Nison, Steve. *Japanese Candlestick Charting Techniques.* New York: John Wiley & Sons, Inc., 1990.

Refenes, Paul. *Neural Networks in the Capital Markets,* (pp. 213–219). New York: John Wiley & Sons, Inc., 1995.

Rotella, Robert P. *The Elements of Successful Trading.* New York: Simon & Schuster, 1992.

Schwager, Jack D. *The New Market Wizards: Conversations with America's Top Traders.* New York: HarperCollins (HarperBusiness), 1992.

Zweig, Martin. *Winning on Wall Street.* New York: Warner Communications Co., 1990.

Index

FOR MORE INFORMATION

INSIDE ADVANTAGE

Inside Advantage is a newsletter edited by Murray A. Ruggiero, Jr. In each issue, he shares statistical research and fully discloses computerized trading systems. On average, every issue of *Inside Advantage* includes three to five systems for trading commodities, mutual funds and stocks. The holding periods of these trading systems range from less than one day to three months or more.

In addition to providing computerized trading systems, *Inside Advantage* also contains interviews with top traders and analysts such as Larry Williams, Linda Raschke and John Murphy.

Subscriptions cost: $85 for six issues; $95 outside U.S.
$140 for twelve issues; $160 outside U.S.

INSIDE ADVANTAGE DISK SERVICE AND TRADING TOOL

This service supplies you with a disk that contains all of the trading systems published in *Inside Advantage* so you can use them in TradeStation or SuperCharts. In addition to the code, we will supply you with other tools that were used when researching these systems.

The cost for six disks, plus a bonus disk containing the extra utilities, is only $99 ($115 outside U.S.)--less than $15 each.

CATALOG FOR COMPUTERIZED TRADERS

Our free catalog contains products that cover all aspects of analysis, from intermarket analysis to candlestick recognition and cycle-based trading. There are products that will help you build neural networks and use genetic algorithms in trading. We specialize in tools and systems that are compatible with Omega Research's TradeStation and SuperCharts.

RUGGIERO ASSOCIATES 1-800-211-9785
18 Oregon Avenue, East Haven, CT 06512